The Politics

of

John F. Kennedy

THE WORLD STUDIES SERIES

General Editor: JAMES HENDERSON, M.A. Ph.D.,
Senior Lecturer in Education with special reference to Teaching of History
and International Affairs, Institute of Education, University of London

Editorial Board: MOTHER MARY de SALES, M.A., Principal Lecturer in
History, Coloma College
JOSEPH HUNT, M.A., Senior History Master, City of London School
JAMES JOLL, M.A., University Lecturer in Modern History and Sub-Warden
of St. Anthony's College, Oxford
ESMOND WRIGHT, M.A., M.P., Professor of Modern History,
University of Glasgow

VOLUMES PUBLISHED

Malaysia and its Neighbours, J. M. Gullick.
The European Common Market and Community, U. W. Kitzinger, Fellow
of Nuffield College, Oxford.

FORTHCOMING VOLUMES

Brazil: The Pattern of National Development, L. M. Bethell, University
College, London.
The Indian-Pakistan Problem, Dr. Peter Lyon, London School of
Economics.
Israel and the Arab World, C. H. Dodd, Department of Social Studies,
University of Durham.
Apartheid, Dr. Edgar Brookes.

The Politics

of

John F. Kennedy

Edmund S. Ions
M.A., B.Litt. (Oxon)
Lecturer in Politics, University of York

LONDON
ROUTLEDGE & KEGAN PAUL

First published 1967
by Routledge & Kegan Paul Limited
Broadway House, 68–74 Carter Lane
London, E.C.4

Printed in Great Britain by
C. Tinling & Co. Ltd
Liverpool, London and Prescot

© *Edmund S. Ions 1967*

SBN 7100 2990 X (C)
7100 2991 8 (P)

Contents

The book is divided into seven parts in order to distinguish various aspects of a large subject. However, documents and articles appearing in one part may be quite relevant to topics occurring elsewhere in the readings. References in the Introduction are to the numbered documents in the main text of the book. The Editor's references in the documents are numbered and given at the end of each reading.

General Editor's Preface

The World Studies Series is designed to make a new and important contribution to the study of modern history. Each volume in the Series will provide students in sixth forms, Colleges of Education and Universities with a range of contemporary material drawn from many sources, not only from official and semiofficial records, but also from contemporary historical writing and from reliable journals. The material is selected and introduced by a scholar who establishes the context of his subject and suggests possible lines of discussion and enquiry that can accompany a study of the documents.

Through these volumes the student can learn how to read and assess historical documents. He will see how the contemporary historian works and how historical judgements are formed. He will learn to discriminate among a number of sources and to weigh evidence. He is confronted with recent instances of what Professor Butterfield has called 'the human predicament' revealed by history; evidence concerning the national, racial and ideological factors which at present hinder or advance man's progress towards some form of world society.

Mr. Ions has made an ingenious blend of what the man, Kennedy, actually said as President and what others said about him before and after his assassination. Perhaps the greatest value of these documents lies in the opportunity they afford the reader to observe steadily and distinctly the difference between person and office during the Kennedy regime.

The selection of documents provides clues to an understanding of that White House incumbent, whose humanity is comparable in interest with Abraham Lincoln's.

JAMES HENDERSON

Volume Editor's Preface

The President of the United States is inevitably a subject of world interest today. Whoever he is and whatever his policies, the effects of his personality and his views reach out to every corner of the globe. Some Presidents of the United States have ranked with the great men of history. Others have been judged mediocre. It is too early to say whether history will include John Fitzgerald Kennedy's name among the truly great Presidents. What is beyond doubt is that his Presidency was one of the most eventful and significant in American history. The readings in this book help to illustrate and explain why this is so.

The book is divided into seven Parts:
Parts One and Two examine the ideas and policies which Kennedy brought with him to the White House when he was elected to the Presidency.
Part Three describes the talented group of men surrounding President Kennedy as his chosen administrators and aides, and also explores Kennedy's method of conducting his high office.
Parts Four and Five deal with the complex problems which tested Kennedy's qualities of leadership at home and overseas, and his response to those problems.
Part Six explores various aspects of the Presidency and further discusses Kennedy's conception of the office.
Part Seven presents three appraisals of the Kennedy Presidency from three different perspectives.

NOTE—In many of the documents in this book readers will encounter American spellings, as all documents are presented in their original format.

E. S. I.

Acknowledgements

The author and publishers wish to thank the following for kind permission to print the extracts included in this collection:

Andre Deutsch Ltd and The Houghton Mifflin Co., *A Thousand Days*, by Arthur M. Schlesinger, Jr., 1965; *Antioch Review*, 'Kennedy in History: An Early Appraisal', by William G. Carleton, 1964; Hodder & Stoughton Ltd and Harper & Row Inc., *Kennedy*, by Theodore Sorensen, 1965; *The Observer*, London, 'Kennedy's New Testament', by Godfrey Hodgson, 1962; *Political Science Quarterly*, 'Kennedy in the Presidency: A Premature Appraisal', by Richard Neustadt, 1964; *The Progressive*, 'The Men around Kennedy', by Karl Meyer, 1960, and 'The Big Issue: a Memorandum', by Arthur M. Schlesinger, 1960; *The Saturday Review*, 'How Powerful is the Presidency?', by Sidney Warren, 1962; *The Sunday Telegraph*, 'A New Power in the White House', by Gore Vidal, 1961; *Virginia Quarterly Review*, 'The Kennedy Style and Congress', by Carroll Kilpatrick, 1963.

Introduction

John Fitzgerald Kennedy was President of the United States for two years, ten months, and two days. His term of office was cut short by assassination on 22 November 1963. Under the American Constitution, a President's term of office lasts four years, and he will normally count on a further term in order to realize many of his policies and legislative proposals. John Kennedy was denied this opportunity by the assassin's act at a time when his re-election for a second term was virtually certain.

During the comparatively short period of his Presidency, however, Kennedy made a remarkable impact. He kindled an extraordinary degree of enthusiasm and a sense of purpose in the American people. He also earned genuine respect not only from the people he led, but all around the world. The explanation for this lay chiefly in the sense of new beginnings and fresh approaches he seemed to bring to old problems. This was allied to the professional competence shown by his Administration in Washington.

The new spirit brought in by the Kennedy government was known collectively as the 'New Frontier' spirit. It was made up of a large number of factors, some of them highly diverse, and care is needed in using the term. There were disappointments in Kennedy's Presidency as there always are in high elective offices which depend on a number of variable factors for sustained success. Kennedy fired the imagination of the American people, but he did not inspire the federal legislature, the United States Congress. It was left to his successor, President Johnson, to realize many of Kennedy's legislative proposals. Again, Kennedy had some notable successes in the conduct of foreign policy, but there were also severe setbacks. There is even an air of paradox in the contrast between Kennedy's remarkable popularity in America and his legislative performance as President. The reasons for this lie in the complex relationships which exist between the President's office and the powers of Congress.

It is not the purpose of the present book to analyse the relationship between Kennedy and the United States Congress during his term of office, but it should be borne in mind that American government is largely a dialogue between the President, the Executive branch of the government, and Congress, the legislative branch. Each has certain well defined powers under the Constitution and guards them jealously. Congress in particular is jealous of encroachments by the Executive branch of the government, and this sets limits to the amount a President can achieve, whatever his appeal or popularity (see Document 27).

With these cautions in mind, however, it remains true that John Kennedy captured the imagination of the American people and went on to gain world-wide esteem for his conduct of affairs as President of the United States of America.

How President Kennedy formulated the ideas and policies summed up in the term 'the New Frontier', how he pursued those policies and how he came to earn a world reputation as a leader is the subject of this book. Documents and extracts have been selected to illustrate these themes. Together, they go some way towards explaining the deep sense of shock felt by many millions of people when the news came that President Kennedy had been assassinated.

A discussion of the 'New Frontier' can be approached through the career and character of John F. Kennedy himself. In many ways, John Kennedy was trained for the Presidency from birth. For two generations on either side of the family, the tradition was one of active participation in politics. Kennedy's maternal grandfather was mayor of the city of Boston and three times elected a United States Congressman. The paternal grandfather, Patrick Kennedy, was closely identified with the political 'bosses' who controlled politics in Boston, and an influential member of the Democratic Party in the same city. Patrick Kennedy's son Joseph, the father of the late President of the United States, maintained the family connection with the Party and counted among his many influential friends President Franklin Roosevelt. By careful investment and speculation,

Joseph Kennedy amassed a large fortune on the stock market and in real estate. Undoubtedly his great wealth eased the path of his sons, John, Robert and Edward, when each in turn sought preferment in national politics. Although he did not enter practical politics himself, Joseph Kennedy was very anxious that at least one of his sons should do so.

The identification of the Irish with politics in America is one of the most interesting parts of American history. It belongs to the social as well as to the political history of the nation, for it can be argued that many, if not most, of the Irish immigrants who sought power, fame, or fortune in American politics were spurred by social aspirations as well as by political ambitions. The two are inextricably bound up in the history of a family like the Kennedys. A brief historical digression will underline the significance of this and provide some insights into the drive and ambition shown by John Fitzgerald Kennedy in his path to the Presidency. It will also provide some clues to the intriguing character John Kennedy presents to the student of politics.

When, towards the middle of the nineteenth century, the Irish began to emigrate to America in large numbers, they tended to congregate in the larger cities of the eastern seaboard of America. Boston, on the north-east coast, received an ever-increasing tide of immigrants. From the first, the Catholic Irish were marked out by their speech, their visible poverty and of course by their religion from the old established families of Protestant orthodoxy and genteel sensibility. The Bostonians often showed an open contempt for the Irish labourers who thronged the waterfront bars, ready to accept the meanest jobs in the city. Like many other immigrant families, the Kennedys of the late nineteenth century often saw job advertisements which stated: 'No Irish need apply'.

In this situation, the Irish knew, or could discover by painful experience, that Boston society and its avenues of advancement were not open to them. Yet in a democracy which gave the vote to every naturalized American citizen, the individual immigrant held a tiny source of power. Moreover (as their natural gregariousness soon demonstrated at election times), Irish immigrants voting together held potential sources of real power. Politics became a possible road to personal advancement. As more and more immigrants swarmed in, those who had already witnessed elections in the wards of cities like Boston recognized the value of political organization.

At the same time, the older established Protestant families of Boston were less and less inclined to play their traditional role in political affairs, which seemed to them increasingly distasteful. Over a period, they largely deserted active politics, especially at the level of the city or the ward, where elections were won and lost. This was the gap which men like Patrick Kennedy were more than ready to fill towards the end of the nineteenth century. If their methods of organizing the vote to win elections in the wards were not always admirable or honest, this was chiefly because in the rough and tumble of ward politics there was little give and take.

Fresh waves of immigration near the end of the century brought further competition from those who sought the same positions of power and influence at the city hall or the state house. By the beginning of the present century, Italian, German, Greek and Jewish immigrants were competing in ward politics in the larger cities of the east coast.

As part of the first big wave of immigrants in the nineteenth century, the Irish were well placed in what became to some degree a fight for survival. The stakes in the game were largely connected with favours the city hall could dispense, especially jobs in the rapidly expanding cities. The ability to influence, or better, to determine, the election result in a particular city or even in a ward was crucial. Here, assisted by their numbers, their knowledge of the language and their natural gregariousness, the Irish eventually dominated the politics of many cities.

A local Irish politician could often satisfy his political ambition at the level of alderman or perhaps with the mayoralty of the city. As their control of local politics extended, however, many Irish immigrants looked towards national politics for the realization of their ambitions. Thus, although John Kennedy's grandfather was proud to be Mayor of Boston, it was as a United States Congressman in Washington that he found greater satisfaction and enjoyed more esteem and influence. These political skills and the instincts developed with them were passed on in the Kennedy family from father to son.

Joseph Kennedy, the father of the late President, used his wealth to give his sons the best education which money, and some influence, could buy. John Kennedy was educated at an expensive preparatory school in New England and then at Harvard, the most illustrious university in the United States.

At first, the young John Kennedy showed little enthusiasm for his studies. Following his father's advice, however, he spent a short time at the London School of Economics, where the brilliant and provocative socialist Harold Laski was lecturing and where other radical thinkers could influence his mind. With the advent of war in Europe, John Kennedy returned to Harvard with a new enthusiasm for studies in politics and history. He was also interested in economics, though he never performed well in the subject. He graduated with honours and wrote a highly commended undergraduate thesis dealing with the British policy of appeasement towards Hitler in the thirties. The thesis was later published under the title *Why England Slept* (see p. 223) and became a best seller on both sides of the Atlantic.

When America entered the European war in 1943, Kennedy was initially debarred from active service by a back injury he suffered at school whilst playing football. When conscripted, he held a number of sedentary jobs in United States naval bases, but by combining his personal initiative with his father's influence in high places he finally realized his ambition to be called for active service. He became commander of a torpedo boat in the Far East and saw a good deal of action there. When the torpedo boat he commanded was rammed by a Japanese destroyer Kennedy showed outstanding heroism in rescuing his comrades and bringing those who survived to safety. He was subsequently decorated for his action.

The war over, his steps turned to journalism, and he reported news from Britain and Europe on a variety of political events. In 1946, he decided to enter politics, and in that year stood for election to the United States House of Representatives in one oft he poorest Congressional Districts in Boston. This gave his father immense satisfaction as it continued the family tradition. The father's hopes had earlier centred on his eldest son Joseph, but those hopes ended when Joseph was killed in the war of 1939–45.

The 1946 election was the first to be fought by the twenty-nine year old John Kennedy, and the professional politicians in

Ions: *The politics of John F. Kennedy*

Boston did not rate his chances highly. Yet Kennedy conducted his campaign with immense drive and built up an extremely efficient political organization for capturing votes. Many professionals paid tribute to his readiness to visit and talk to almost everyone in the Congressional District. Others confirmed that he was closely advised by his father. When Kennedy took his seat in the House of Representatives in Washington he was the youngest Congressman in the House.

After serving for three terms in Congress, his political ambitions turned to the upper house, the United States Senate. There, with their six year term of office (by contrast to the Congressman's two year term), the Senators visibly enjoyed much more power and influence than a Congressman could normally attain. In 1952, Kennedy stood for election to the Senate. His opponent, it is interesting to note, was a scion of an old-established Boston Protestant family, Henry Cabot Lodge. Kennedy's maternal grandfather had opposed the grandfather of Henry Cabot Lodge for the Senate seat in 1916. On that occasion, the genteel Protestant had defeated the Irish candidate. In 1952, the Irish candidate triumphed and John Kennedy took his seat as a United States Senator for the State of Massachusetts. There can be no doubting the pleasure this gave to the Boston Irish.

Within four years of his election to the Senate, John Kennedy gained national prominence in the Democratic Party. At the National Party Convention in 1956 he very nearly gained the Party's nomination for the office of Vice-President of the United States. The voting was close, and only after a number of delegates switched their votes on a second ballot was Kennedy forced to concede to an older member of the Senate, Estes Kefauver. Despite this defeat, Kennedy had made a remarkable impact at the national level as a young Senator still in his first term.

The Democratic 'ticket' of Adlai Stevenson and Estes Kefauver was easily defeated in the November 1956 elections when the incumbent President Eisenhower stood for re-election. Nevertheless from then on, John Kennedy planned to seek nomination once more at the next Democratic Convention in 1960. This time, however, he would not be seeking the second place on the Democratic ticket: he was determined to gain the

Presidential nomination and then go on to win the Presidency in November 1960.

As he organized and began to seek support for his candidacy, several factors counted heavily against him. These factors were less important for a candidate seeking the Vice-Presidency, but it was soon evident that they counted a great deal for the Presidency.

First among these was the fact that he was a Roman Catholic. No Roman Catholic had ever been elected President of the United States. When in 1928 the Democratic Party nominated Al Smith, a Roman Catholic, as their candidate for President of the United States, his defeat in the subsequent election was widely attributed to his religion. The memory of this in the minds of the Democratic king-makers of the 1950s was a formidable obstacle to John Kennedy's hopes (see Document 12).

Kennedy's undoubted wealth was also a source of difficulty. The Democratic Party has traditionally identified itself with the poorer immigrants in American society. The old tradition in American politics, that any poor boy could rise to be President ('from log cabin to White House'), did not fit well on a Harvard-educated Senator whose father had settled more than a million dollars on him before he was twenty-one.

Kennedy's youth and comparative inexperience also told against him. As one of his opponents for the 1960 Democratic nomination liked to point out, the American people prefer the man in the White House to have 'a touch of grey in his hair'. It must be remembered that the American President is a father figure for the nation, and in moments of crisis the people turn instinctively to the President for guidance and leadership. A conspicuously youthful millionaire from Massachusetts, it was widely felt, could hardly fit this important role. Again, in the vital encounters with other world leaders, most of whom were old enough to be his father, how would John Kennedy fare? These and other doubts were in the minds of the powerful men who influenced the choice of the Democratic Party in 1960 as the national elections for the Presidency approached.

The account of how John Kennedy met these various challenges to his candidacy, and how he surmounted each one, makes an exciting story full of lessons for the student of politics, though it is too long and too detailed to recount here. A full account is given in the extremely readable book by Theodore White, *The Making of the President, 1960* (see p. 222). There the author shows how Kennedy won the nomination of the Democratic Party by a combination of dynamic energy, great eloquence and by brilliant political organization.

The qualities Kennedy showed in that campaign were those which made his Presidency so interesting and often exciting to follow. Within weeks of his inauguration as President of the United States in January 1961 a sense of excitement, of new beginnings, of new policies and purposes began to transmit itself from Washington to the American nation, and then beyond America to a watching world. That spirit can best be summed up in the term 'The New Frontier', and though earlier cautions about the use of the term need to be recalled in order to distinguish the optimism of 1961 from the final achievements of Kennedy's Presidency, there can be no doubt that his Administration brought new hopes and fresh energies to an American people which seemed to have lost its confidence in itself.

The Kennedy years must be introduced against the last years of the Eisenhower Presidency in order to appreciate this change. During the last four years of Eisenhower's eight years as President, the United States experienced a period of national drift. There was a sense of confusion but also of alarm in the face of increasing evidence that Russia was forging ahead of the United States in vital areas of technology—particularly rocketry and space exploration. This sense of national drift seemed to be epitomized in the person of a President who clearly preferred a game of golf to the cares of office. It became the pointed custom of some newspaper editors to provide yet another photograph of President Eisenhower on the golf-course, juxtaposed to a column reporting domestic problems in the United States, such as labour troubles, civil rights disturbances, and other examples of America's many unsolved domestic problems.

Eisenhower was saved from a good deal of public criticism because of the gratitude felt by the nation towards this war-time general whose exploits had been fully (and carefully) recorded in published form. Also, Eisenhower's health suffered so much from the many inescapable burdens of the Presidential office that he twice experienced serious physical breakdowns. At times there was some doubt that he would survive. Meanwhile, however, Presidential leadership languished. Authority and initiative tended to lie more and more with the President's close advisers, especially Vice-President Richard Nixon, who was very willing to gain first-hand experience of the office he intended to seek at the 1960 election, when Eisenhower retired.

During the last two years of Eisenhower's Administration, criticism mounted. Much of it could be seen to originate from the date when, to the astonishment of all Americans, Russian scientists succeeded in sending up the first man-made satellite, a propaganda victory which was soon reinforced when the Russians sent up heavier, and more sophisticated, satellites as proof of their superiority in this field of technology. In America, a number of articles and writings by eminent men drew attention to the dismal irony that America could produce large cars adorned with much superfluous chromium plate, yet at the same time poverty existed for millions of Americans left behind in the race. The more concerned, articulate Americans voiced the urgent need for channelling the energies and the expertise of the American people to real purpose, rather than senseless 'conspicuous consumption', which added nothing to the wealth or health of the nation.

Kennedy's call for a new sense of purpose came in at this point. At an early stage of his campaign for the Presidency, he called for a real effort 'to get this country moving again'. Though it might take great effort and impose many burdens, Kennedy stressed, the effort was vital if drift and stagnation were not to lead to a national decline in the struggles which surely lay ahead (see Documents 3 and 5).

Kennedy appealed for a new sense of national purpose and a new set of priorities in order to meet the challenge not only of Soviet competition but also of many other problems facing America in a troubled world. His call to action provides the core of that 'New Frontier' spirit which he brought to the Presidency. The documents in this book show how Kennedy was addressing himself to this theme and calling to the attention of Americans the stark facts of the international situation as early as 1958, two years before he stood for the Presidency. In this he was assisted by others, especially keen students of affairs in America, who wrote forthrightly about the dangers America was courting by cosy indifference to the problems of emerging nations, to the challenge contained in Soviet progress, and to the appeal of communism among the poorer nations of the world (see Document 4).

Kennedy's dynamic appeal to the good sense of the American people began to take effect as he travelled around America in 1960 making scores of speeches to audiences great and small. His audiences were also impressed by the energy, the handsomeness and the wit of the candidate. Nor was his campaign hindered by the occasional appearance on the hustings of his beautiful young wife, Jacqueline. But perhaps the chief reason for Kennedy's victory over the Republican candidate Richard Nixon was the superbly efficient organization he built up and maintained. Here was an old maxim of the Irish in city politics showing itself at the level of Presidential politics: the need for good political organization. Kennedy accepted this maxim completely, and just as his superior organization won him a seat in the House of Representatives in 1946 and the United States Senate in 1952, so a much extended organization helped largely to 'engineer' the Presidency for Kennedy against formidable opposition.

An idea of the skill and expertise of the Kennedy organization is given in Document 9: *The Men around Kennedy* by Karl Meyer. Political analysts of the 1960 election recognized that Kennedy had brought something new to the history of Presidential contests in the United States. In future, it may be, a candidate cannot hope to win unless he goes some way towards matching the professional skills shown by the Kennedy forces in 1960. In that campaign, the use of computers for the analysis of opinion polls; of wireless communication and the mass media; of brilliant staff work in the creation and then the exploitation of a favourable 'image' of the candidate in all the states of the Union, all contributed vitally to the final result.

Kennedy did not disband his political organization when he entered the White House as President. Rather, he seemed to carry it into the White House with him, to assist him in the enormous task of fulfilling the duties and responsibilities of the Presidency. An American writer who was also a friend of the President visited the White House a few months after Kennedy was installed, and he reported eloquently on the 'intellectual mafia' he found there. In Document 10, an article by Gore

Vidal, the writer recaptures some of the excitement felt in Washington in the Spring of 1961.

The new note was sounded most eloquently by John Kennedy himself in his inaugural address to the American nation. The inaugural address of a new President is always a noteworthy occasion. Some inaugurals have been dull and uninspiring, a portent of the Presidency which followed. John Kennedy's speech will undoubtedly be recalled as one of the most dramatic and inspiring addresses in the history of Presidential inaugurals. In its clear summons to the American people to recover their historic purpose; in its confident assertion to the whole world that the torch had been handed to a new generation, 'tempered by war, disciplined by a hard and bitter peace', the address served notice to every nation, 'whether it wishes us well or ill, that we shall pay any price, bear any burden, meet any hardship, support any friend, oppose any foe to assure the survival and success of liberty'. There were other striking passages in President Kennedy's inaugural to claim the attention of the world community, and the full text printed here, Document 6, deserves careful study for the qualities of boldness, determination but also of sagacity, prudence and political wisdom it displays.

Apart from these invaluable qualities, Kennedy also brought to the Presidency a zest for politics. No doubt this was partly inherited from his father and his grandfathers, but his ability actually to enjoy the burdens of the office struck many close observers as remarkable. He enjoyed the exercise of power, and did not hesitate to accept the responsibilities it thrust upon him. The Presidency of the United States is a lonely eminence, and many Presidents have testified to the awesome, at times terrifying responsibilities it thrusts upon the holders of the office (see Document 24). President Harry Truman accepted the logic of his high office when he placed on his office desk in the White House a small notice which read: 'The buck stops here'. There are some minor decisions a President can delegate, but the important decisions of high policy, particularly in times of crisis, are his alone. At times of crisis he must act quickly or be overtaken by disaster. The documents in this book dealing with the Cuban problem (18 and 19) illustrate the point. Reading his nation-wide address to the American people at the height of the missile crisis in Cuba, one senses the lonely hours the

President must have spent as he prepared to take the responsibility of issuing an ultimatum to the Soviet leaders, thus bringing the world to the brink of nuclear war (see Document 18).

Yet domestic issues in American politics also bring moments of crisis, and the continuing problem of civil rights for Negroes in many parts of the United States requires decisive action from a President. Part IV, dealing with this large and complex problem, shows how President Kennedy faced the difficult challenge presented by the white majority of the southern states in defying the President and also the Supreme Court of the United States (see Documents 13 and 14).

The problems which await a new President of the United States are thus manifold, at times overwhelming. Many expert political analysts have argued that the office carries too much responsibility and imposes too many burdens for one man. There is certainly much evidence in the recent history of the Presidency to justify the view that the office impairs and finally cripples the emotional, mental, or physical capabilities of the President.

Throughout his Presidency, Kennedy was troubled with his back injury. Long hours of work and hard campaigning often brought acute pain, and at times he had to resort to crutches. He never complained about this recurrent burden, and he did not allow it to affect his performance as President or as campaigner for the causes he furthered. Among his qualities was that of courage.

There were other qualities which fortified him for the burdens of office. No political portrait of John Kennedy would be complete without mention of his wit and sense of humour. His brand of humour was a special one, and it was effective because he intuitively grasped the sources of American wit. More often than not his quips were turned against himself when fate, or the American electorate, had given him a sharp knock. His humour was usually ironic, quick to find an amusing side in a human situation where humour was not intended. When he was not guying himself, he would often guy his immediate friends and supporters. His humour could also take the form of a witty turn of phrase in a speech. Usually, the source of the wit was both social and political, skilfully based on the aspirations of his audience. Here he touched one of the richest veins of American humour. Audiences throughout America were quick to appreciate it, and it contributed greatly to his popularity.

Some further qualities of John Kennedy also deserve notice, for they helped to give a certain 'style' to his Presidency and his Administration which had much to do with his immense popularity. John Kennedy was in a certain sense an 'intellectual'. That is to say he enjoyed the world of ideas, of books, of informed opinion, and of political argument on a high plane. However, he was not the sort of intellectual who prefers the inactivity of the scholar's den to the world of action where men strive, compete, argue, and even fight. Kennedy managed to combine the virtues of the man of ideas with those of the man of action. The combination is invaluable in high political office where qualities of vision, but also of decision, are called for (see Document 23).

As a man of ideas who appreciated intellectual qualities in others, Kennedy welcomed the company of those who possessed such qualities. Hence the intellectual entourage which surrounded him in Washington, at some cost to his popularity with members of the United States Congress. Together, however, the group of talented men who joined President Kennedy's Administration in Washington brought a new style to the life of the nation's capital. These men and their wives liked the good things of life. They enjoyed books, music, art, the theatre, good food, and intelligent conversation. Furthermore the President's wife Jacqueline was an ideal hostess for the distinguished gatherings of artists and musicians who were attracted to the life of the capital. The grace, charm, and artistic talent of Mrs. Kennedy did much to make the White House a natural setting for occasions of the utmost elegance. The White House, it should be noted, had not previously been accustomed to such gatherings.

As journalists reported the new Washington scene (or new 'style', to use the current term), the popularity of the Kennedys reached great heights. Clearly, the majority of the American people liked and admired the 'Kennedy style' in Washington, for here was sophistication, wealth and talent (see Document 10).

But the men who gathered about Kennedy were also hard-working, dedicated men. They brought to their allotted tasks a high degree of professional skill. Whether at work or play, they revealed themselves as tough-minded, hard-headed, business-like, professional. These were the men President Kennedy liked to have about him. The President himself, it must be stressed, was more at home with the hard-working and hard-headed side of the new regime than with the musicians and artists who gathered at the White House for elegant soirées. Kennedy was essentially a political animal. He retained an aloofness, a detachment and a capacity for chilly reserve which, taken together, provide some of the answers to how he became President (see Documents 12 and 22).

He enjoyed power, as he freely confessed. He even liked the job of President, though he could on occasion complain, as most individual. One of many continuing demands, for instance, was the need to sift through a mountain of paper work. For this task, however, he possessed special gifts. He had a remarkable ability, as many different witnesses have confirmed, to extract very swiftly the essential ideas or the main argument in a long memorandum. As one journalist observed at the time: 'The guy eats up paper like a termite. . . .'

This unusual ability to extract essential information from a flood of paper work was paralleled by a similar ability in discussion. Many have testified to the remarkable power of President Kennedy to glean from any of his advisers, or from visiting diplomats, precisely the amount of information the visitor could usefully offer. Here again, it was his unusual gift for detecting the essential and a resolute refusal to waste time on inessentials which made Kennedy an efficient instrument for discharging the office of President. These qualities, allied to his ability to take quick, though calculated decisions, went some way towards providing him with the ideal equipment for his high office.

There were other qualities he possessed which, in other contexts, might be thought distasteful. He could be ruthless, as some of his attacks on President Eisenhower make plain. He could also employ other skills and techniques, such as adroitness, cunning, the ability to manoeuvre and the readiness to compromise when he deemed it expedient. Some would deplore these techniques of the successful politician, yet they are part of the stuff of politics and must be accepted as such. John Kennedy accepted them just as he accepted that politics is primarily concerned with power—how it is secured, how retained, how it is used and how it may be abused.

Fortunately, he possessed much more than the average politician's skills for the play of power he was forced to engage in as a head of state. Some observers were quick to note, for instance, that at the time of the Cuban missiles crisis, Kennedy's ultimatum to Soviet Russia left room for manoeuvre to the Russian leaders. Here was a political lesson he had absorbed many years earlier; that if you corner your opponent, it is often wise to leave him an avenue of escape. If you do not, he is forced to hit back at you. In nuclear terms, of course, this would lead to world disaster (see Document 18).

Such political skills John Kennedy possessed in good measure. Yet he also possessed qualities of prudence, caution, of wisdom even, and they emerge in many of the documents in this book. He was a complex man, and he cannot easily be typed. He was a highly intelligent, deeply thoughtful person who was nevertheless not an intellectual in the ordinary sense of that term. He could charm an audience with a polished turn of phrase or a recondite allusion drawn from his wide reading, but he was also an Irish politician with an intuitive flair for exploiting any weakness in his opponent's position. At times he was ruthless, and at other times he was magnanimous. He joked frequently; more often he was deadly serious.

Perhaps the most perceptive observation on John Kennedy was made when he told his wife on one occasion that he was 'an idealist without illusions'. The paradox this suggests is perhaps the central clue for understanding the late John Kennedy's politics. He loved the clash of opposites. His best speeches show this, with their frequent use of strong antithesis. One of the most characteristic phrases in President Kennedy's inaugural address was his succinct call: 'Let us never negotiate out of fear. But let us never fear to negotiate. . . .'

In the storms and stresses of American politics, John Kennedy found just that clash of principles, persons and pursuits which could satisfy this part of his nature. He was a man of ideals who shed his illusions as he struggled to win the highest elective office in a democratic, egalitarian society of nearly two hundred million people.

The methods he used, the speeches he made, and the qualities he evinced are illustrated in the documents given in this book. Taken together, they help to account for the deep sense of shock the world experienced when John Kennedy's career was summarily ended by a senseless act on 22 November 1963.

For students who wish to make a further study of the subjects which occur in this book, the following suggestions may be useful. They are noted under separate headings, but it must be stressed that the subjects are not mutually exclusive. Politics is a total process. Discussions or explanations under one heading often relate to other topics. For the topics suggested below, students may wish to refer first to the documents named. Other documents elsewhere in the book may then be studied for further evidence.

There is now a vast literature on all aspects of American politics, and any good library will contain some of the books. To assist those who wish to have definite suggestions for further reading, a short list of books is given on page 222.

1. *The Office of the President*
Although the Presidential office is nominally filled by one person, the President must rely on a large number of advisers and specialists. This produces various problems in American government. (See Documents, 10, 22, 23.) Despite these many advisers, however, the Presidency is a lonely eminence, and many argue that the office carries far too much responsibility for one person. It can be argued that the office is urgently in need of drastic reforms. (See Documents 25, 27, 18.)

2. *The Mass Media in Politics*
The influence of television, press and the radio at election times provokes much comment today. Is this influence good or bad? Does television play a decisive part in the modern campaign? Can a candidate for office abuse the different media for his own ends? A number of important discussions lead off from these questions. They may be considered separately before a general

discussion on the effects of the mass media is attempted. (See Documents 9, 11, 12, 24.)

3. The Conduct of Foreign Policy

Different systems of government have different methods for the formulation and the conduct of foreign policy. This is of course one of the most vital—if not the most vital—area of governmental responsibility today. The American method for the formulation and conduct of foreign policy is often criticized. What are its strengths and weaknesses? (See Documents 2, 3, 25, 26.)

4. Political Leadership

What qualities do we look for in national leaders today? Could we draw up a list of the ideal qualities for a President of the United States? The difficulties, and perhaps the dangers of attempting to do this can be explored. (See Documents, 4, 6, 10, 12.)

5. Civil Rights in the United States

This problem continues to be one of the most serious and intractable problems in American society. Why is there no easy solution? What progress can be noted during the Kennedy Presidency? (See Documents 13, 14, 27, 28.)

6. What Was the New Frontier?

The question is not an easy one. Was it a programme of action? A group of individuals? A set of campaign promises? A certain 'style' of politics in Washington D.C.? (See Documents 3, 4, 5 and other documents throughout the book.)

7. The 'Crisis' of Democracy

Much writing in recent years has suggested that democracy is going through a crucial phase. The word 'crisis' is sometimes used to refer to this phase. How has this come about? Is it a question of outdated institutions, or lack of leadership, or a lack of participation on the part of the people? (See Documents 1, 4, 8, 25.)

8. *The Meaning of Democracy*

Many definitions of 'democracy' have been offered in the past and in the present. What is *your* definition? Defenders of the American system of government argue that, for all its faults, it is a thoroughly democratic system. What is the evidence for this? (See Documents 2, 4, 14, 16, 26.)

PART I

The Locust Years

The New Frontier spirit did not begin with President Kennedy's inauguration in January 1961. It can be found in his speeches and writings several years before he was elected President. Two examples of those speeches are given in the following pages.

At Loyola College, Maryland in 1958 Senator John Kennedy called for a new set of national priorities and a new direction of the national effort to meet the challenge of Soviet competition in science and technology. The Sputnik series of artificial satellites in 1957 had demonstrated Russian superiority in space exploration. In other areas of technology and science there were further examples of Soviet superiority. Kennedy drew a sharp contrast between the education system of the Soviet Union and that of the United States. Here, as elsewhere, he showed a mastery of the facts.

Clearly, his first task in promoting the call for a new set of national priorities was to show the urgent need for change. Kennedy did so by the frequent use of statistics in his speeches. As a politician, he knew how to use—and he could occasionally misuse—statistics to support his arguments. In this case, the statistics were very unflattering to the United States.

The second speech was given before the Democratic Party of Wisconsin in 1959. Kennedy began with a phrase Sir Winston Churchill once used to underline the failures of the British government in the thirties when Nazism threatened Europe. In Churchill's phrase, the thirties were 'years the locusts have eaten'. Similarly, Kennedy urged in his speech to the Wisconsin Democrats, the years of the Eisenhower Administration were 'years the locusts have eaten'. It will be noticed, however, that Kennedy's speech on that occasion was strongly partisan. He spoke as a Democratic politician to members of the Democratic

Party. In calling for radical changes and a new sense of purpose in America, it was equally part of Kennedy's aim to discredit the legacies of the other party. If he had not succeeded in this, Kennedy's New Frontier might have remained empty rhetoric.

DOCUMENT I. SPEECH BY SENATOR JOHN F. KENNEDY. LOYOLA COLLEGE, BALTIMORE, MARYLAND, 18 FEBRUARY 1958.

We have been assuming that our superior wealth would obtain a superior education for our children. But we have failed to devote more than a tiny fraction—at most 3 per cent—of our national income for this purpose, as contrasted to the Soviets' 10 per cent. We have taken pride in our American inventive genius, but we have too often applied it to gadgets and luxuries, while the Soviets intensified their basic research. We now realize that their traditions of scientific genius are as fully developed as our own. We have comfortably assumed that Marxist dogma and totalitarian repression would produce only stultified minds and ridiculous theories. . . . But tonight we are not laughing at the Sputniks.

There are still others who are convinced that every Russian achievement is simply a crude imitation of our own. But the truth of the matter is that in many areas we are seeking to imitate the Russians. A year ago an American firm asked the Soviets for the right to manufacture a Russian-developed turbo-drill. It could dig oil wells through hard rock ten times as fast as any American drill. Our scientists admire the Soviet Sputniks. Our aeronautical engineers envy their inter-continental jet bombers. Our atomic physicists were impressed by their atomic reactors which produce 5,000 kilowatts of commercial electric power and were in operation nearly four years ago.

In short, we have badly deceived ourselves about Russian intellectual achievements. We have been complacent about our own supposed monopoly of know-how. We have been mistaken about their supposed ignorance, and we have completely failed to understand the crucial importance of intellectual achievements in the race for security and survival.

Our lack of educational achievement is not only costly in terms of scientific weapons. The millions of uncommitted people who hold the key to the future live in the so-called underdeveloped areas. Their greatest need is not arms or propaganda or treaties. They need technicians and technical assistance. They want 'know-how' and they want results. 'We shall see,' Mr. Khrushchev told Southeast Asia during his 1956 tour, 'who has more engineers, the United States or the Soviet Union.'

Students from all of these areas are thronging to the University of Moscow and other excellent Russian institutions. We can hardly expect them to return home as dedicated missionaries for Western ideals. And Russian science may score an even more spectacular success if it devises and exports new ways of irrigating the desert, of exploiting the ocean bed, harnessing jungle rivers, changing the weather, or conquering the plagues afflicting these peoples for centuries.

Who has the best system of education today—the U.S. or the U.S.S.R.? Direct comparisons are difficult and in many ways meaningless, but let us at least be aware of what we are facing.

American students who finish high school complete twelve years of instruction; comparable Russian students receive only ten years. But in those ten years they receive more hours of instruction than American students do in twelve. They attend classes six days a week, ten months a year. They do not enjoy the long summer vacations originated in our system in response to the needs of an agricultural community.

They have approximately seventeen pupils per teacher; we have twenty-seven. Aside from some choice in the selection of foreign languages, they have no elective subjects. The ten-year curriculum includes, on a compulsory basis, five years of physics, five years of biology, four years of chemistry, one year of astronomy and ten years of mathematics up to trigonometry and elementary calculus. Few, if any, twelve-year curricula in America cover as much.

[United States] Atomic Energy Chairman Strauss has stated: 'I can learn of no public high school in our country where a student obtains so thorough a preparation in science and mathematics, even if he seeks it—even if he should be a potential Einstein, Edison, Fermi or Bell.' Only a small fraction of our high school graduates have had even one year of chemistry. An even smaller proportion have had one year of physics. In fact, more than half of our high schools do not teach any physics at all. In the last year for which statistics are available, we produced only 125 new physics teachers—although we have at least 28,000 high schools.

Our lag in mathematics is even more shocking. A Russian child learns how to use a slide-rule in the fifth grade.[1] Their schools last year produced roughly 1·5 million graduates with a thorough training in arithmetic, algebra, geometry, astronomy, trigonometry, and elementary calculus. But we graduated less than 100,000 students with any background of advanced mathematics at all. A survey of 211 prospective elementary school teachers has found that 150 of them had always hated arithmetic. A large proportion of our high schools offer no classes in advanced mathematics or even geometry at all. In the words of Admiral Rickover: 'It is time we faced up to the fact that few American students at age twenty-one or twenty-two know as much after a four-year college course as most European secondary school students know at age eighteen or nineteen.'

What are the facts on the college level? Russian college students receive on the average twice as many instruction hours as Americans. Their students are paid for going to college. Their college education is furnished by the state, and their professors receive pay several times above that awarded most other occupations. As a result Soviet enrollments in institutions of higher learning already exceed our own; and they are growing faster.

The Russians are graduating ten times as many engineers as they did a generation ago—and at a rate two and one-half times greater than the United States. They have enrolled and are graduating more scientists. In addition, their technical institutions turn out tremendous numbers of engineering technicians. Though not fully-fledged engineers, these technicians are invaluable in both the Soviet defense effort and foreign aid program.

What do we do to begin now? We can sit back and wait for the Russian system to collapse. We can hope that education will prove to be their undoing. We can believe that our system will prevail in the long run because our side is right, or because we have more money, or because we have more brains.

On the other hand, we could compete with the Russians by imitating them. We *could* force students to go into science and engineering whether they wish it or not. We *could* draft scientists for governmental research. We *could* arbitrarily restrict the production of consumer goods while we develop new scientific weapons. We could pour unlimited money into special projects without regard to other needs. We could reserve our universities for only those whose talents we seek. We could impose upon our students a workload injurious to their health and personality. We could remove all elements of choice in our high schools and colleges, all influence of public opinion, all vestiges of academic freedom.

I do not say that either of these courses would be doomed to failure. We have followed the course of complacency up to now—and have survived. The Communists have followed the course of control—and they have done well. But I cannot believe that anyone of us believes *either* course should be followed. . . .

The Federal Government must be willing to put into the construction of new schools each year for the next several years at least as much as the cost of one aircraft carrier. But emphasis must not be on quantity alone. Nor must we correct our deficiencies only in the areas of mathematics and science. We are colossally ignorant today about other countries, other languages, other cultures and religions. This is especially true of the Middle East, Africa, Asia and Ceylon and Russia.

We must reverse those trends that see only four out of five of our top students finishing high school—and only two out of the five going on to college. We cannot continue to pay our college faculties and schoolteachers less for improving the minds of our children than we pay plumbers and steam fitters for improving our homes.

Much of the responsibility rests with the Federal Government: for the construction of new facilities on the school and college level, for the financing of new scholarships, teaching materials, and the rest. But the basic responsibility rests with [the] parents of our future leaders and citizens of a democracy under fire. If you prefer more effective detergents or longer [car] tail fins over sending technicians to Latin America, our scientists will be meeting with your requests. If you agree with our former Secretary of Defense that in pure research 'you don't know what you are doing', then our scientists will emphasize more practical gadgets. If you scoff at intellectuals, harass scientists, and reward only athletic achievements, then the future is very dark indeed.

But if, on the other hand, you and I and all of us demand a better education for all, the politicians as well as scientists, for diplomats as well as engineers, for all citizens in all occupations, then we may face the future with hope and with confidence. Let us not despair but act.

Let us not seek the Republican [Party] answer or the Democratic [Party] answer but the right answer. Let us not seek to fix the blame for the past. Let us accept our own responsibility for the future.

NOTE

(1) In the American state school system, children in the fifth grade are aged nine to ten.

THE YEARS THE LOCUSTS HAVE EATEN

In his speech at Wisconsin which follows, Kennedy began with the Churchill phrase and continued his call for a new direction of the national effort. He also used a telling phrase of the great Democratic President Franklin Roosevelt, who referred to the twenties in America as 'eight gray years'. Those years were marked by Republican ascendancy in American politics and featured the Presidencies of Warren Harding, Calvin Coolidge and Herbert Hoover. The decade ended with the most disastrous economic slump in American history.

Kennedy deliberately and carefully fostered in the minds of his audiences a sense that the nineteen fifties in America resembled the nineteen twenties. The twenties were a period of false prosperity and cosy indifference to world problems: three Republican Presidents had lulled Americans into the conviction that all was well and would continue to go well. The crash of 1929 ended the illusion. Similarly, Kennedy argued, the fifties had lulled Americans into a feeling of security and indifference. But international statistics, Kennedy reminded his audiences, showed another picture.

DOCUMENT 2. SPEECH BY SENATOR JOHN F. KENNEDY TO THE
DEMOCRATIC PARTY OF WISCONSIN. MILWAUKEE, WISCONSIN,
13 NOVEMBER 1959.

Twenty-three years ago, in a bitter debate in the House of
Commons, Winston Churchill charged the British Government
with acute blindness to the menace of Nazi Germany, with
gross negligence in the maintenance of the island's defenses,
and with indifferent, indecisive leadership of British foreign
policy and British public opinion. The preceding years of drift
and impotency, he said, were 'the years the locusts have eaten'.

Since January 1953, this nation has passed through a similar
period. When we should have been decisive we, too, were in
doubt. When we should have sailed hard into the wind, we,
too, drifted. When we should have planned anew, sacrificed,
and marched ahead, we, too, stood still, sought the easy way
and looked to the past.

And these, too, were precious years, vital years, to the greatness of our nation, as the thirties were to Great Britain. For on
the other side of the globe another great power was not standing
still and she was not looking back and she was not drifting in
doubt. The Soviet Union needed these years to catch up with
us, to surpass us, to take away from us our prestige and our
influence and even our power in the world community. They
want to 'bury' us, as Mr. Khrushchev says, not necessarily by
war but by possessing the most powerful military establishment,
by boasting the most impressive scientific achievements, by
dominating the most markets and trade routes, by influencing
the most needy or neutral nations through aid and trade and
diplomatic penetration. That is how they hope to 'bury' us—
to extend their sphere of influence, to build respect for the
Communist system, and to prove to the under-developed
countries that their route, the Communist route, is the better
route to industrial development.

And that is what the Soviets have been working on these last
seven years of American drift—'the years the locusts have
eaten'.

I do not say that all was perfection in 1952, under the last
Democratic Administration. But we were in 1952 the unchallenged leaders of the world in every sphere—militarily,

economically, and all the rest. We were building strength and friendships around the world. We were successfully containing the spread of Communist imperialism. And we were the leaders of a Free World community that was united, dynamic, and growing stronger every day.

And now it is 1959. The Russians beat us into outer space. They beat us around the sun. They beat us to the moon. Half of Indo-China has disappeared behind the Iron Curtain. Tibet and Hungary have been crushed. For the first time in history, Russia has its long-sought political foothold in the Middle East —and even an economic foothold in Latin America. And meanwhile we have been forced to abandon the Baghdad Pact, to send Marines to Lebanon and our fleet to Formosa, to endure our Vice-President being spat upon by our former 'Good Neighbors', and to forget our plans for a meaningful NATO.[1]

But all these more dramatic, more publicized events only symbolize what has happened. The seven-year record of Russian gains and American gaps is not a pleasant one. But let us total up the balance sheet. Let us face the facts.

1. *Militarily.* I would not say that the Russians possess an over-all superiority. But we have fallen behind the Soviet Union in the development and production of ballistic missiles—both intercontinental and those of intermediate range. They have surpassed us in the thrust of rocket engines, jet engines, and new types of fuel. They now have more long-range modernized submarines than we do—more in fact, than Nazi Germany had entering World War II—and they may well be pulling ahead of us in numbers of long-range jet bombers with a nuclear bomb capacity. Their continental air defense is thought to be superior, their installations better dispersed, better concealed, and better protected.

There is no doubt, of course, of their superiority in numbers of military manpower, both mechanized and otherwise. All of NATO possesses 21 divisions; the Soviet Union has 175 divisions—2·5 million men. They develop new weapons, General Gavin estimates, twice as fast. They devote twice as much of their resources to military efforts as we do—even though we are twice as rich. They have passed us in the production of military end items, and caught up with us in total military expenditures. They make decisions faster. They seem to utilize their military intelligence better. And they have the largest espionage network in the world's history.

All this they have done—while we, for seven years, have cut our forces, reduced our budgets, held back our missile programs, wasted our money and time and scientific talent, and all the while assuring the American people that we could never be second-best. Democrats in the Congress tried to fight these trends. But we did not control the Defense Department, or the Budget Bureau, or the White House.

2. *In education, science and research,* the story under this Administration has been the same. We harassed our scientists. We overcrowded our schools, we cut back our research. We underpaid our teachers. We let brilliant students drop out after high school. The President would not support an adequate program to construct desperately needed classrooms, at either the public school or college level.

But meanwhile, in the Soviet Union, the Russians were putting twice as much of their resources into education. Their teachers commanded top salaries. Their classrooms contained fewer pupils per teacher. Their curricula were stronger in terms of science, mathematics, physics, and languages. Their most talented students were kept in school. The new Soviet budget puts its biggest increases in science and education.

And as a result, it is estimated that they will soon have three times as many scientists, technicians, and engineers as we do. They are already graduating more. And their brilliant scientific achievements are not only aimed at capturing headlines—they are aimed at capturing the hearts and minds of men. The Philippine Ambassador to the U.N., Carlos Romulo, stated the blunt truth in these words: 'The masses of Asia and Africa have remained quiet for several generations (believing) . . . that the west was invincible. (But) this belief has been shattered. . . . The Soviets sent a satellite into orbit around the earth, another around the sun, and then landed a space rocket on the moon. To under-developed countries these achievements, plus Soviet advances in technology, education, economic and military power, have been little short of miraculous'.

I am convinced that American education and American science, given the necessary funds and effort and leadership, can also work miracles—miracles that could well surpass any the

Russians have ever envisaged. But it will take a new Administration to do the job.

3. The third vital area of competition is *in economic power.* 'Development of Soviet economic might,' said Mr. Khrushchev to the Twenty-first Communist Party Conference, 'will give Communism the decisive edge in the international balance of power.' No area of competition is more vital to our leadership and prestige. But for seven years we have kept our sights low, fluctuating between inflation and recession, handicapped by serious pockets of high unemployment, low purchasing power, and declining farm income, hamstrung by high interest rates and tight money. While our annual average rate of growth was thus roughly 3%, the Russians were up to 6%, twice as high. Their industrial capacity is expanding nearly three times as fast as ours at an annual rate of 9·5%. To be sure, they started a lot further back and they still have a long way to go—but thirty years ago this was a relatively backward nation. If these trends continue, they could increase their defense budget by over 50% in the next seven years with no new strain. Today, despite our greater wealth, they roughly match our contribution for defense, foreign aid, industrial investment and research and development—and their new 1960 budget, a peacetime record, continues this emphasis. In 1958, for example, Russia produced four times as many machine tools as the United States; but we produced fifty times as many automobiles. *We* were way ahead in washing machines, refrigerators, freezers, and TV sets.

Much of our steel output—which has been declining—goes into these autos and appliances, into our homes, office buildings and shopping centers. But practically all of Russia's growing steel capacity—expanding 9% every year—goes into heavy steel shapes and plates—for missiles, planes, and satellites, for submarines and guns, for machinery and tools to expand their own industry at home and those of hopeful nations abroad. Unlike our own, their steel output since 1951 has nearly doubled—and another 50% increase is expected by 1965.

Similar statistics could be cited for Soviet coal, oil and lumber —three American industries with chronic problems that have been badly neglected or postponed under this Administration. Similar data could be cited for Soviet fuel and energy output, and their use of commercial atomic power—and yet we in this country continue to waste great hydro-electric dam sites and delay an already dawdling atomic power program. By 1965 they aim to outproduce us in cement. Already their transportation system is growing faster than ours. They are investing more in their railroads. Soviet jet transports were in operation three years before our Boeing jets began their first commercial service —and Moscow, controlling as it does so many of the best air routes, is rapidly becoming one of the air capitals of the world.

4. *In agriculture*, while we are weakening our farm economy and penalizing our farmers for their increased efficiency and productivity,[2] the Russians—as Mr. Khrushchev made clear— are determined to pass us. Already their agricultural production is expanding faster than their population. Their grain production is up an estimated 30%. Their production of fertilizer has expanded, on the average some 11% every year since 1951. And now they are out to match us in meat, butter, and milk. If our agricultural economy collapses, if our so-called surpluses remain a liability to the taxpayers instead of a blessing to a hungry world, then they, not we, may become the world's greatest arsenal of food. But this need not happen—and I am hopeful that a new Administration and a new Secretary of Agriculture, would see that it does not happen.

5. Finally, look at the contrasting changes *in aid and trade abroad*. When we abruptly abandoned the Aswan Dam in Egypt as economically unfeasible, the Russians went ahead to finance it. When we refuse Latin-American countries loans for their oil development programs, because we think it should be left up to private enterprise, the Russians move in and make the loan. While we starve the Development Loan Fund—our best tool to help the underdeveloped world get on its own feet—the Sino-Soviet bloc has already actually passed us in economic assistance to selected key areas, the potential trouble spots of the world; Indonesia, Ceylon, the United Arab Republic States of Egypt and Syria, Afghanistan, Yemen—and, more recently—Iraq, Nepal and Ethiopia.

The number of Red technicians in other countries has increased at twice the rate of our own. The loans available to underdeveloped nations are at an interest rate below that of any Western source. They sell machinery below cost—they buy strategic commodities above the world price. With less expenditure but more direction, their economic offensive continues to score.

Their cultural program is a part of this. They have spent more than one-half billion dollars over the past few years to send their artists, dancers, and other entertainers all over the world—we have allotted $2 to $3 million a year for this purpose. They spent $50 million on their exhibit at the Brussels World's Fair—we spent $14 million.

This is what has been going on—for seven long years . . . and that is why I say they are 'years the locusts have eaten'. I do not say the picture is all bad. I do not say that the other side of the ledger is all blank. But neither can we afford to ignore these facts and their implication any longer.

I do not think the American people have been made aware of these facts. We have been complacent, self-contented, easy-going. It brings to mind the words of Franklin Roosevelt in 1928, after two terms of Harding and Coolidge. 'The soul of our country,' said F.D.R., 'lulled by material prosperity, has passed through eight gray years.'

'Eight gray years'—'years that the locusts have eaten.' Years of drift, of falling behind, of postponing decisions and crises. And, as a result, the burdens that will face the next Administration will be tremendous. The gaps between ourselves and the Soviet Union will be many—and dangerous—and are still growing. 'If they succeed and we fail,' Mr. Allen Dulles has warned, 'it will only be because of our complacency—and because they have devoted a far greater share of their power, skill, and resources to our destruction than we have been willing to dedicate to our own preservation.'

But it is not too late. For we have in this country all the strength and all the vision and all the will we need—if we will only use them. And perhaps these seven gray years, and these spectacular Russian gains, have awakened us from our sleep. The Russian pennant on the moon has shown us our task. Mr. Khrushchev's confident boasts have outlined our challenge. And I think we can live up to it. I think we can make up for the 'years the locusts have eaten'. I think we can close the gaps and pull ahead.

But to do this we must put an end to this depression of our

national spirit—we must put these dull, gray years behind us and take on the rendezvous with destiny that is assigned us. We must regain the American purpose and promise and become again the creative and purposeful people which, except when we have duped ourselves, we really are. Let us, then, with full production and full employment at home, begin to play our full part in the development of a world of peace and freedom. Let us join the human race.

NOTES

(1) 'Good Neighbors': the Latin American nations of South America. When Vice-President Richard Nixon visited several of the Latin American countries on a goodwill tour in April 1958, he was spat on in Caracas, Venezuela. See Richard Nixon, *Six Crises* (1962), p. 204. Kennedy was somewhat rhetorical in this part of his speech. The United States was never a member of the Baghdad Pact, which collapsed when Iran dropped out in 1959. The United States supported the pact, but also supported the succeeding pact, CENTO (Central Treaty Organisation) embracing Turkey, Iran, Pakistan and Britain.

(2) An over-simplification which nevertheless was likely to appeal to an audience in Wisconsin, part of the great farming belt of the United States. Kennedy implied that when American farmers increased productivity, the Eisenhower government made this the opportunity for taking away farm subsidies, thus raising farm prices.

A CALL TO ACTION

Kennedy made the following speech on the first day of 1960, the year in which he would seek election to the Presidency. The speech was dramatic and challenging, but again shrewdly political. His audience contained a large number of experienced journalists, and it was perhaps no accident that he quoted approvingly from two of the most respected journalists in the United States—Walter Lippmann and Edward R. Murrow.

He also drew skilfully on the more illustrious periods of American history in order to underline once more the drabness of the Eisenhower period. The main purpose of the speech was to stress the need for leadership in the years ahead. That leadership, he implied, was distinctly lacking in the present Administration. Here, and at other points in the speech, the reader can detect that John F. Kennedy was already declaring his 'availability' for the Presidential contest in November of that year.

DOCUMENT 3. SPEECH BY SENATOR JOHN F. KENNEDY. WASHING-
TON, D.C., 1 JANUARY 1960.

Certainly it is time for a change—time for us, in the words of
Walter Lippmann, 'to come alive and to be alert and to show
vigor, and not to keep mouthing the same old slogans, and not
to dawdle along in the same old ruts'.

But the primary point is that, whether we like it or not, this
is a time of change. As a people that set out to change the world
I think we should like it, however difficult the challenges. For
no nation is at its best except under great challenge. The question for us now is whether in a changing world we will respond
in a way befitting 'the land of the free and the home of the
brave'—whether we will measure up to the task awaiting us.

That task is to do all in our power to see that the changes
taking place all around us—in our cities, our countryside, our
economy, within the Western world, in the uncommitted world,
in the Soviet empire, on all continents—lead to more freedom
for more men and to world peace. It is only when the iron
is hot that it can be molded. The iron—the new world—being
forged today is now ready to be molded. Our job is to shape
it, so far as we can, into the world we want for ourselves and
our children and for all men.

This will require that we recapture our national purpose and
redouble our energy. For we seem to have lost both the sense
of the promise of America and the will to fulfil it.

Our Declaration of Independence gave hope to all the world
because it spoke in terms of liberty for 'all men', and not for just
the privileged few. And in every succeeding statement of
American purpose—the Gettysburg Address, Wilson's 'Fourteen
Points', the 'Four Freedoms', the Preamble to the Marshall
Plan legislation, the Preamble to the 'Point Four' legislation—
that same emphasis on the rights and needs of 'all men' has been
present. In different contexts we gave these testaments of
national faith and purpose a specific meaning which led a
grateful humanity everywhere to raise monuments in their
hearts where they honored the very word 'American'. Yet we
cannot rest on those monuments today.

The world is now waiting for us to re-apply the faith we
inherited from our fathers, and to give them a new creative

validity in the uncharted world that surrounds us. The road ahead, to be sure, is a hard road, a road that man has never traveled before, a road full of great obstacles. But America has never long faltered in the face of new challenges.

It is true that in the 1920s we retreated into isolation and stagnation, keeping out new immigrants and new ideas, winking at corruption at home and ignoring dictators abroad—and then finally collapsing into a deep economic depression.

But in the first one hundred days of the New Deal this nation recovered faith in itself and its future. 'Governments can err,' [President] Franklin Roosevelt said, 'Presidents do make mistakes; but the immortal Dante tells us that divine justice weighs the sins of the cold-blooded and the sins of the warm-hearted in different scales. Better the occasional faults of a Government that lives in a spirit of charity than the consistent omissions of a Government frozen in the ice of its own indifference.'

History repeats itself and once again we have lived through a temporary period of national retreat. On too many pressing issues we have had 'a Government frozen in the ice of its own indifference'. Some of these are old problems which we had no excuse to ignore. For so long as there are slums in which people have to live, so long as there are schools that are overcrowded or antiquated or inadequate, so long as there are men in search of decent jobs and homes, so long as there are sick people in need of medical care, so long as anyone suffers discrimination by reason of color, race, religion, or national origin, the work of America is not done. What makes the neglect of these old domestic problems even more inexcusable are the new problems in the world, to meet which a strong, healthy America is so necessary.

'No nation has ever been great that was not called to greatness by its leaders,' Edward R. Murrow has remarked. The signs of our lack of national leadership—of our loss of national vision—are all too clear and present. Not having been called to greatness, not having been shown the great goals and the great dangers ahead, we have, as a nation, gone soft—physically, mentally, spiritually soft. With a tough test facing us for a generation or more, we seem to be losing our will to sacrifice and to endure. We are in danger of betraying our traditions. We have altered our national scale of values.

The slow corrosion of luxury—the slow erosion of our courage—is beginning to show. Nearly one out of every two young American men is rejected by Selective Service today as mentally, physically, or morally unfit for any kind of military service. Still more are screened out after induction. And those taken have been described by one general as 'a disappointing lot' on the whole. The Navy releases statistics showing more men in [our] naval prisons than [in] the entire Norwegian and Danish navies combined—and showing enough men branded deserters to supply a full crew for an aircraft carrier.

What has happened to us as a nation? Profits are up—our standard of living is up—but so is our crime rate. So is the rate of divorce and juvenile delinquency and mental illness. So are the sales of tranquilizers and the number of children dropping out of school.

We are, I am afraid, in danger of losing something solid at the core. We are losing that Pilgrim and pioneer spirit of initiative and independence—that old-fashioned Spartan devotion to 'duty, honor, and country'. We don't need that spirit now, we think. Now we have cars to drive and buttons to push and TV to watch—and pre-cooked meals and prefab houses. We stick to the orthodox, to the easy way and the organization man. We take for granted our security, our liberty, and our future—when we cannot take any one of them for granted at all. The words of Omar Khayyam have become our slogan: 'Take the cash and let the credit go, nor heed the rumble of a distant drum.'

I do not say that we have all weakened. There was, in Korea, a young prisoner of war who was singled out of the line-up upon capture and asked his opinion of General Marshall. 'General George C. Marshall,' he replied, 'is a great American soldier.' Promptly a rifle butt knocked him to the ground. Then he was stood up again to face his captors—and again he was asked: 'What do you think of General Marshall?' And again he gave the same steadfast reply—only this time there was no rifle butt, no punishment at all. They had tested his will, his courage to resist, his manhood—and now they knew where to classify him.

Where will we be classified when our own will and spirit are tested? Among the weak or the tough-minded? Among the

34

lovers of comfort or the lovers of liberty? In this next decade there are not going to be any easy answers. There are not going to be any convenient escapes. There are no lazy ways to place the blame and burden on anyone else. It is all up to us—up to each and every one of us.

In the last few years I have been saying all this to many groups of fellow Americans . . . and everywhere I have found people ready to be shown the new dimensions of our problems, ready to face the full facts of this crisis, ready to pay the price of survival. Travelling around the country, I have become convinced that the American people are ready to enter into full partnership with the newly developing free peoples, ready to accept the Soviet challenge to compete peacefully on all levels, ready to resume, on earth and in space, the pioneering that made America great. I believe that we Americans are ready to be called to greatness.

In 1960 as in 1932 the American people can, as I hope they will, turn from the party of memory to the party of hope. But the fundamental call to greatness is coming not from any party or any person but from history and the hard logic of events. From the lessons we have learned in two world wars, one world depression, and the Cold War, as well as from the history of this republic, the American people will now, I trust, be granted the vision of a new America in a new world. This is the vision without which our people will perish.

THE BIG ISSUE OF THE 1960 ELECTIONS

In July 1960 Senator John F. Kennedy gained the nomination of the Democratic Party for the November Presidential election. The Republican Party selected Richard Nixon, then Vice-President of the United States.

Many political observers and analysts thought that John Kennedy stood little chance of defeating Nixon. There was the question of his Catholic religion, his comparative youth and his apparent lack of experience, all of which contrasted with the experience and most of all the incumbency (as Vice-President) of the Republican candidate. A further period of Republican rule in the White House thus seemed a distinct possibility.

This prospect alarmed many Americans, and not simply

members of the Democratic Party. Many liberals and intellectuals in the United States were acutely concerned at the state of American society, at the lack of direction they associated with the Eisenhower Presidency, and thus at the spectacle the United States presented before world opinion.

Arthur Schlesinger, Junior, has been one of the most articulate liberals in the United States for several years. He was formerly a Harvard professor of history and has always identified himself with the liberal wing of the Democratic Party. In 1960 he wrote a memorandum on what he felt was the crucial issue in the forthcoming election. Originally written for private circulation, the memorandum soon found its way into print and appeared in the American journal *The Progressive* (September 1960) which has always identified itself with forward-looking policies and ideas.

The extracts which follow are taken from that article. The writer's eloquent contrast of the Republican 'consumer-spending' thesis with the true needs of the American nation in 1960 deserves careful note. The argument contained there found its way into several speeches Kennedy gave in the election campaign which won him the Presidency.

DOCUMENT 4. EXTRACTS FROM 'THE BIG ISSUE: A MEMORANDUM' BY ARTHUR M. SCHLESINGER, JR. (FROM *The Progressive*, MADISON, WISC., 3, SEPTEMBER 1960).

On 8 November, the American people will choose a new President. In choosing a new President, they will choose the direction in which they want the United States to move in the next four years.

Now it is widely said that there are no real issues between the two parties—that Democrats and Republicans are in substantial agreement on national policies—that, so far as the main thrust of our national development goes, it really won't make much difference which party is in power after 1960.

It is the contention of this memorandum that there is a profound issue between the parties—an issue of national policy as clear-cut, as far reaching, and as urgent as the one the nation faced in 1932—and that the electorate's decision in 1960 will therefore be of fateful import to our national future.

We are told, of course, that we have prosperity and that we

have peace and that America is the richest and most powerful nation in the world, and that, in the words of Vice-President Nixon, these have been 'the best seven years' of our lives. Yet an increasing number of thoughtful Americans are not satisfied with this cheery statement of our national situation. More and more people have forebodings about the position and prospects of the United States in the decade ahead.

For one thing, the American people are growing restlessly aware that the United States is losing ground in the great world competition with the Soviet Union. We are still ahead in many ways, but this is mainly because we had an earlier start. As fast as we continue to move, the Communists seem to be moving even faster. As a result, they are steadily narrowing the gap between us. Even more alarming, in certain decisive categories of national strength—in new weapons, in the contest for space, in technical education, and in the rate of economic growth—the Soviet Union appears already (in Prime Minister Khrushchev's favorite phrase) to have 'overtaken and surpassed' us.

The Communist competition is a hard fact of life, but it should not by itself be the determining motive of our national policy. We degrade ourselves when we permit the Communist challenge to drive us to do things which we ought to be doing anyway for our own sake. The determining motive of our national policy should be our own ideals and objectives; it should be the pursuit of excellence in our own way of life. This surely is the second source of our anxiety—the spreading awareness that we are even falling behind in making adequate provision for the welfare and opportunity of our own people and for the future of our children and thus of our nation.

Our national population has increased by nearly thirty million since 1950. Recollect for a moment that the total population of the United States in 1860 was only about thirty-one million. We have grown in the last decade by an amount nearly equal to our entire population one hundred years ago.

The annual appearance of three million new boys and girls automatically creates needs for new houses, new schools, new hospitals, new communities; the relentless expansion is straining our facilities to the utmost. And these new boys and girls constitute our most valuable natural resource. Our future will

D
37

depend on their knowledge, their education, their health, their strength, on the opportunities open to them to develop their abilities. From the viewpoint not just of humanity but of national power, these children should be a major object of national investment.

It is precisely these new boys and girls who have been most forgotten during this decade. The Eisenhower Administration has made no systematic effort to enlarge our public services and facilities to keep pace with population growth. Quite the contrary: it has moved in the opposite direction. As a result of deliberate policy, the national government is spending a smaller share of our gross national product on public services and facilities today than it was a decade ago. While our population billows, our national leadership has made only the most feeble effort to enlarge our social overhead—education, medical care, housing, slum clearance, urban and suburban planning, social security, provision for the sick and aging, roads, recreation, water, assistance to distressed classes and areas, resources and energy development—to assure decent opportunities for these new children. The whole quality of our national life is threatened by deterioration.

The sense of bafflement over these slippages at home and abroad is compounded by the fact, constantly reaffirmed to us by our leaders as if it should silence all our doubts, that we remain the richest country known to human history. We are indeed stupefyingly rich. But is this enough? We seem to be dismayingly poor where it counts. We are approaching an annual gross national product of an unimaginable $500 billion a year. Yet out of this we are apparently unable to meet elementary national needs in either our foreign or our domestic policy.

Why is it that our fantastic abundance cannot enable us to remain safely ahead of the Communist world in national power?

Why is it that our fantastic abundance cannot enable us to provide decently for the education, health, and welfare of our own population and the quality of our national existence?

Why are we increasingly tormented as a nation by a series of 'gaps'—the missile gap, the educational gap, the health gap, the poverty gap, the gap between our community life and our national hopes?

What is essential to understand is that these gaps are not separate and unrelated questions. They are all aspects of the underlying issue on which the nation must make its decision in November [1960].

What is this underlying issue? It can be most conveniently tagged by a useful but forbidding phrase cherished by economists. That phrase is the *allocation of resources*. It refers to the uses to which we put our national income. The reason our wealth, staggering as it is, does not give us security in the world or welfare and opportunity at home or hope for our future is to be found in the priorities according to which we allocate that wealth.

There need be no question about the theory which has governed the allocation of resources during most of the last decade. The Eisenhower Administration has again and again stated its conception of our proper national priorities. Dr. Raymond J. Saulnier, chairman of the President's Council of Economic Advisers, recently told the Joint Economic Committee his theory of the American economy: 'Its ultimate purpose is to produce more consumer goods. This is the goal. This is the object of everything that we are working at: to produce things for consumers.' Not to produce better people or better schools or better health or better communities or better opportunities for cultural and spiritual development; not even to produce better guided missiles—but to produce more things to be sold at a profit—more gadgets and gimmicks to overwhelm our bodies and distract our minds.

The President of the United States has repeatedly identified himself with this position. In 1954 he laid down as a major goal of his Administration: 'We will reduce the share of the national income which is spent by the government.' He has been faithful to this pledge. One of the first consequences was the Revenue Act of 1954, which resulted in the transfer of some $7 billion ($10 billion in current dollars) from public to private spending.

President Eisenhower has lost few opportunities to reiterate this belief. As he put it last year: 'Our federal money will never be spent so intelligently and in so useful a fashion for the economy as will the expenditures that would be made by the private taxpayer, if he hadn't had so much of it funneled off into the federal government.' If this statement means anything, it means that the President of the United States seriously thinks that it is more 'intelligent' and 'useful' for the individual consumer to spend money for luxuries and frills, for a second car and a third television set, than for his government to spend it for education, for the fight against poverty, for national defense.

Vice-President Nixon reaffirmed this position in his address of 27 January 1960 in Chicago. He then said, after outlining his view of national objectives, 'We Republicans have unshakable faith that the way to achieve these goals is by the free choice of millions of individual consumers'.

The Eisenhower-Nixon thesis is definite and explicit. It is that the allocation of our resources should be determined by the way the consumer chooses to spend his money; or, to put it another way, that the production of goods and services for sale to consumers properly enjoys first claim on the great bulk of our national wealth and talent.

In saying this, Eisenhower and Nixon imply that responsibility for any subsequent trouble lies with the individual consumer. This implication is characteristically unfair: the individual consumer is the victim, not the cause, of the situation. The moving force behind the Administration thesis is the alliance between the big producers, who live by the creation of consumer wants, and the big advertisers, who have mastered the technology of creating wants where none existed before. It is this alliance which finances and controls the Republican party. Naturally a Republican Administration adopts its view that everything should be sacrificed to the sale of goods on the consumer market.

The Eisenhower Administration seems to have two other reasons for adopting the consumer-spending thesis.

One reason presumably is that the Administration approves of the allocation of resources that results from this thesis; i.e., that it considers our greatest national need today, not more public services, but more things for businessmen to sell to consumers, and consequently favors steering most of our talent and our resources into devising things for consumers and means to persuade consumers to accept them.

The second reason is that the Administration evidently feels that any deviation from the policy of maximizing private consumption would mean the end of a free economy and the destruction of the American way of life. President Eisenhower, in a recent press conference, seemed to say that there was no alternative to the present theory of resources allocation except totalitarianism. 'If you take our country and make it an armed camp and regiment it, why, for a while you can—you might do it with great morale, too, if you could get people steamed up like you did in wars; you might do this thing most—well, in very greater tempo than we are now doing it. . . . Now, I think our people ought to have greater faith in their own system, go ahead on their own.'

There is nothing wrong about wanting to do things for consumers. One great pride of the industrial age is the democratization of comfort. Today all can aspire to decencies and amenities of life which were once reserved for aristocratic and wealthy élites. This represents one of the massive triumphs of history. No one would propose to end all that. Austerity as an end in itself is economic puritanism and to be avoided in all sensible nations.

And free consumer choice is fine. The ideal society would surely be one based on the greatest possible amount of unfettered individual choice.

These objectives are not at issue. The question is rather whether these should be the *dominating* objectives of our society in the next decade as they have been in the last—whether at this moment in history the United States is wise in acting as if the production and consumption of things for sale to consumers should be the central and all-absorbing end of our national existence, to which everything else is to be subordinated. Consumer goods as the underpinning of life are one thing: as the main object of life, quite another. We must decide whether we really want consumer spending to dictate our national priorities.

There are two main objections to the Eisenhower-Nixon thesis that the overriding purpose of our national life ought to be to increase consumer spending.

The first is the *moral* objection. The basic premise of the consumer spending philosophy is that the needs of life are to be fulfilled through material opulence—that the way to achieve the promise of the Declaration of Independence and the

American Revolution is to guarantee to every American pro-
ducer and advertiser, before anything else, the sacred right to
stampede consumers into buying their products. Under the
consumer spending infatuation, we have almost worked ourselves into the state of mind that what cannot pay for itself in
the market is hardly worth doing at all. Emerson summed up
the consumer spending philosophy a century ago when he
wrote, 'Things are in the saddle/And ride mankind'.

Is this really what the Founding Fathers fought the American
Revolution for? Is this what the promise of American life is all
about? Such a view surely represents a debasement of the
American tradition, which is essentially a spiritual tradition.
The ultimate point of American life is not the choking of people
with material luxury. It is the development of the character of
man and of the quality of the life he lives. Our concern has
been not with *things* but with *people*—their identity, welfare,
opportunity, and dignity.

When our President and Vice-President tell us that money
is spent more 'intelligently' and 'usefully' for things rather than
for people, for private indulgence than for public need, and
when one hears those same leaders go on to denounce the
godless materialism of the Communists, it makes one wonder
whether they are not doing so in the name of a godly materialism of our own.

If we accept their view of what America is all about, we will
find ourselves in the condition feared by Walt Whitman: 'It is
as if we were somehow being endow'd with a vast and more and
more thoroughly-appointed body, and then left with little or
no soul.'

The second objection to the Administration thesis is the
policy objection. We are the wealthiest nation in the world; and
some people think that this is enough to insure our strength
and our survival. They could not be more wrong. The true
question is not how much we have, but the uses to which we
put it.

What have been the practical consequences of letting, in
Vice President Nixon's words . . . 'the free choice of millions
of individual consumers' determine the allocation of our
resources and talent?

It is precisely this theory which has produced the contemporary American paradox of public poverty in the midst of private plenty. It is precisely this theory which has given the Eisenhower-Nixon Administration the weird and intolerable conviction that the richest nation in human history cannot 'afford' to do what must be done to maintain national strength and opportunity. . . .

Under the Eisenhower dispensation, where private interests have priority over public interest and everyone's making a fast buck [dollar] is supposed to insure the common good, the public sector takes second place. While consumer goods heap up in our attics and basements, while our advertising system knocks itself out trying to create new wants which will require more and more private goods and services, while more and more of our resources are absorbed in the 'style racket' and 'designed obsolescence' and the consumer-spending merry-go-round, the public framework of society, on which everything else rests, is overstrained by population growth and undercut by neglect. Our cities rot away, our suburbs grow more chaotic, our schools more overcrowded, our teachers more underpaid, our roads more dangerous, our national parks more unkept, our air and our streams more polluted, our law enforcement more harried and unsatisfactory, a sixth of the nation lingers in scandalous poverty, our weapons development and foreign aid grow more tragically inadequate.

To sum up, under the Eisenhower-Nixon philosophy—

We have used our wealth as much as possible for individual purposes and as little as possible for national purposes.

We have used our wealth as much as possible for private purposes and as little as possible for community purposes.

We had dedicated a major share of our national energy to inventing and satisfying consumer 'wants' and expect to build national health, intelligence, and power out of what is left over. . . .

PART II

The New Frontier

Following his nomination by the Democratic Party in July 1960, Presidential candidate John F. Kennedy gave the traditional 'acceptance' speech to the convention. In the course of that speech he introduced the 'New Frontier' theme. The New Frontier, it should be stressed, was announced as a set of challenges to the American people and not as a set of political promises. 'The New Frontier,' Kennedy said, 'sums up not what I intend to offer the American people but what I intend to ask of them. . . .'

His acceptance speech covered many other points suited to the occasion, and accordingly the New Frontier theme was not elaborated in any detail. However on 29 October when the campaign was at its height, Kennedy spoke at length and in considerable detail on the challenges of the New Frontier. That speech is given here and deserves careful study. It will be noted that it was designed to appeal to all sorts of Americans across the fifty States of the Union: to the young and the old; to the town dweller and the farmer; to the industrialist and the worker. The speech also shows how the strategy of the Kennedy campaign for the Presidency had now turned from the essentially negative task of discrediting the Republican record to the positive and more constructive task of presenting a programme to the American people for the many challenges they would face in the future.

DOCUMENT 5. EXTRACTS FROM A SPEECH BY SENATOR JOHN F. KENNEDY AT VALLEY FORGE, PENNSYLVANIA, 29 OCTOBER 1960.

I have said in this campaign that we stand today on a new frontier, a frontier that will demand of us all, in each individual

44

home as well as the White House, qualities of courage and conviction.

For we are moving into the most challenging, the most dynamic, the most revolutionary period of our existence—the 1960s. The next 10 years will be years of incredible growth and change—years of unprecedented tasks for the next President of the United States. . . .

What are the new frontiers of the 1960s? We can foresee earthshaking revolutions abroad—new nations, new weapons, new shifts in the balance of power and new members of the nuclear club. But equally earthshaking, equally fraught with both danger and opportunity, are the new frontiers we face here at home.

First is the new frontier of population. Nineteen hundred and sixty will conclude the largest 10-year growth in the history of our country, a growth which equals the entire population of Poland or Spain. By 1970, our population will have grown to 208 million people, and to maintain an advancing standard of living for that many people, we will have to increase our gross national product to three-quarters of a trillion dollars. That requires a rate of growth no less than 5 per cent a year, and we are not growing at that rate today. To secure full employment to that growing labor force, we will have to find 25,000 new jobs a week. We are not finding those jobs today. To adequately house that tremendous population, we will have to build double the homes we are building today. The new frontier of population holds out the promise of a greater country, greater markets, and greater prosperity, but to meet those opportunities we will have to do better than we have been doing in the past eight years.

Second is the new frontier of longevity. Already nearly 10 per cent of our population is over the age of 65. And medical research, if properly encouraged, is on the verge of new breakthroughs in learning the cause and the cure of cancer, hardening of the arteries, and other diseases that take their toll in the later years of life. But will these extra years be a blessing or a curse? Will they be years of loneliness, poverty, high doctors' bills, and low income? Or will they be years of dignity and security and recognition? Forcing a retired worker to get by on an average social security check of $72 a month or forcing him to take a pauper's oath before he can receive assistance on his medical bills is not the way to meet this challenge. I think we can do better.

Third is the new frontier of education. Pouring into our schools in the next 10 years will be the nearly 51 million children who were born in this country between 1946 and 1958—a number greater than our entire population in 1880. They are already creating the most critical classroom shortage in the history of our public [state] schools. In the 1960s, as that problem grows even more acute, and as this wave grows older, it will spread into our colleges and universities as well. We will need, in this period immediately ahead, to recruit more new teachers for our public schools than all those presently in service combined. We will need to build more college classrooms and dormitories than we have built in the last 200 years. We will need to spend, as a nation, nearly twice as much on education as we are spending today. There is hardly a family in America that does not look forward to a son or daughter in college. But already our colleges are being overcrowded, their costs are rising, and some 50 per cent of our top students do not receive a higher education. There is an old saying that civilization is a constant race between education and catastrophe. In a democracy such as ours, in an age such as this, we must make sure that education wins that race.

Fourth is the new frontier of suburbia, the fastest growing sector of the American population. Most suburban areas have gained more residents in the last 10 years than in the previous century, and that growth will be increased in the sixties. But they are not prepared. Their property tax can ill afford more schools and community facilities. Their transportation network into the city is overloaded already. Their patchwork growth cuts across the jurisdiction and ability of outmoded local government units to meet these problems. But as this urban sprawl continues to consume surrounding lands at a voracious rate, our older cities are already witnessing a tragic phenomenon: suburban slums. The next administration must meet these problems head on.

Fifth are the new frontiers in science and space. We are already racing from the jet age to the space age before meeting the safety, airport development, and other problems of the former. Space exploration that unravels the secrets of our universe, reconnaissance satellites that can replace a hundred U-2 planes watching over all the world, civilian travel in space vehicles, and the rule of law and disarmament in space itself, all these lie ahead of this generation. But we need not look only to the skies for new horizons. The wonders of atomic energy, if properly pursued, promise new miracles in medicine, refrigeration, communication, and power for our homes and factories. The conversion of salt water to fresh water—a project widely neglected in recent years—could end for ever the domestic squabbles between the States of this Nation and the peoples of this earth, and, if we develop it first, mean more to our prestige than all the Soviet moonrockets combined in those under-developed nations where great deserts border great oceans. We must find ways in the sixties of obtaining an endless supply of food and power from the ocean depths themselves and of replacing our dwindling resources of energy from the granite that lies beneath every continent. And, if we can fulfil our hopes for peace, instead of beating our swords into plough-shares, and our spears into pruning hooks, we can convert our bombs into power reactors that will electrify the frontier and the jungle.

Sixth is the new frontier of automation. In every kind of endeavor, in office work as well as industry, in skilled labor as well as common tasks, machines are replacing men, and men are looking for work. And this same revolution of technology is taking place on our farms, where the smallest number of farmers on the smallest acreage in our time has produced the largest crop, and the largest surplus, in our history. Our task is to harness the wonders of automation, to make it a blessing instead of a curse, to use its abundance wisely and generously. We cannot reverse the tide of technology, but lest we become its slave, let us make certain it serves the people.

Seventh and finally is the new frontier of leisure time. The coming of automation, the expansion of labor force, the extension of the lifeline, and the speed of modern transportation, all contribute to the amount of time available to Americans outside of work. What will we do with that time? If we continue to ignore the polluting of our streams, the littering of our national parks, and the waste of our national forests, we will be denying to ourselves and our children a part of their rightful heritage. If more and more cars on more and more super-highways, requiring more and more parking places replace parks and playgrounds and scenic routes, if we permit the great medium of television to occupy more and more of our time with poorer and poorer programs appealing to the lowest common denominator, then we will be failing the public interest on this frontier in the same way that the quality of the old frontier was hurt by those who selfishly seized public lands or razed our great forests.

Twenty-four years ago, Franklin Roosevelt told the Nation: 'I, for one, do not believe that the era of the pioneer is at an end; I only believe that the area for pioneering has changed.' The new frontiers of which I speak call out for pioneers from every walk of life—in the White House in Washington, but in the country at large as well. The challenge can be concealed for a little while, but it cannot be ignored, and it cannot be met by a soft complacency, a satisfaction with things as they are, or a commitment to the past. . . .

The new frontier of which I speak is not too hard for us, neither is it far off. No one need bring it to us; it is here, both its dangers and its opportunities, and we must meet its challenges here, in our hearts.

PRESIDENT KENNEDY'S INAUGURAL ADDRESS

The inaugural address of a newly elected President of the United States is an important State occasion. The President delivers it before the assembled members of Congress, justices of the United States Supreme Court, foreign ambassadors and many dignitaries from all walks of life.

In his inaugural address the President will normally reveal his hopes and intentions concerning the many burning problems he will surely encounter on taking office. The address is thus an occasion for estimating the character and the calibre of a new President.

President Kennedy's inaugural address was widely praised as one of the most eloquent, but also one of the most wise and hopeful ever delivered. Given at a time of international tensions, with a host of unsolved problems at home and abroad, the address combined a spirit of confidence and determination with prudence and caution. President Kennedy quickly dispelled any feelings of easy optimism among his fellow Americans by promising them '. . . the burden of a long twilight struggle, year in and year out . . .' Here, as elsewhere, Kennedy almost seemed to borrow the eloquence of Winston Churchill, the historic figure he so much admired.

In his address, Kennedy spoke not only to his fellow Americans, but also to the poorer nations of the world and to the new states emerging from colonial rule. He also spoke to any 'potential adversaries' of the United States, urging 'that both sides begin anew the quest for peace . . . remembering on both sides that civility is not a sign of weakness, and sincerity is always subject to proof. . . .'

Almost all of Kennedy's qualities can be detected in his inaugural address. In it there was realism, toughness, shrewdness; but also vision, statesmanship and historical depth.

DOCUMENT 6. PRESIDENT KENNEDY'S INAUGURAL ADDRESS. WASHINGTON, D.C., 20 JANUARY 1961.

We observe today not a victory of a party but a celebration of freedom—symbolizing an end as well as a beginning—signifying renewal as well as change. For I have sworn before you and Almighty God the same solemn oath our forebears prescribed nearly a century and three-quarters ago.

The world is very different now. For man holds in his mortal hands the power to abolish all forms of human poverty and all forms of human life. And yet the same revolutionary beliefs for which our forebears fought are still at issue around the globe —the belief that the rights of man come not from the generosity of the state but from the hand of God.

We dare not forget today that we are the heirs of that first revolution. Let the word go forth from this time and place, to friend and foe alike, that the torch has been passed to a new generation of Americans—born in this century, tempered by war, disciplined by a hard and bitter peace, proud of our ancient heritage—and unwilling to witness or permit the slow undoing of those human rights to which this Nation has always been committed, and to which we are committed today at home and around the world.

Let every nation know, whether it wishes us well or ill, that we shall pay any price, bear any burden, meet any hardship, support any friend, oppose any foe to assure the survival and success of liberty.

This much we pledge—and more.

To those old allies whose cultural and spiritual origins we share, we pledge the loyalty of faithful friends. United, there is little we cannot do in a host of co-operative ventures. Divided, there is little we can do—for we dare not meet a powerful challenge at odds and split asunder.

To those new states whom we welcome to the ranks of the free, we pledge our word that one form of colonial control shall not have passed away merely to be replaced by a far more iron tyranny. We shall not always expect to find them supporting our view. But we shall always hope to find them strongly supporting their own freedom—and to remember that, in the past, those who foolishly sought power by riding the back of the tiger ended up inside.

To those peoples in the huts and villages of half the globe struggling to break the bonds of mass misery, we pledge our best efforts to help them help themselves, for whatever period is required—not because the Communists may be doing it, not because we seek their votes, but because it is right. If a free society cannot help the many who are poor, it cannot save the few who are rich.

To our sister [Latin American] republics south of our border, we offer a special pledge—to convert our good words into good deeds—in a new alliance for progress—to assist free men and free governments in casting off the chains of poverty. But this peaceful revolution of hope cannot become the prey of hostile powers. Let all our neighbors know that we shall join with them to oppose aggression or subversion anywhere in the Americas. And let every other power know that this hemisphere intends to remain the master of its own house.

To that world assembly of sovereign states, the United Nations, our last best hope in an age where the instruments of war have far outpaced the instruments of peace, we renew our pledge of support—to prevent it from becoming merely a forum for invective—to strengthen its shield of the new and the weak—and to enlarge the area in which its writ may run.

Finally, to those nations who would make themselves our adversary, we offer not a pledge but a request: that both sides begin anew the quest for peace, before the dark powers of destruction unleashed by science engulf all humanity in planned or accidental self-destruction.

We dare not tempt them with weakness. For only when our arms are sufficient beyond doubt can we be certain beyond doubt that they will never be employed.

But neither can two great and powerful groups of nations take comfort from our present course—both sides overburdened by the cost of modern weapons, both rightly alarmed by the steady spread of the deadly atom, yet both racing to alter that uncertain balance of terror that stays the hand of mankind's final war.

So let us begin anew—remembering on both sides that civility is not a sign of weakness, and sincerity is always subject to proof. Let us never negotiate out of fear. But let us never fear to negotiate.

Let both sides explore what problems unite us instead of belaboring those problems which divide us. Let both sides, for the first time, formulate serious and precise proposals for the inspection and control of arms—and bring the absolute power to destroy other nations under the absolute control of all nations.

Let both sides seek to invoke the wonders of science instead of its terrors. Together let us explore the stars, conquer the deserts, eradicate disease, tap the ocean depths and encourage the arts and commerce.

Let both sides unite to heed in all corners of the earth the command of Isaiah—to 'undo the heavy burdens . . . [and] let the oppressed go free'.

And if a beach-head of co-operation may push back the jungle of suspicion, let both sides join in a new endeavor, not a new balance of power, but a new world of law, where the strong are just and the weak secure and the peace preserved.

All this will not be finished in the first one hundred days. Nor will it be finished in the first thousand days, nor in the life of this Administration, nor even perhaps in our lifetime on this planet. But let us begin.

In your hands, my fellow citizens, more than mine, will rest the final success or failure of our course. Since this country was founded, each generation of Americans has been summoned to give testimony to its national loyalty. The graves of young Americans who answered the call to service surround the globe.

Now the trumpet summons us again—not as a call to bear arms, though arms we need—not as a call to battle, though embattled we are—but a call to bear the burden of a long twilight struggle, year in and year out, 'rejoicing in hope, patient in tribulation'—a struggle against the common enemies of man: tyranny, poverty, disease and war itself.

Can we forge against these enemies a grand and global alliance, North and South, East and West, that can assure a more fruitful life for all mankind? Will you join in that historic effort?

In the long history of the world, only a few generations have been granted the role of defending freedom in its hour of maximum danger. I do not shrink from this responsibility—I welcome it. I do not believe that any of us would exchange places with any other people or any other generation. The energy, the faith, the devotion which we bring to this endeavor will light our country and all who serve it—and the glow from that fire can truly light the world.

And so, my fellow Americans: Ask not what your country can do for you—ask what you can do for your country.

My fellow citizens of the world, ask not what America will do for you, but what together we can do for the freedom of man.

Finally, whether you are citizens of America or citizens of the world, ask of us here the same high standards of strength and sacrifice which we ask of you. With a good conscience our only sure reward, with history the final judge of our deeds, let us go forth to lead the land we love, asking His blessing and His help, but knowing that here on earth God's work must truly be our own.

EARLY MESSAGES TO CONGRESS

President Kennedy sent several messages to Congress in the first months of his Administration. Among the earliest were those containing his proposals for legislation on medical care

for the aged and for federal (that is, government) aid to
education. Both sets of proposals were typical of the 'welfare'
type of legislation Kennedy favoured. But to many members
of the Congress these measures smacked of 'creeping socialism'
and they were vigorously opposed by the many members of
both parties who believed firmly in the virtues of free enterprise and the competitive capitalist system.

The two messages to Congress included here show something
of President Kennedy's techniques for urging the Congress to
consider favourably the legislation he was about to introduce.
He shows his knowledge of the facts, uses official statistics
persuasively and seeks to enlist the co-operation of members
of Congress. He is also concerned to suggest that his proposals
are not in essence 'socialistic' but combine government help
with the traditional American reliance on self-help through
personal endeavour.

President Kennedy's Medical Care for the Aged bill which
followed his message of 9 February was defeated in Congress.
However an amended 'Medicare' bill was passed by Congress
after his death and enacted into law on 30 July 1965. Much
of the New Frontier programme of legislation was realized
only after the President's death. Federal Aid to Education
Acts were also passed in 1965, and reflected the main proposals
outlined in the message to Congress printed here.

DOCUMENT 7. SPECIAL MESSAGES TO CONGRESS FROM PRESIDENT
KENNEDY: I. HEALTH AND HOSPITAL CARE, 9 FEBRUARY 1961.

To the Congress of the United States:
The health of our nation is a key to its future—to its economic
vitality, to the morale and efficiency of its citizens, to our
success in achieving our own goals and demonstrating to others
the benefits of a free society. Ill health and its harsh consequences are not confined to any state or region, to any race,
age, or sex or to any occupation or economic level. This is a
matter of national concern.

More than twenty-five billion dollars a year—over 6 per
cent of our national income—is being spent from public and
private funds for health services. Yet there are major deficiencies in the quality and distribution of these services.

The dramatic results of new medicines and new methods—opening the way to a fuller and more useful life—are too often beyond the reach of those who need them most.

Financial inability, absence of community resources, and shortages of trained personnel keep too many people from getting what medical knowledge can obtain for them.

Those among us who are over 65—16 million today in the United States—go to the hospital more often and stay longer than their younger neighbors. Their physical activity is limited by six times as much disability as the rest of the population. Their annual medical bill is twice that of persons under 65—but their annual income is only half as high.

The nation's children—now 40 per cent of our population—have urgent needs which must be met. Many still die in infancy. Many are not immunized against diseases which can be prevented, have inadequate diets or unnecessarily endure physical and emotional problems.

These and other problems of health care can and must be met. Only a part of the responsibility rests with the federal government. But its powers and resources make its role essential in four areas for improving health care: social insurance, facilities, personnel and research.

Health Insurance for the Aged

Twenty-six years ago this nation adopted the principle that every member of the labor force and his family should be insured against the haunting fear of loss of income caused by retirement, death or unemployment. To that we have added insurance against the economic loss caused by disability. But there remains a significant gap that denies to all but those with the highest incomes a full measure of security—the high cost of ill health in old age. One out of five aged couples drawing Social Security benefits must go to the hospital each year. Half of those going to hospitals incur bills in excess of $700 a year. This is over one-third of the total annual income of a typical couple, more than a modest food budget for an entire year. Many simply do not obtain and cannot afford the care they need.

. . . Congress last year recognized the problem of those needy aged requiring welfare assistance to meet their medical costs.

But now we must meet the needs of those millions who have no wish to receive care at the taxpayers' expense, but who are nevertheless staggered by the drain on their savings—or those of their children—caused by an extended hospital stay.

In our Social Security and [some] Retirement systems we have the instruments which can spread the cost of health services in old age over the working years—effectively, and in a manner consistent with the dignity of the individual. By using these proved systems to provide health insurance protection, it will be possible for our older people to get the vital hospital services they need without exhausting their resources or turning to public assistance. The self-supporting insurance method of financing the cost of such health services is certainly to be preferred to an expansion of public assistance, and should reduce the number of those needing medical care under the public assistance program. The state and local money thus freed should be further used to help provide services not included in this proposal, and to assist those not covered.

For it should be stressed that this is a very modest proposal, cut to meet absolutely essential needs, and with sufficient 'deductible' requirements to discourage any malingering or unnecessary overcrowding of our hospitals.

In essence, I am recommending enactment of a health insurance program under the Social Security system that will provide the following benefits:

First, in-patient hospital services up to 90 days in a single spell of illness, for all costs in excess of $10 per day for the first 9 days (with a minimum of $20), and full costs for the remaining 81 days. Because hospital costs place by far the heaviest and most unmanageable burden on older persons, it is these services that should receive major emphasis in any health insurance program.

Second, skilled nursing home services up to 180 days immediately after discharge from a hospital. To provide an incentive for use of these less expensive facilities, an individual could, in short, receive two days of skilled nursing home care in place of one day of hospital care when this satisfies his requirements.

Third, hospital out-patient clinic diagnostic services for all costs in excess of $20. These services, too, will reduce the need for hospital admissions and encourage early diagnosis.

Fourth, community visiting nurse services, and related home health services, for a limited period of time. These will enable many older people to receive proper health care in their own homes.

I propose that these insurance benefits be available to all persons aged 65 and over who are eligible for Social Security benefits.

This program would be financed by an increase in Social Security contributions of one-quarter of one per cent. each on employers and employees, and by an increase in the maximum earnings base from $4,800 a year to $5,000 which would amply cover the cost of all insurance benefits provided. The system would be self-supporting and would not place any burden on the general revenues.

This program is not a program of socialized medicine. It is a program of prepayment of health costs with absolute freedom of choice guaranteed. Every person will choose his own doctor and hospital.

No service performed by any physician at either home or office, and no fee he charges for such services, would be involved, covered or affected in any way. There would be no supervision or control over the practice of medicine by any doctor or over the manner in which medical services are provided by any hospital. The program is a sound one and entirely in accordance with the traditional American system of placing responsibility on the employee and the employer, rather than on the general taxpayers, to help finance retirement and health costs.

II. FEDERAL AID TO EDUCATION, 20 FEBRUARY 1961.

To the Congress of the United States:
Our progress as a nation can be no swifter than our progress in education. Our requirements for world leadership, our hopes for economic growth, and the demands of citizenship itself in an era such as this all require the maximum development of every young American's capacity.

The human mind is our fundamental resource. A balanced Federal program must go well beyond incentives for investment in plant and equipment. It must include equally determined measures to invest in human beings—both in their basic education and training and in their more advanced preparation for professional work. Without such measures, the Federal Government will not be carrying out its responsibilities for expanding the base of our economic and military strength.

Our progress in education over the last generation has been substantial. We are educating a greater proportion of our youth to a higher degree of competency than any other country on earth. One-fourth of our total population is enrolled in our schools and colleges. This year 26 billion dollars will be spent on education alone.

But the needs of the next generation—the needs of the next decade and the next school year—will not be met at this level of effort. More effort will be required—on the part of students, teachers, schools, colleges and all 50 states—and on the part of the Federal Government.

Education must remain a matter of state and local control, and higher education a matter of individual choice. But education is increasingly expensive. Too many state and local governments lack the resources to assure an adequate education for every child. Too many classrooms are overcrowded. Too many teachers are underpaid. Too many talented individuals cannot afford the benefits of higher education. Too many academic institutions cannot afford the cost of, or find room for, the growing numbers of students seeking admission in the sixties.

Our twin goals must be: A new standard of excellence in education—and the availability of such excellence to all who are willing and able to pursue it. . . .

[The President's legislative proposals in outline:
1. A three-year programme of federal assistance for elementary and secondary school construction and teachers' salaries, to the amount of more than $700 million per annum.
2. A five-year programme of housing loans for State colleges, on the basis of $250 million per annum.
3. A five-year programme of state scholarships for 'talented and needy students' with 25,000 awarded in the first year, rising to 50,000 per annum.

4. Expansion of student loan facilities to increase and extend loans to students.]

GOVERNMENT AND THE PEOPLE

At first glance, President Kennedy's speech at Yale University on 11 June 1962 may appear fairly routine and unimportant. Yet he attached great importance to this speech and spoke in earnest. One of his major concerns as President was to bring the people into closer touch with the government. One of the first tasks, he felt, was to demolish certain myths in the mind of the public concerning the government—its size, its cost, its apparent remoteness. He was also anxious to maintain business confidence in America, on which so much depends. In this speech, therefore, he was also speaking to businessmen at all levels when he distinguished between a mythical element in business confidence and the reality on which it should be based. He was hinting, in fact, that business confidence may easily be based on irrational and superstitious beliefs rather than on the facts.

The speech is therefore a very good example of Kennedy's efforts to tackle persistent problems of American society and of the American economy at their source. It also shows his ability to argue cogently yet clearly on several difficult problems at the same time. It is interesting to conjecture the tortuous length of such a speech had it been attempted by one less gifted than President Kennedy.

DOCUMENT 8. MYTHS RESPECTING AMERICAN GOVERNMENT. SPEECH BY PRESIDENT KENNEDY AT YALE UNIVERSITY, NEW HAVEN, CONNECTICUT, 11 JUNE 1962.

... Mythology distracts us everywhere—in government as in business, in politics as in economics, in foreign affairs as in domestic policy. But today I want particularly to consider the myth and reality in our national economy. In recent months many have come to feel, as I do, that the dialogue between the parties—between business and government—is clogged by illusion and platitude and fails to reflect the true realities of contemporary American society.

I speak of these matters here at Yale because of the self-evident truth that a great university is always enlisted against the spread of illusion and on the side of reality. No one has said it more clearly than your President Griswold: 'Liberal learning is both a safeguard against false ideas of freedom and a source of true ones.' Your role as university men, whatever your calling, will be to increase each new generation's grasp of its new duties.

There are three great areas of our domestic affairs in which, today, there is a danger that illusion may prevent effective action. They are first, the question of the size and shape of government's responsibilities; second, the question of public fiscal policy; and third, the matter of confidence—business confidence or public confidence, or simply confidence in America. I want to talk about all three, and I want to talk about them carefully and dispassionately—and I emphasize that I am concerned here not with political debate, but with finding ways to separate false problems from real ones. ...

Let us take first the question of the size and shape of government. The myth here is that government is big and bad—and steadily getting bigger and worse. Obviously this myth has some excuse for existence. It is true that in recent history each new administration has spent much more money than its predecessor. Thus President Roosevelt outspent President Hoover and, with allowances for the special case of the Second World War, President Truman outspent President Roosevelt. Just to prove that this was not a partisan matter, President Eisenhower outspent President Truman by the handsome figure of $182 billion. It is even possible something of this trend may continue.

But does it follow that big government is growing relatively bigger? It does not, for the fact is for the last fifteen years the federal government—and also the federal debt, and also the federal bureaucracy—has grown less rapidly than the economy as a whole. If we leave defense and space expenditures aside, the federal government since the Second World War has expanded less than any other major sector of our national life—less than industry, less than commerce, less than agriculture, less than higher education, and very much less than the noise about 'big government'.

The truth about big government is the truth about any

59

other great activity: it is complex. Certainly it is true that size brings dangers, but it is also true that size can also bring benefits. Here at Yale, which has contributed so much to our national progress in science and medicine, it may be proper for me to mention one great and little-noticed expansion of government which has brought strength to our whole society: the new role of our federal government as the major patron of research in science and in medicine. Few people realize that in 1961, in support of all university research in science and medicine, three dollars out of every four came from the federal government. I need hardly point out that this has taken place without undue enlargement of government control, that American scientists remain second to none in their independence and in their individualism. . . .

Next, let us turn to the problem of our fiscal policy. Here the myths are legion and the truth hard to find. But let me take as a prime example the problem of the federal budget. We persist in measuring our federal fiscal integrity today by the conventional or administrative budget, with results which would be regarded as absurd in any business firm, in any country of Europe or in any careful assessment of the reality of our national finances. The administrative budget has sound administrative uses. But for wider purposes it is less helpful. It omits our special trust funds; it neglects changes in assets or inventories. It cannot tell a loan from a straight expenditure; and worst of all, it cannot distinguish between operating expenditures and long-term investments. . . .

Still in the area of fiscal policy, let me say a word about deficits. The myth persists that federal deficits create inflation and budget surpluses prevent it. Yet sizable budget surpluses after the war did not prevent inflation, and persistent deficits for the last several years have not upset our basic price stability. Obviously deficits are sometimes dangerous, and so are surpluses. But honest assessment plainly requires a more sophisticated view than the old and automatic cliché that deficits automatically bring inflation.

There are myths also about our public debt. It is widely supposed that this debt is growing at a dangerously rapid rate. In fact, both the debt per person and the debt as a proportion of our Gross National Product have declined sharply since the

Second World War. In absolute terms the national debt increased only 8 per cent, while private debt was increasing 305 per cent and the debts of state and local governments increased 378 per cent. Moreover, debts, public and private are neither good nor bad, in and of themselves. Borrowing can lead to over-extension and collapse, but it can also lead to expansion and strength. There is no single, simple slogan in this field that we can trust.

Finally, I come to the problem of confidence. Confidence is a matter of myth and also a matter of truth, and this time let me take the truth of the matter first.

It is true—and of high importance—that the prosperity of this country depends on assurance that all major elements within it will live up to their responsibilities. If business were to neglect its obligations to the public; if labor were blind to all public responsibility; above all, if government were to abandon its obvious, and statutory, duty of watchful concern for our economic health—if any of these things should happen, then confidence might well be weakened and the danger of stagnation would increase. This is the true issue of confidence.

But there is also the false issue; and its simplest form is the assertion that any and all unfavorable turns of the speculative wheel, however temporary and however plainly speculative in character, are the result of—and I quote—'lack of confidence in the national administration'. This, I must tell you, while comforting, is not wholly true. Worse, it obscures the reality, which is also simple. The solid ground of mutual confidence is the necessary partnership of government with all of the sectors of our society in the steady quest for economic progress.

Corporate plans are not based on a political confidence in party leaders, but on an economic confidence in the nation's ability to invest and produce and consume. Business had full confidence in the administrations in power in 1929, 1954, 1958 and 1960, but this was not enough to prevent recession when business lacked full confidence in the economy. What matters is the capacity of the nation as a whole to deal with its economic problems and its opportunities.

The stereotypes I have been discussing distract our attention and divide our effort. These stereotypes do our nation a disservice, not just because they are exhausted and irrelevant, but above all because they are misleading, because they stand in the way of the solution of hard and complicated facts. It is not new that past debates should obscure present realities. But the damage of such a false dialogue is greater today than ever before simply because today the safety of all the world—the very future of freedom—depends as never before upon the sensible and clear-headed management of the domestic affairs of the United States. . . .

PART III

The Kennedy Style in Washington

The New Frontier was many things. It was a set of ideas, policies and attitudes: it was also a group of men who approached their allotted tasks with unusual skills and expertise. Many of those who assisted John Kennedy in 1960 in his campaign for the Presidency joined him as members of his Administration or as aides in the White House. President Kennedy also recruited others in order to form his Administration, and it was widely noted that the criterion for selection was excellence, not the re-payment of political debts.

These highly talented men reflected different aspects of the President himself. There was the cool, calculating Kennedy who scrutinized opinion polls and who knew how and where to mend his political fences. There was the ex-journalist with an instinct for a good news story and who knew the art of timing if, as President, he was about to release important news. There was the Harvard product with a genuine interest in ideas and in the great figures of history. And there was the hardworking executive who knew how to organize his day—and his leisure —in order to get through a mountain of work or an impossible schedule. Beyond that, there was always the witty, occasionally profane Irishman who enjoyed the good things of life and whose sense of humour lurked at the most solemn state occasions.

The extracts in this section are selected in order to convey different aspects of the Kennedy 'style' in Washington, as journalists currently described it. The reader may find a number of the names mentioned in the following extracts unfamiliar. This is to some extent unavoidable, but the identities are less important here than the *characteristics* of the men Kennedy chose to assist him. The first piece, by Karl Meyer, describes the men around Kennedy in 1960, many of whom joined him in the White House later.

DOCUMENT 9. 'THE MEN AROUND KENNEDY', BY KARL E. MEYER (FROM *The Progressive*, MADISON, WISC., SEPTEMBER 1960).

The first thing you notice in Senator John F. Kennedy's office are the books. In his suite in the Old Senate Office Building . . ., the clutter of books on desk-tops and shelves conveys the flavor of the seminar and school room. The titles are in odd juxtaposition; *The Blowing Up of the Parthenon,* by Salvador de Madariaga (with an author's inscription), leans uncomfortably against John F. Parker's *1001 Jokes, Stories, Gems of Wisdom by and about Politicians.*

But the combination, though it might jar a librarian, is wholly congruous in the office which serves as the nerve centre for the Democratic Presidential nominee's campaign staff. The men behind Kennedy, and the campaign they are waging, compose a study in the artful coexistence of scholarship and political savvy, of sweaty electioneering and intellectual detachment.

Those in Washington who have been reporting politics since the days of Coolidge can recall nothing quite like the cadre of intense and earnest young men who are advance agents for Kennedy's New Frontier. There is little of the amateur zest that enlivened (and plagued) Adlai Stevenson's two Presidential campaigns, and the smell of Kansas City cigar smoke which trailed the Truman camp is equally absent.

Instead, the advisers around Kennedy are very much like the candidate himself. 'His would probably be a no-nonsense type of Administration,' wrote Kennedy's biographer, James Mac-Gregor Burns, 'run by men young, dedicated, tough-minded, hard-working, informed, alert, and passionless. The place would be quiet, taut, efficient—sometimes, perhaps, even dull.'

At this moment, it is not dull. . . . Amid the clatter of typewriters, the jangle of telephones, and the parade of petitioners, a momentary disorder masks the inner discipline of what is probably this century's best organized Presidential campaign. . . .

But the sense of order and discipline should not deceive. This is not an organization built along military lines. As President

Eisenhower has so well tutored the nation, the methods of the military mean that subordinates have formidable powers of discretion, and that the Chief is to be vexed only by the weightiest problems on which his adjutants cannot agree. In contrast, the Kennedy organization seems to be modelled on that of an efficient corporation in which the president is in full command of his junior executives (and of those relatives who confuse the business with a family firm). Each department—sales, personnel, public relations—is headed by an alert official who handles his chores with a maximum of rationalism and a minimum of fuss. But the department heads cannot commit the top executive, as drill sergeants so often have seemed to commit the Commander-in-Chief in the Eisenhower years. 'There is nobody that can commit the Senator,' an aide stresses, 'except the Senator himself. . . .'

The nearest thing to a general manager in the campaign organization is the candidate's brother, Robert Kennedy. Television has made the thirty-four-year-old Bobby familiar, and there is no need to belabor his mastery of hearing-room technique, his knowledge of the arcana of the Teamsters Union, and his terrier-like relentlessness in pursuit of prey.[1] The degree of his determination to elect his brother President has sometimes awed and sometimes dismayed bystanders. But with all his virtues as an organizer, Bobby has his limitations, and they have been concisely summed up by Richard Rovere.

'Good political staff work,' wrote Rovere in *The New Yorker* 'is always a joy for politicians to behold, but in essence it is a virtue that has more in common with neat bookkeeping than it has with the more serious and interesting aspects of politics. Much of the efficiency for which Bobby is admired is the product of neat bookkeeping and little else.'

Working in tandem with Bobby is the organization's chief policy and planning executive, Theodore Sorensen, who has been irreverently dubbed by some reporters as the Keeper of the Image. In some ways Sorensen affords a fascinating contrast with the Senator. His roots are in the farmbelt state of Nebraska, his lineage is a melting-pot composite of Danish and Russian, his political heritage is the Republican progressivism of the late George Norris, and his religion is Unitarian. But the similarities between Ted Sorensen and his chief are a measure of how the

65

intellectual distance between Nebraska and Massachusetts has shrunk. Since he joined the Kennedy staff in 1953, Sorensen has acquired influence because he has an almost intuitive affinity with the thinking of the Senator. His admirers relate that it is almost impossible to distinguish his speech-writing prose from that of the Senator.

The thirty-two-year-old Sorensen, who is listed only as a 'clerk' on the Senate payroll, shares with Kennedy a coolness of demeanor, a brisk efficiency, a detached liberalism, and a deep involvement in the game of politics. As a much-traveled organizer in the field, and as the Senator's chief speech writer, he has made many friends, but his single-minded devotion to his chief has made some enemies who do not hesitate to call him tough and ruthless.

There is less controversy about Lawrence F. O'Brien, the skilled professional who heads up the sales force. O'Brien, who at forty-five is practically the Methuselah of the group, is a one-time advertising and public relations man from Springfield, Massachusetts. A veteran of the 1952 and 1958 Kennedy Senatorial campaigns, O'Brien manages everything from campaign buttons and tea parties to the larger problems of organizational policy. It is he who presides over the field headquarters in the IBM building, where presumably 'Elect!' has replaced the 'Think!' placards. As author of [a] fourteen-page *Kennedy for President, State Organization Procedure*, O'Brien has won praise from discerning students of such matters.

The chief of public relations is Pierre Salinger, age thirty-five, who lends the only note of raffishness to the upper echelons of the Kennedy organization. In a fine old tradition, Salinger works in an atmosphere of exuberant confusion. One reporter described him as a 'rather frenetic figure surrounded by cigar stubs and notes on the backs of envelopes'. While the Harvard Business School might disapprove, the working Press has developed an affection for this onetime night editor of the San Francisco *Chronicle* who retains something of the rumpled tradition of the city room.

Salinger's offbeat quality is neatly balanced by Archibald Cox, a pipe-smoking, tweedy figure who looks every bit a Harvard professor, which he is. In the jargon of industrial personnel, Cox's role might be described as research and development, or perhaps as new product promotion. He is the official envoy to the campus, and his task is to corral both scholars and ideas into the Kennedy fold. At forty-eight, Cox is another old-timer in the organization, a senior citizen who worked in both the Justice and Labor Departments under Franklin D. Roosevelt. . . .

An impressive-looking roster of intellectuals works with and under Cox, but appearances can be misleading. Although Republican oratory is already dwelling on the diabolic powers of Professors John Kenneth Galbraith and Arthur M. Schlesinger, Jr., both of Harvard, there is little evidence that either wields great influence at the summit. To be sure, Kennedy has extended a tactful welcome to these and other eminent academicians, but the power of the professors has been largely overstated. Certainly they enjoy nothing like the status of such Roosevelt brain trusters as Berle, Tugwell, and Moley, and they have less influence than they had in the Stevenson campaigns.

In the Kennedy organization, as in any efficiently run corporation, it is the hardheads and not the eggheads who are in charge. The decisive, day in, day out influence is exercised by a group of junior executives with special expertise who are close to the center of power. Mike Feldman is typical of the group in background and temperament. He joined the Senator in 1957, after serving apprenticeship as a law professor, a Securities and Exchange Commission official, and as counsel for the Senate Banking and Currency Committee.

Working closely with Feldman is Richard N. Goodwin, who is following a familiar New Deal itinerary. He came to Washington two years ago from Harvard Law School to serve as law clerk to Supreme Court Justice Felix Frankfurter. Goodwin, twenty-eight years old, joined Kennedy as a kind of utility infielder after working on the staff of the House Legislative Oversight Committee, where he did most of the legwork on the exposé of rigged television quiz shows. Nonetheless, he is surprisingly unjaundiced and is widely regarded as one of the ablest and best-natured of the Kennedy crew.

The specialist in labor and immigration problems has been Ralph Dungan, 37, who after a season in the fusty offices of the Bureau of the Budget became a Kennedy appointee on the Senate Labor Committee. Dungan has now been detailed to organizational work. One of the key advisers on civil rights questions is Harris L. Wofford, Jr., thirty-four, a widely-travelled law professor at Notre Dame who has been a legal assistant to the Civil Rights Commission. Timothy E. J. (Ted) Reardon, Jr., who has been with Kennedy since his days in the House, is administrative assistant. A onetime advertising man, Reardon handles the mail and is a stickler for keeping [political] fences trim in Massachusetts.

This sampling of Kennedy associates—the list could go on *ad tedium*—is not intended as a 'who's who' or as an inside dopester's key to Kennedy confidential. Rather, it is meant to point to a question: Does the ascent of the Kennedy star herald something new in American politics?

The answer is an emphatic and incontrovertible yes. . . .

[Yet] it is not age that sets the Kennedy men apart. Rather it is that the Senator's young pros have taken the skills and attitudes found in sophisticated managerial circles and have applied them to the most backward of the social arts, politics.

To start with, there is the matter of education. In times past, professional politicians looked with scorn or amused tolerance on the airs of the educated, and in campaigns, professorial advisers might be hustled out of sight as if they were run-down relatives. But prevailing attitudes have changed, and Kennedy has turned against the anti-intellectual tradition with a vengeance. Not only does the candidate himself look as if he strolled to the hustings straight from Harvard Yard, but his predominantly Ivy League staff contains enough former football prayers to assemble a respectable scrimmage.[2] One Kennedy organizer, Byron 'Whizzer' White, was an All-American at the University of Colorado—but, characteristically, 'Whizzer' was also a Rhodes scholar at Oxford.

Unlike the hacks and ward-heelers of bygone days, Kennedy's men have brought to politics a zeal for professionalism, a respect for learning, and a capacity for mastering intricate legislative problems. The seriousness and high purpose of the Kennedy forces command respect. But there is an important added ingredient: in sharp contrast to other eggheads in politics, the Kennedy men also display an unnerving tough-mindedness concerning the means and ends of politics.

As to methods, the young pros show an almost brutal realism

about the techniques of mass communication. The whole apparatus of persuasion and manipulation—opinion polls, Trendex ratings, and market research—holds few secrets from the Senator's staff. Although there is a healthy skepticism based on experience regarding the accuracy of polls, there is also a healthy respect for the power of television (in the language of the trade) 'to project an image.'

Something of the same hard realism extends to the organization's thinking on the ends of politics. The approach is pragmatic and problem-solving, and there is a marked distrust for the doctrinaire enthusiast. In many ways the approach is admirable and refreshing because of its flexibility and candor. But it is a managerial approach. As in a corporation, problems are seen primarily in a technical rather than a moral light, and the response is distinctly in terms of the head, not the heart. Significantly, 'cool' is the ubiquitous adjective used to describe Kennedy and his staff.

In terms of conviction, the broad consensus is liberal in the Northern Democratic sense of the word. In both foreign and domestic policy, the Kennedy men lean more to the views of Adlai Stevenson than to those of either Dean Acheson or Senator Lyndon Johnson. . . .

It is liberalism expressed without florid rhetoric—or for that matter, without noticeable passion. It reflects a world that despairs of 'final solutions' and confronts the future less with youthful ardor than with stoic resolve. . . .

NOTES

(1) The President's brother Robert earned a national reputation for his work as a lawyer investigating charges of racketeering in the labour unions of the United States. Many of the hearings were on television. President Kennedy appointed his brother Attorney General of the United States in 1961. He is now a United States Senator for the State of New York.

(2) *Ivy League.* The term is commonly applied to eight men's colleges near the east coast of the United States, each of them distinguished and together forming an elite among eastern universities. They are Harvard, Yale, Princeton, Cornell, Brown, Dartmouth, Columbia and the University of Pennsylvania.

THE NEW MAN IN THE WHITE HOUSE

In the following article Gore Vidal, an American playwright and a friend of the President, described the atmosphere in the

White House in the Spring of 1961. Naturally the writer's style is literary in flavour, but Vidal stood for election to Congress on one occasion and shows some keen insights into politics in the article.

DOCUMENT 10. 'A NEW POWER IN THE WHITE HOUSE', BY GORE VIDAL (FROM *The Sunday Telegraph*, LONDON, 9 APRIL 1961).

Until last month, I had not been at the White House since 1957 when I was asked to compose a speech for President Eisenhower.

At that time the White House was as serene as a resort hotel out of season. The corridors were empty. In the various offices of the Executive Branch (adjacent to the White House) quiet grey men in waistcoats talked to one another in low-pitched voices.

The only colour, or choler, curiously enough, was provided by President Eisenhower himself. Apparently, his temper was easily set off; he scowled when he stalked the corridors; The Smile was seldom in evidence. Fortunately, Eisenhower was not at the White House often enough to disturb that tranquility which prevailed, no matter what storms at home, what tragedies abroad.

Last month I returned to the White House . . . to find the twentieth century, for good or ill, installed. The corridors are filled with eager youthful men, while those not young are re-vitalised.

As Secretary of Commerce Luther Hodges (at 62 the oldest member of the Cabinet) remarked: 'There I was a few months ago, thinking my life was over. I'd retired to a college town. Now . . . well, that fellow in there,' (he indicated the President's office) 'he calls me in the morning, calls me at noon, calls me at night: why don't we try this? Have you considered that? Then to top it all he just now asks me: where do you get your suits from? I tell you I'm a young man again.'

In the White House Press room reporters are permanently gathered. Photographers are on constant alert and television cameramen stand by, for news is made at all hours.

The affection of the Press for Kennedy is a phenomenon, unique in Presidential politics. There is of course the old saw that he was a newspaperman himself (briefly) and also that he is a bona fide intellectual (on the other hand, the working Press is apt to be anti-intellectual); but, finally, and perhaps more to the point, Kennedy is candid with the Press in a highly personal way. He talks to them easily. There is no pomp; there is little evasion; he involves them directly in what he is doing. His wit is pleasingly sardonic.

Most important, until Kennedy it was impossible for anyone under 50 (or for an intellectual of any age) to identify himself with the President. The intellectual establishment of the country opted for 'alienation,' the cant word of the '40s and '50s, and even those who approved of this or that President's deeds invariably regarded the men set over us by the electorate as barbarians (Truman's attack on modern painting, Roosevelt's breezy philistinism, Eisenhower's inability to express himself coherently on any subject.)

For 20 years the culture and the mind of the United States ignored politics. Many never voted; few engaged in active politics. Now everything has changed. From Kenneth Galbraith to Robert Frost the intellectual establishment is listened to and even, on occasion, engaged to execute policy.[1]

Close to, Kennedy looks older than his photographs. The outline is slender and youthful, but the face is heavily lined for his age. On the upper lip are those tiny vertical lines characteristic of a more advanced age.

He is usually tanned from the sun, while his hair is what lady novelists call 'chestnut', beginning to go grey. His eyes are very odd. They are, I think, a murky, opaque blue, 'interested' as Gertrude Stein once said of Hemingway's eyes, 'not interesting'; they give an impression of flatness, while long blond eyelashes screen expression at will. His long fingers tend to drum nervously on tables, on cups and glasses. He is immaculately dressed; although, disconcertingly, occasional white chest hairs curl over his collar.

The smile is charming even when it is simulated for the public. Franklin Roosevelt set an unhappy tradition of happy warriors and ever since his day our politicians are obliged to beam and grin and simper no matter how grave the occasion. Recently, at a public dinner, I had a thoughtful conversation with Harry Truman. He was making a particularly solemn point when suddenly, though his tone did not change, his face jerked abruptly into a euphoric grin, all teeth showing. I thought he had gone mad, until I noticed photographers had appeared in the middle distance and it was the old politician's unconscious reflex to smile.

As for Kennedy's personality, he is very much what he seems. He is withdrawn, observant, icily objective in crisis, aware of the precise value of every card dealt him. Intellectually, he is dogged rather than brilliant.

Over the years I've occasionally passed on to him books (including such arcana as Byzantine economy) which I thought would interest him. Not only does he read them but he will comment on what he's read when I see him next. . . .

After his defeat for the Vice-Presidential nomination in 1956, he was amused when I suggested that he might feel more cheerful if every day he were to recite to himself while shaving the names of Vice-Presidents of the United States, a curiously dim gallery of minor politicians. Also somewhat mischievously, I suggested he read *Coriolanus* to see if he might find Shakespeare's somewhat dark view of democracy consoling. Mrs. Kennedy and he read it aloud one foggy day at Hyannisport. Later he made the point with some charm that Shakespeare's knowledge of the democratic process was, to say the least, limited.

On another occasion, I gave him the manuscript of a play of mine whose setting was a nominating convention for the Presidency. He read the play with interest; his comments were shrewd. I recall one in particular, because I used it.

'Whenever,' he said, 'a politician means to give you the knife at a convention, the last thing he'll say to you as he leaves the room is, "Now look, Jack, if there's *anything* I can do for you, you just let me know!" That's the euphemism for "you're dead".'

Kennedy's relationships tend to be compartmentalized. There are cronies who have nothing to do with politics whom he sees for relaxation. There are advisers whom he sees politically but not socially.

The only occasion where personal friendship and public policy appear to have overlapped was in his appointment of the perhaps-not-distinguished Earl Smith (our envoy to Cuba at the time of the débâcle) as Ambassador to Switzerland. The Swiss, who are acting for the United States in Havana, complained loudly. To save the President embarrassment, Earl Smith withdrew.

With chilling correctness, Kennedy is reported to have called in the Swiss Ambassador to Washington and given him a lesson in international diplomacy (i.e. you do not criticise publicly an ambassadorial appointment without first apprising the Chief of State privately). The Ambassador left the White House shaken and bemused.

Kennedy is unique among recent Presidents in many ways. For one thing, he has ended (wistfully, one hopes for ever) the idea that the Presidency is a form of brevet rank to be given to a man whose career has been distinguished in some profession other than politics or, if political, the good years are past and the White House is merely a place to provide some old pol [politician] with a golden Indian Summer.

Yet the job today is, literally, killing, and despite his youth, Kennedy may very well not survive. A matter, one suspects, of no great concern to him. He is fatalistic about himself. His father recalls with a certain awe that when his son nearly died during the course of a spinal operation he maintained a complete serenity: if he was meant to die at that moment he would die and complaint was useless.

Like himself, the men Kennedy has chosen to advise him have not reached any great height until now. They must prove themselves *now*. Government service will be the high point of their lives, not an agreeable reward for success achieved elsewhere. Few men have the energy or capacity to conduct successfully two separate careers in a lifetime, an obvious fact ignored by most Presidents in their search, often prompted by vanity or a sense of public relations, for celebrated advisers.

Nearly half the electorate was eager to find Kennedy and his regime 'Intellectual' (in the popularly pejorative sense), given to fiscal irresponsibility and creeping socialism. There is, by the way, despite the cries of demagogues, no operative Left in the United States. We are divided about evenly between conservatives and reactionaries. But now, having experienced his Administration, it is evident even to the most suspicious of the Radical Right that Kennedy is not an adventurous reformer of the body politic, if only because this is not the time for such a reformation, and he knows it.

73

Essentially, he is a pragmatist with a profound sense of history, working within a generally liberal context. Since the United States is in no immediate danger of economic collapse, and since there is no revolutionary party of Left or Right waiting to seize power, our politics are firmly of the Centre. The problems of the nation are lagging economic growth, which under an attentive Administration can be corrected, and foreign affairs, where the United States vis-à-vis Russia remains a perhaps-insoluble problem, but one Kennedy is addressing with coolness and a commendable lack of emotion. . . .

Perhaps the most distressing aspect of the last Administration was President Eisenhower's open disdain of politics and his conviction that 'politician' was a dirty word. This tragic view is shared even now by the majority of the American electorate, explaining the General's continuing appeal. Time and time again during those years one used to hear: 'O.K., so he is a lousy President, but thank God he isn't a politician!'

Kennedy, on the other hand, regards politics as an honourable, perhaps inevitable, profession in a democracy. Not only is he a master of politics, but he also takes a real pleasure in power. He is restless; he wants to know everything; he wanders into other people's offices at odd hours; he puts in a 10-hour office day; he reads continuously; even, it is reported, in the bathtub.

Most interesting of all, and the greatest break with tradition, have been his visits to the houses of friends in Washington, many of them journalists. Ever since the first protocol drawn up for George Washington, the President seldom goes visiting and never returns calls. Kennedy has changed that. He goes where he pleases; he talks candidly; he tries to meet people who otherwise might never get through the elaborate maze of the White House, in which, even during the most enlightened Administration, unpleasant knowledge can be kept from the President.

Inevitably, the President is delivered into the hands of an inner circle which, should he not be a man of considerable alertness and passion, tends to cut him off from reality. Eisenhower was a classic case. It was painfully evident at Press conferences that he often had no knowledge of important actions taken by the Government in his name; worse still, he was perhaps the only President not to read newspapers. The result was that when crises occurred, despite all his good intentions he was never sufficiently aware of the nature of any problem to have a useful opinion on its solution.

Only by constant study and getting about can a President be effective. As Harry Truman once remarked, despite the great power of the office, it was remarkably difficult to get anything done. 'You tell 'em what you want and what happens? Nothing! You have to tell 'em five times.'

The reason for this seeming disobedience is due, partly, to the hugeness of the Federal Government and, partly, to the fact that no matter what a President wants there are those who will oppose him within his own Administration. Most Presidential staffs inevitably take advantage of their President, realising that in the rush of any day's business he will make many decisions and requests which he cannot possibly follow up. Kennedy, however, has already shown an unusual ability to recall exactly what he requested on any subject and the impression he gives is of a man who means to be obeyed by his staff.

'He is deliberately drawing all the threads of executive power to himself,' remarked one close adviser. The cumbersome staff system of the Eisenhower Administration has been abandoned in favour of highly personal relationships between President and advisers. No one's function is ever clearly defined. The President moves men from project to project, testing them, extracting new points of view.

Not only is this a useful way of getting the most out of his staff, but it also ensures, rather slyly, Kennedy's own unique position at the centre of the web of power: he alone can view and manipulate the entire complex of domestic and international policy. No one in his Administration may circumvent him because none can master more than a part of the whole.

This ultimate knowledge of the whole is power, and finally, the exercise of power is an art like any other. There is no doubt of John Kennedy's mastery of that art. He is a rare combination of intelligence, energy and opportunism. Most important, he is capable of growth. He intends to be great.

What he will accomplish depends largely upon his ability to rally the bored and cynical Western world, to fire the imagination of a generation taught never to think of 'we' but only of 'I'. There are fragile signs (the warm response to the 'Peace Corps'), and favourable omens (popular approbation reflected in polls)

that a torpid society has at last been stirred by its youthful
leader. If true, in the nick of time. Civilisations are seldom
granted so vivid a second chance.

(1) Kenneth Galbraith. A Harvard professor of economics who accepted the
post of Ambassador to India in President Kennedy's Administration. A
prolific writer with the characteristic New Frontier interest in literature and
the arts.
Robert Frost. President Kennedy invited the late Robert Frost, one of
America's best loved poets, to read a poem at the Presidential inaugural
ceremonies on 20 January 1961. Although snow and bitter weather marred
the reading, the ageing poet recited his poem from memory rather than read
it. The presence of the poet at the inaugural was symbolic of the new attitude
in the White House towards literature and the arts.

KENNEDY'S RELATIONS WITH THE PRESS

The importance of good press relations for a modern President
need hardly be stressed. As an ex-journalist himself, Kennedy
had a particular interest in the Press, not only in the United
States, but in Europe and elsewhere. Some of President
Kennedy's techniques for maintaining good relations are shown
in the following pages. The reader will see that despite his
unusual knowledge of the American Press, John Kennedy was
not always successful in maintaining good relations.

Theodore Sorensen, from whose book *Kennedy* (1965) the
following extract was taken, served as a close adviser to John
Kennedy from 1953 to 1963. He was a legislative assistant and
speech writer for Senator Kennedy up to 1960 and from 1961
to the President's death was a Special Counsel to the President.
Sorensen was undoubtedly closer to the late President than any
other adviser or consultant, with the possible exception of the
President's brother Robert. In the following extract and elsewhere in this book, Sorensen's intimate knowledge of President
Kennedy is everywhere apparent.

The book *Profiles in Courage* mentioned in the first paragraph
was written by Senator Kennedy in 1955, when he was con-
valescing from a serious operation to his back. The work is a
series of essays on examples of political courage in history. The
essays deal chiefly with men who stood against their own friends

and supporters or against public opinion in defence of what they held to be right. When it appeared in 1956 the book was an instant best seller.

DOCUMENT 11. EXTRACTS FROM *Kennedy*, BY THEODORE SORENSEN (HODDER & STOUGHTON AND HARPER & ROW, 1965): I. KENNEDY'S RELATIONS WITH THE PRESS. (CHAP. XII, PP. 310–316.)

The gap between public opinion and the public interest, which had been the theme of *Why England Slept* and *Profiles in Courage*, became a theme of John Kennedy's campaign, Inaugural and first State of the Union Message in what he regarded as an age of dangerous complacency. He recognized his obligation to 'lead, inform, correct and sometimes even ignore constituent opinion, if we are to exercise fully that judgment for which we were elected.' And no problem of the Presidency concerned him more than that of public communication—educating, persuading and mobilizing that opinion through continued use of the political machinery, continued travelling and speaking and, above all, continued attention to the mass media: radio, television and the press.

John Kennedy knew the newspaper profession as few politicians knew it. He had served two brief stints as a working reporter. He often considered purchasing a newspaper once he left public life. He discussed with a reporter how the low quality of most typography could be improved. He numbered several Washington newsmen among his closest friends. He mingled with them informally and formally, socially and professionally, and enjoyed both joking with them and talking seriously with them, just as he did with fellow politicians. His wife was a former newspaperwoman for the old Washington *Times Herald*, and his father had passed on to him a flair for public relations and some painful lessons of experience. Many of John Kennedy's good friends in the journalism fraternity, in fact, had been his father's harshest critics, and many of his father's newspaper friends became the President's harshest critics.

During his long quest for the Presidency, Kennedy had been helped by his unusual accessibility to reporters. He knowingly timed his major campaign releases to meet their a.m. and p.m.

deadlines, sometimes evaluated a speech draft as if he were writing the headlines, and subjected himself to more interviews, press conferences, 'backgrounders' and assorted other news gatherings than his opponents in both parties combined. Political reporters were impressed by his candid and never exaggerated review of the potential delegate and electoral count. In the White House Pierre Salinger was superb, but Kennedy was his own best Presidential press secretary. His activities, aims, announcements and family dominated the news, and exclusive interviews with the President, once a rare event in journalism, took place almost daily.

Yet there remained a curious dichotomy in his attitude towards the press. He regarded newsmen as his natural friends and newspapers as his natural enemies. He was more concerned about a news column read by thousands than a newscast viewed by millions. He both assisted and resented the press corps as they dogged his every footstep. He had an inexhaustible capacity to take displeasure from what he read, particularly in the first half of his term, and an equally inexhaustible capacity to keep on reading more than anyone else in Washington. He always expected certain writers and publications to be inconsistent and inaccurate, but was always indignant when they were. While he fortunately grew insensitive to old critics, he remained unfortunately too sensitive to new ones. He could find and fret over one paragraph of criticism deep in ten paragraphs of praise. He dispensed few favors to his journalistic friends, but ardently wooed his journalistic foes. He had an abhorrence of public relations gimmicks, but was always acutely aware of what impression he was making.

Few, if any, Presidents could have been more objective about their own faults or objected more to seeing them in print. Few, if any, Presidents could have been so utterly frank and realistic in their private conversations with reporters and so uncommonly candid in public—but few, on the other hand, could have been so skilful in evading or even misleading the press whenever secrecy was required. Finally, few, if any, Presidents could have been more accessible and less guarded with individual reporters and editors—or more outraged when anyone else 'leaked' a story.

If there is a logical inconsistency in these attitudes, it stems from similar inconsistencies in political life. The President knew that the fairness, if not the favoritism, of the reporters covering his campaign had helped to elect him—but he also knew that the overwhelming proportion of editors and publishers had been out to defeat him. He valued the role of the press in calling his shortcomings to his attention—but that did not make him enjoy it any more than any proud man.

This was not simply a matter of 'image'. The public and posterity would judge him and his program on the basis of the 'news', and, he felt, more on the basis of the written than the spoken word. He needed to know, therefore, what was being written and how he could make it, if not more favorable, at least more objective and accurate.

At the heart of it all was an attitude he had expressed to me as Senator when complimenting me on my friendships with Massachusetts reporters. 'Always remember,' he had added, 'that their interests and ours ultimately conflict.' From 1957 through 1960 through 1963, John Kennedy's tide of favorable publicity, only some of which he stimulated, helped build his popularity. Certainly it irritated his opponents. But gradually the conflict to which he referred, which had nothing to do with partisan loyalties or charges of a 'one-party press', grew clearer to both of us, particularly in the White House:

. As President, in order to promote his program and his re-election, he was required to use the newspapers and other media, and the newsmen resisted and resented the feeling of being used. 'He wants us as a cheering squad,' complained one reporter. Indeed he did.

. As President he sought to control the timing of his announcements with a view to obtaining maximum effectiveness. His best interests, even on many nonsecurity matters, often required at least temporary secrecy, either to protect proposals that were still in the discussion stage, and too weak to face public fire, or to give a helpful element of surprise and initiative to his actions. But the best interests of the news media, even on many security matters, required penetration of that secrecy. They had to publish something every day or week, regardless of whether it was speculative, premature or wholly invented.

. As President he preferred to correct his errors before they were exposed—the press preferred to expose them before they could be corrected. 'We're looking for flaws,' was the way one White House reporter summed up his role, 'and we'll find them. There are flaws in anybody.' When the newspapers erred, however, as they sometimes did, Presidential corrections or even press retractions rarely had the impact of the original story.

. As President he wanted as much privacy as possible for his personal family life, but these were subjects on which the press wanted as much publicity as possible, and his attractive, photogenic family and his own good looks had led to much of his favorable publicity in the pre-Presidential days.

. As President his progress in many areas was often characterized by small, dull or complex steps, but newspaper headlines in the same areas more often dwelt on the simple, the sensational and the controversial. Good news, when printed, would reflect more favorably on a President—but 'bad news is news,' he said ruefully, 'and good news is not news, so [the American people] get an impression always that the United States is not doing its part.' The press was far more interested in finding out, for example, who in the government or among our allies had disagreed with the President than who had agreed. Criticism and dissent invariably made bigger and better headlines and columns than praise; and two and one-half million honest civil servants were not nearly so newsworthy as one sinner.

. As President, finally, he preferred to decide for himself which were the major issues requiring decision and when, but newspaper stories could blow up minor, premature, past or even nonexistent subjects into issues in the national mind. Kennedy never doubted the accuracy of Oscar Wilde's observation: 'In America the President reigns for four years, but Journalism governs forever.'

All these differences of perspective posed a conflict of interest, and, with a greater degree of tolerance each year, the President philosophically made up his mind to accept it. 'I think that they are doing their task, as a critical branch,' he smilingly said of the press one day, 'and I am attempting to do mine; and we are going to live together—for a period—and then go our separate ways.'

The President shrugged off many but by no means all critical stories with a favorite phrase: 'They have to write something.' Those who wrote in 1961 that he was enamored with power, he noted, were writing in 1962 that he was pre-occupied with its limitations. Those who wrote in 1962 that he was not spending his popularity were writing in 1963 that he had taken on too many fights. The reporter who purported to discover 'Kennedy's Grand Strategy' for an article in 1962 wrote another article, in the same magazine one year later, entitled 'The Collapse of Kennedy's Grand Design.'

Moreover, he never lost sight of the invaluable assistance to him of a free and critical press. While Mr. Khrushchev's 'totalitarian system has many advantages as far as being able to move in secret,' he said,

> . . . there is a terrific disadvantage in not having the abrasive quality of the press applied to you daily. . . . Even though we never like it, and even though we wish they didn't write it, and even though we disapprove, there isn't any doubt that we could not do the job at all in a free society without a very, very active press.

. . . His White House and other aides were also directly accessible to the press. In addition we found it necessary, in order to answer the President's inquiries intelligently, to read a number of newspapers and read them early. JFK—as he persuaded the headline writers to call him, not to imitate FDR but to avoid the youthful 'Jack'—read (actually, in about half of these, skimmed) all the Washington newspapers (*Post, Star, News*), most of the New York newspapers (*Times, News, Wall Street Journal*, at one time the *Herald Tribune* and frequently most of the others), the Baltimore *Sun*, the Boston *Globe* and *Herald*, the Miami *Herald*, the Chicago *Sun-Times*, the Chicago *Tribune*, the Philadelphia *Inquirer* and the St. Louis *Post-Dispatch*. When he had time, he read the sports page as well as the front page, social news as well as financial news, and gossip columnists as well as political columnists. He liked the political cartoonists—Herblock, he remarked, was 'very gentle' with him—and he enjoyed the humor and 'inside dope' columns, at times using privately but never maliciously nicknames he had read in those columns such as 'Nose McCone' and 'By George McBundy'.

His magazine reading was equally omnivorous, covering at least sixteen periodicals ranging from the *New Republic* to *Sports Illustrated*, from *The New Yorker* to *Look*. He read several British newspapers and journals as well, and regarded *Le Monde* in Paris as one of the world's finest. But he did not read everything. He almost never read *U.S. News & World Report*, for example, on the grounds that it had little news and less to report. Yet he read *Time* and *Newsweek* faithfully, and felt their condensed hindsight often influenced their readers more than daily newspaper stories. He had his disagreements with *Newsweek*, particularly on the inaccuracies in its political gossip column in the front, but *Time* was a source of special despair. For, unlike *U.S. News & World Report*, it was well written. Unlike the Chicago *Tribune*, it gave an impression of objectivity. And unlike its White House correspondent, Hugh Sidey, unlike its sister publication *Life*, and unlike what he regarded to be its general pre-1961 attitude toward his efforts, it was in John Kennedy's opinion consistently slanted, unfair and inaccurate in its treatment of his Presidency, highly readable but highly misleading.

II. KENNEDY AND TELEVISION. (CHAP. XII, pp. 328–331.)

A good 'image' on television is also of the utmost importance to a modern President. Kennedy was well aware that he owed a great deal of his popularity with the American people to his favourable television 'image'. The following section from Theodore Sorensen's book *Kennedy* shows how concerned Kennedy was to maintain this. As Sorensen shows, the President was also aware that 'over-exposure' might reduce his effectiveness on television, and that 'selectivity' was the best technique.

His greatest weapon, [President Kennedy] said more than once, was television. In addition to his televised press conferences and major speeches, the President frequently issued short statements on television from the White House and frequently granted special television interviews. The most successful of these was the unprecedented interview conducted by the three White House correspondents for the major networks, carried by all three to a vast audience in December, 1962. The President did not influence the choice of either questioners or questions. Relaxed in his White House rocker, with no crowd of reporters and with the cameras concealed, he spoke with astonishing candor—almost as if he thought it was a private interview— about his views of the office, his problems and prospects.

Receiving a tremendously favorable response, he planned to make such an appearance an annual affair, and scheduled a repeat performance for December 17, 1963, the anniversary of the first.

The President, along with his office, his family and the White House, also became the focal point of numerous television (and illustrated magazine and newspaper) presentations which took the public behind the scenes. Reporters and cameramen stayed with the President in the course of his duties to record 'a typical day at the White House,' 'the actual conduct of Presidential business' or 'how a decision is made.' These were not simulated conferences of the types staged in the previous administration. The reporters or cameramen were simply there when one of us walked into the President's office for a wholly unrehearsed meeting.

At times some of his associates were less comfortable than he with a camera crew observing their deliberations, and at times we found it necessary to make somewhat oblique references to sensitive subjects. Some critics worried that the presence of cameramen or reporters might interfere with the natural flow of business. But the President never permitted their presence when it might do so.

Kennedy wearied of hearing how much more often Roosevelt had used the 'fireside chat,' and he discovered with much satisfaction that the faulty memory of its advocates had greatly exaggerated its frequency. The largest number of 'fireside chats' FDR ever made in one year was a total of four in his first year, at the depth of the depression and the height of his influence. He made only four more during the rest of his entire first term, and throughout his whole tenure averaged fewer speeches from his office than Kennedy.

The danger which limited both men was not too much 'exposure', as commonly assumed, but too little selectivity. 'The public psychology,' wrote Roosevelt, expressing sentiments which Kennedy shared, 'cannot . . . be attuned for long periods of time to a constant repetition of the highest note in the scale.'

I do not believe it is possible to 'overexpose' a President like Kennedy. Nevertheless he could not, with any effectiveness, go on the air to denounce Big Steel, or announce a Cuban quarantine, or deliver some momentous message, every month of the year. Selectivity was the key—selecting the right time and the right issues. As a commander saves his biggest guns for the biggest battles, so Kennedy limited his direct national appeals to situations of sufficient importance to demand it and sufficiently fluid to be helped by it. 'I made a speech,' he reminded a press conference pressing him for a 'fireside chat' on the Birmingham race conflict, 'the night of [the] Mississippi [crisis] at Oxford, to the citizens of Mississippi and others, that did not seem to do much good. But this doesn't mean we should not keep on trying. . . . If I thought it would [be helpful], I would give one.'

At a time when the international scene and the narrow Congressional margins required all the national unity possible, John Kennedy saw no sense in dividing the country, or alienating the Congress, or squandering his limited political capital, or feeding the fires of extremism, or wearing out his welcome and credibility, by making major appeals for public support on too many hopeless or meaningless causes. 'I will,' he said early in his term, 'at such time as I think it most useful and most effective . . . use the moral authority or position of influence of the Presidency. . . . [But] I want to make sure that whatever I do or say does have some beneficial effect.'

The most frequent complaint concerned Kennedy's refusal to employ more 'fireside chats' on behalf of legislation.[1] He employed them where he thought they would help vital measures, such as the Test Ban Treaty, tax cut and civil rights bill and in his constant televised plugs for foreign aid, and he was also willing to fight for his program in press conference statements and speeches around the country. But he had to consider the legislative and political consequences of opening a 'cold war' with a Congress that was in fact passing, even though it was very slowly passing, most of the important Kennedy items and that was nominally a Democratic Congress. If the public response, in the form of letters to the Congress, turned out to be light—as it usually is—he would have laid his full prestige on the line for little gain and possibly a loss.

The fact is that a large proportion of the public will not listen to a Presidential speech on legislation. Many of those who do listen will resent being deprived of their regular TV entertainment. Very few of the rest feel sufficiently affected to write their Congressmen, and very few Congressmen feel sufficiently flexible to change their votes on the basis of such letters. Most members of Kennedy's bipartisan opposition in Congress were either irrevocably committed by the time a speech was in order or permitted by their seniority and safe districts to disregard both the President and any petitions he might stir up. No speech could have sprung the Department of Urban Affairs free from the House Rules Committee, for example. No speech could have obtained passage of an education bill which lacked a hundred or more votes, or made the Senate Finance Committee move faster, or forced Louisiana's Otto Passman to like foreign aid.

Whether on TV or the public platform, John Kennedy's major speeches were an important tool of his Presidency. He often used them to define administration decisions in specific terms and to convey those decisions throughout the government as well as the rest of the world. We had more experts from whom to seek ideas, facts and first drafts than we had in pre-Presidential years. Next-to-final drafts were usually submitted to the agencies concerned for their views, and this process was so slow on foreign policy speeches that McGeorge Bundy would gather all concerned around a table in his office to go over the draft in one sitting. We also had more pressures for completing authorized texts well ahead of time for advance distribution and foreign-language translation. . . .

He took pains to have a hand in every major Presidential paper—not only speeches but letters, messages and proclamations—and he still chose his words and their arrangement with great care. His Inaugural, State of the Union, American University, United Nations, Berlin, Irish Parliament and other addresses, including those televised from the White House on Cuba and civil rights, earned him the title of one of the most articulate and eloquent Presidents since Lincoln. . . .

NOTE

(1) Actually Roosevelt had rarely used his 'fireside chats' to put pressure on the Congress, and often delivered them when Congress was out of session.

THE MIND OF JOHN KENNEDY

Arthur Schlesinger Junior, from whose book *A Thousand Days* the following extracts are taken, is specially qualified to record the Presidency of John Kennedy. He was formerly a Harvard professor and has an outstanding reputation as the historian of President Franklin Roosevelt's New Deal in the thirties. He thus brings the historian's perspective and a scholar's intellect to the task of recording the Presidency.

Apart from this, Arthur Schlesinger has been an active liberal Democrat for many years. In 1960 he supported Kennedy for President and was often asked to contribute drafts for speeches during the campaign. In 1961 Kennedy invited Schlesinger to serve in the White House as Special Assistant to the President. From then on Schlesinger was a close adviser as well as a personal friend of the President. The following extracts from Arthur Schlesinger's book on the Presidency of John Kennedy deal with the qualities of mind the author observed in the President, together with illuminating insights into Kennedy's complex character. Because of his close association with the late President, Arthur Schlesinger states in the Foreword to his book that his account does not claim to be a definitive history but rather a personal memoir. Students of history may note that there are advantages to this as well as drawbacks.

DOCUMENT 12. EXTRACTS FROM *A Thousand Days: John F. Kennedy in The White House*, BY ARTHUR M. SCHLESINGER, JR. (ANDRE DEUTSCH and HOUGHTON MIFFLIN, 1965). (CHAP. IV, PP. 104–113.)

The Kennedy Mind: I
Kennedy was called an intellectual very seldom before 1960 and very often thereafter—a phenomenon which deserves explanation.

One cannot be sure what an intellectual is; but let us define it as a person whose primary habitat is the realm of ideas. In this sense, exceedingly few political leaders are authentic intellectuals, because the primary habitat of the political leader is the world of power. Yet the world of power itself has its intellectual and anti-intellectual sides. Some political leaders find exhilaration in ideas and in the company of those whose trade it is to deal with them. Others are rendered uneasy by ideas and uncomfortable by intellectuals.

Kennedy belonged supremely to the first class. He was a man of action who could pass easily over to the realm of ideas and confront intellectuals with perfect confidence in his capacity to hold his own. His mind was not prophetic, impassioned, mystical, ontological, utopian or ideological. It was less exuberant than Theodore Roosevelt's, less scholarly than Wilson's, less adventurous than Franklin Roosevelt's. But it had its own salient qualities—it was objective, practical, ironic, skeptical, unfettered and insatiable.

It was marked first of all by inexhaustible curiosity. Kennedy always wanted to know how things worked. Vague answers never contented him. This curiosity was fed by conversation but even more by reading. His childhood consolation had become an adult compulsion. He was now a fanatical reader, 1200 words a minute, not only at the normal times and places but at meals, in the bathtub, sometimes even when walking. Dressing in the morning, he would prop open a book on his bureau and read while he put on his shirt and tied his necktie. He read mostly history and biography, American and English. The first book he ever gave Jacqueline was the life of a Texan, Marquis James's biography of Sam Houston, *The Raven*. In addition to *Pilgrim's Way*, *Marlborough* and *Melbourne*, he particularly liked Herbert Agar's *The Price of Union*, Samuel Flagg Bemis's *John Quincy Adams*, Allan Nevins's *The Emergence of Lincoln*, Margaret Coit's *Calhoun* and Duff Cooper's *Talleyrand*. He read poetry only occasionally—Shakespeare and Byron are quoted in a looseleaf notebook he kept in 1945–46—and by this time fiction hardly at all. His wife does not remember him reading novels except for two or three Ian Fleming thrillers, though Kennedy himself listed *The Red and the Black* among his favorite books and, at some point in his life, had read most of Hemingway and a smattering of contemporary fiction—at least *The Deer Park*, *The Fires of Spring* and *The Ninth Wave*. His supposed addiction to James Bond was partly a publicity gag, like Franklin Roosevelt's supposed affection for 'Home on the Range.' Kennedy seldom read for distraction. He did not want to waste a single second.

He read partly for information, partly for comparison, partly for insight, partly for the sheer joy of felicitous statement. He delighted particularly in quotations which distilled the essence of an argument. He is, so far as I know, the only politician who ever quoted Madame de Staël on 'Meet the Press'.[1] Some quotations he carried verbatim in his mind. Others he noted down. His loose-leaf notebook of 1945–46 contained propositions from Aeschylus ('In war, truth is the first casualty'), Isocrates ('Where there are a number of laws drawn up with great exactitude, it is a proof that the city is badly administered; for the inhabitants are compelled to frame laws in great numbers as a barrier against offenses'), Dante ('The hottest places in Hell are reserved for those who, in a period of moral crisis, maintain their neutrality'), Falkland ('When it is not necessary to change it is necessary not to change'), Burke ('Our patience will achieve more than our force'), Jefferson ('Widespread poverty and concentrated wealth cannot long endure side by side in a democracy'), de Maistre ('In all political systems there are relationships which it is wiser to leave undefined'), Jackson ('Individuals must give up a share of liberty to preserve the rest'), Webster ('A general equality of condition is the true basis, most certainly, of democracy'), Mill ('One person with a belief is a social power equal to ninety-nine who have only interest'), Lincoln ('Public opinion is everything. With it nothing can fail, without it nothing can succeed'), Huck Finn on *Pilgrim's Progress* ('The statements are interesting—but steep'), Chesterton ('Don't ever take a fence down until you know the reason why it was put up'), Brandeis ('Unless our financial leaders are capable of progress, the institutions which they are trying to conserve will lose their foundation'), Colonel House ('The best politics is to do the right thing'), Churchill ('The whole history of the world is summed up in the fact that, when nations are strong, they are not always just, and when they wish to be just, they are often no longer strong. . . . Let us have this blessed union of power and justice'), Lippmann ('The political art deals with matters peculiar to politics, with a complex of material circumstances, of historic deposit, of human passion, for which the problems of business or engineering do not provide an analogy'), Hindu proverbs ('I had no shoes—and I murmured until I met a man who had no feet'), Joseph P. Kennedy ('More men die of jealousy than cancer') and even John F. Kennedy:

> To be a positive force for the public good in politics one must have three things; a solid moral code governing his public

actions, a broad knowledge of our institutions and traditions and a specific background in the technical problems of government, and lastly he must have political appeal—the gift of winning public confidence and support.

There emerges from such quotations the impression of a moderate and dispassionate mind, committed to the arts of government, persuaded of the inevitability of change but distrustful of comprehensive plans and grandiose abstractions, skeptical of excess but admiring of purpose, determined above all to be effective.

His intelligence was fundamentally secular, or so it seemed to me. Of course, this was not entirely true. As Mary McCarthy wrote in her *Memories of a Catholic Girlhood*, 'If you are born and brought up a Catholic, you have absorbed a great deal of world history and the history of ideas before you are twelve, and it is like learning a language early; the effect is indelible'. Though Kennedy spent only one year of his life in a Catholic school, he assimilated a good deal of the structure of the faith, encouraged probably by his mother and sisters. He often adopted the Catholic side in historical controversy, as in the case of Mary Queen of Scots; and he showed a certain weakness for Catholic words of art, like 'prudence', and a certain aversion toward bad words for Catholics, like 'liberal'. Nor could one doubt his devotion to his Church or the occasional solace he found in mass.

Yet he remains, as John Cogley has suggested, the first President who was a Roman Catholic rather than the first Roman Catholic President. Intellectual Catholicism in American politics has ordinarily taken two divergent forms, of which Senator Thomas J. Dodd of Connecticut and Senator Eugene McCarthy of Minnesota were contemporary representatives. Kennedy was different from either. Unlike Dodd, he lived far away from the world of the Holy Name Societies, Knights of Columbus and communion breakfast. He discussed the princes of the American Church with the same irreverent candor with which he discussed the bosses of the Democratic party. When a dispatch from Rome during the 1960 campaign suggested Vatican doubts about his views of the proper relationship between church and state, Kennedy said, 'Now I understand why Henry VIII set up his own church'. His attitude toward life showed no traces of the black-and-white moralism, the pietistic rhetoric, the clericalism, the anti-intellectualism, the prudery, the fear of Protestant society, which had historically characterized parts of the Irish Catholic community in America. On the other hand, he did not, like Eugene McCarthy, seek to rescue Catholic doctrine from fundamentalism and demonstrate its relevance to the modern world. Catholic intellectuals recognized his indifference to the scholastic tradition, and some disdained him for it.

Kennedy's religion was humane rather than doctrinal. He was a Catholic as Franklin Roosevelt was an Episcopalian—because he was born into the faith, lived in it and expected to die in it. One evening at the White House he argued with considerable particularity that nine of the ten commandments were derived from nature and almost seemed to imply that all religion was so derived. He had little knowledge of or interest in the Catholic dogmatic tradition. He once wrote Cogley, 'It is hard for a Harvard man to answer questions in theology. I imagine my answers will cause heartburn at Fordham [University] and B. C. [Boston College]'.[2] One can find little organic intellectual connection between his faith and his politics. His social thought hardly resulted from a determination to apply the principles of *Rerum Novarum* to American life. He felt an immense sense of fellowship with Pope John XXIII, but this was based more on the Pope's practical character and policies than on theological considerations. Some of his Protestant advisers probably knew the encyclicals better than he did. Once during the 1960 campaign I handed him a speech draft with the comment that it was perhaps too Catholic. He said with a smile, 'You Unitarians'—meaning Sorensen and myself—'keep writing Catholic speeches. I guess I am the only Protestant around here'.

Still, his basic attitude was wholly compatible with the sophisticated theology of Jesuits like Father John Courtney Murray, whom he greatly admired. In the notebook he kept during his sickness, he wrote down some lines from Barbara Ward: 'What disturbs the Communist rulers is not the phraseology of religion, the lip-service that may be paid to it, or the speeches and declarations made in its favor. . . . Religion which is a mere adjunct of individual purpose is a religion that even the Soviets can tolerate. What they fear is a religion that transcends frontiers and can challenge the purpose and performance of the nation-state.' This was not in the mid-fifties the typical attitude of American Catholics; but, if Kennedy was not a typical American Catholic, his example helped create the progressive and questing American Catholicism of the sixties. Above all, he showed that there need be no conflict between Catholicism and modernity, no bar to full Catholic participation in American society.

His detachment from traditional American Catholicism was part of the set of detachments—detachment from middle-class parochialism, detachment from the business ethos, detachment from ritualistic liberalism—which gave his perceptions their peculiar coolness, freshness and freedom, and which also led those expecting commitments of a more familiar sort to condemn him as uncommitted. In fact, he was intensely committed to a vision of America and the world, and committed with equal intensity to the use of reason and power to achieve that vision. This became apparent after he was President; and this accounts in part for the sudden realization that, far from being just a young man in a hurry, a hustler for personal authority, a Processed Politician, he was, as politicians go, an intellectual and one so peculiarly modern that it took orthodox intellectuals a little time before they began to understand him.

Another reason for the change in the intellectuals' theory of Kennedy was their gradual recognition of his desire to bring the world of power and the world of ideas together in alliance—or rather, as he himself saw it, to restore the collaboration between the two worlds which had marked the early republic. He was fascinated by the Founding Fathers and liked to harass historians by demanding that they explain how a small and under-developed nation could have produced men of such genius. He was particularly fascinated by the way the generation of the Founders united the instinct for ideas, and the instinct for responsibility. 'Our nation's first great politicians,' he wrote, '—those who presided at its birth in 1776 and at its christening in 1787—included among their ranks most of the nation's first great writers and scholars.' But today the gap between the intellectual and politician seems to be growing. . . . today this link is all but gone. Where are the scholar-statesmen? The

American politician of today is fearful, if not scornful, of entering the literary world with the courage of a Beveridge. And the American author and scholar of today is reluctant, if not disdainful, about entering the political world with the enthusiasm of a Woodrow Wilson.

His summons to the scholar-statesman went largely unnoticed by the intellectual community in the fifties, perhaps because he chose such improbable forums as *Vogue* and a Harvard Commencement. Only when he began as President to put his proposition into practice did the intellectual community take a fresh look at him.

The Kennedy Mind: II

The character of his reading and quoting emphasizes, I think, the historical grain of his intelligence. Kennedy was in many respects an historian manqué. The historical mind can be analytical, or it can be romantic. The best historians are both, Kennedy among them. *Why England Slept*, with its emphasis on impersonal forces, expressed one side; *Profiles in Courage*[3], with its emphasis on heroes, expressed the other. But, even in his most romantic mood, Kennedy never adopted a good-guys *vs.* bad-guys theory of history. He may have been a Whig,* but he was not a Whig historian. He had both the imagination and the objectivity which enabled him to see the point in lost causes, even in enemy fanaticisms. In a review of Liddell Hart's *Deterrent or Defense* in 1960, he praised the author's credo: 'Keep strong, if possible. In any case, keep cool. Have unlimited patience. Never corner an opponent, and always assist him to save his face. Put yourself in his shoes—so as to see things through his eyes. Avoid self-righteousness like the devil—nothing is so self-blinding.' Liddell Hart was addressing these remarks to statesmen; they work just as well for historians. . . .

He liked to quote Lincoln: 'There are few things wholly evil or wholly good. Almost everything, especially of Government policy, is an inseparable compound of the two, so that our best judgment of the preponderance between them is continually

---

* In the English sense, that is; in the American sense of believing in a strong Congress and a weak executive, he often emphasized to James MacGregor Burns and others, 'I am no Whig!'

demanded.' When something had enough steam behind it to move people and make an impression on history, it must have some rational explanation, and Kennedy wanted to know what that rational explanation was. The response of the fifties that it was all a struggle between good and evil never satisfied him.

But it was not a case of *tout comprendre, tout pardonner*. Though he saw the human struggle, not as a moralist, but as an historian, even as an ironist, irony was never permitted to sever the nerve of action. His mind was forever critical; but his thinking always retained the cutting edge of decision. When he was told something, he wanted to know what he could do about it. He was pragmatic in the sense that he tested the meaning of a proposition by its consequences; he was also pragmatic in the sense of being free from metaphysics. In his response, too, to the notion of a pluralist universe, Kennedy was a pragmatist— if one may make sensible use of this word, which came into political vogue in the first years of the Kennedy administration and then was oddly revived in the first years of the Johnson administration with the implication that the Kennedy years had not, after all, been pragmatic but were somehow ideological. They were not ideological, though they could perhaps be termed intellectual.

The historical mind is rarely ideological—and, when it becomes so, it is at the expense of history. Whether analytical or romantic, it is committed to existence, not to essence. Kennedy was bored by abstractions. He never took ideology very seriously, certainly not as a means of interpreting history and even not as part of the material of history. If he did not go the distance with de Gaulle in reducing everything to national tradition and national interest, he tended to give greater weight in thinking about world affairs to national than to ideological motives. Like de Gaulle, but unlike the ideological interpreters of the cold war, he was not surprised by the split between Russia and China.

If historic conflict infrequently pitted total good against total evil, then they infrequently concluded in total victory or total defeat. Seeing the past with an historian's eyes, Kennedy knew that ideals and institutions were stubborn, and that change took place more often by accommodation than by annihilation. His cult of courage was in this sense ethical rather than political; he saw the courage of 'unyielding devotion to absolute principle' as the moral fulfillment of the individual rather than as necessarily the best way of running a government. Indeed, he took pains to emphasize in *Profiles* that politicians could also demonstrate courage 'through their acceptance of compromise, through their advocacy of conciliation, through their willingness to replace conflict with co-operation'. Senators who go down to defeat in vain defense of a single principle 'will not be on hand to fight for that or any other principle in the future'. One felt here an echo of St. Thomas: 'Prudence applies principles to particular issues; consequently it does not establish moral purpose, but contrives the means thereto.'

The application of principle requires both moral and intellectual insight. Kennedy had an unusual capacity to weigh the complexities of judgment—in part because of the complexities of his own perceptions. The contrast in *Profiles* between the courage of compromise and the courage of principle expressed, for example, a tension deep within Kennedy—a tension between the circumspection of his political instinct and the radicalism of his intellectual impulse; so too the contrast between the historical determinism, the deprecation of the individual and the passive view of leadership implied in *Why England Slept* and the demand in *Profiles* that the politician be prepared, on the great occasions, to 'meet the challenge of courage, whatever may be the sacrifices he faces if he follows his conscience'. All this expressed the interior strain between Kennedy's sense of human limitation and his sense of hope, between his skepticism about man and his readiness to say, 'Man can be as big as he wants. No problem of human destiny is beyond human beings'.

All these things, coexisting within him, enabled others to find in him what qualities they wanted. They could choose one side of him or the other and claim him, according to taste, as a conservative, because of his sober sense of the frailty of man, the power of institutions and the frustrations of history, or as a progressive, because of his vigorous confidence in reason, action and the future. Yet within Kennedy himself these tensions achieved reunion and reconciliation. He saw history in its massive movements as shaped by forces beyond man's control. But he felt that there were still problems which man could resolve; and in any case, whether man could resolve these problems or not, the obligation was to carry on the struggle of existence. It was in essence, Richard Goodwin later suggested, the Greek view where the hero must poise himself against the gods and, even with knowledge of the futility of the fight, press on to the end of his life until he meets his tragic fate.

NOTES

(1) A regular television feature in the United States where politicians or other notables answer questions put by journalists in the studio.

(2) Fordham and Boston College. Two Catholic universities.

(3) *Profiles in Courage* by John F. Kennedy (1956). See p. 233 in this book.

PART IV

Civil Rights and Civil Liberties

Foremost among America's domestic problems is that of civil rights. The denial of civil rights to Negroes in many areas of the United States, and discriminatory practices in other parts of the country produce severe tensions in American society.

Among the rights denied or withheld are the effective right to vote (as distinct from the nominal right to vote) and the right to educational opportunities equal to those of the white majority in America. Apart from the denial of these basic rights, discrimination on grounds of race and colour continues in many parts of American society, despite continued efforts to eradicate it, and despite some real progress in recent years.

The problem of civil rights is extremely complex, and has its roots deep in American history. The southern states have always had a particular problem here, for the institution of Negro slavery supported the plantation economy of the deep south for two centuries. The American Civil War of 1861 to 1865 was fought over this issue, and with the defeat of the southern states by the north, slavery was declared unconstitutional and illegal. Henceforth, Negroes were to enjoy the same rights and privileges as the white man in the United States.

It is one thing to issue such a proclamation, or to install it in the constitution of the United States, and another to give it practical effect throughout a federal union of states. The refusal or, at best, the reluctance of the southern states in America to accept the new status of the Negro largely accounts for the continued struggle over civil rights.

This is not to say, however, that discrimination against the Negro is confined to the southern states. Leaders of civil rights movements in the United States often point out that a great deal of less obvious but very potent discrimination is practised in the richer north-east states of the Union. This may take a variety of forms—among them discriminatory hiring practices in the labour market, where white-dominated unions are often more to blame than the management; or restaurants where no colour bar is stated, but where a Negro is made to feel extremely unwelcome by the management.

Discussions on civil rights are therefore not confined to the right to vote at a particular election, though Negro leaders are of course vitally concerned with this matter. They are more concerned, however, with achieving equal opportunity free from all types of discrimination, and for the effective realization of these opportunities. This is also the ultimate aim of all genuine supporters of Negro rights.

There is no easy or quick solution to the problem, and the responsible leaders of civil rights movements in the United States realize this. An enormous amount of irrational, yet deeply-ingrained, often unconscious prejudice must be overcome. Prejudice has been the common experience of so many Negroes for so long that the Negro community is itself prejudiced against the white American community in many areas, and this does not simplify the problem. Again, the sheer lethargy of the majority of the nation in face of the problem is perhaps the biggest single obstacle to progress.

A President of the United States can do a great deal to affect the atmosphere in which these problems are encountered. He can give a lead and use the authority of his office, as well as his powers of appointment, to further the cause of Negro and civil rights movements. Or he can attempt to evade the issue, and do little more than give ritual statements in vague terms about the need for some progress at some future time. The actions of a President of the United States on this thorny issue provide many clues to his Presidential calibre.

Kennedy had special problems here for a number of reasons. Firstly, a chorus of Negro protest had been building up during the previous years, accompanied by many incidents of violence. The non-violent aims and policies of the chief civil rights organization, the National Association for the Advancement of Colored People (NAACP) under their leader, Rev. Martin Luther King, were increasingly affected by new militant movements among the Negro community—notably the Black Muslim movement whose leaders have demanded an all-out war against the white man. Incidents involving brutality by white policemen in their treatment of Negro demonstrators in the south did not improve the situation.

Secondly, Kennedy was nominally the leader of the Democratic Party in the country. Yet the southern wing of the Democratic Party represents the most entrenched opposition to the advance of the Negro, and in the deep south the party is largely held together by an inflexible opposition to full civil rights for Negroes. It is there, in the Democratic one-party South, that Negroes are virtually denied all participation in the political process. Again, the fact that Kennedy was a young, rich, north-eastern Democrat did not commend him to the southern Democrats, who have long sought for a President drawn from their own ranks, only to be denied this every four years by the heavy voting power of the northern states.

For all these reasons, and others which lie in the bartering processes of Congressional politics in Washington, Kennedy's task as President and leader of the Democratic Party was not an easy one. Some argued that his record as a Senator and Congressman on this issue was spotty. Certainly his voting record was not as clear-cut as those of other liberal Congressmen and Senators. After his nomination as Presidential candidate in July 1960, however, and with the invaluable support of Lyndon Johnson of Texas as the candidate for the Vice-Presidency, Kennedy made several speeches where his support for the Negro cause was unequivocal.

When Kennedy was elected President and took office in January 1961, this did not mean, of course, that the problem was soon to be solved. The South was ready to resist any attempt by a northern Democratic President to compel them to integrate the white and Negro communities there. Cases continued to come before the federal courts in southern districts where discriminatory practices were charged by the leaders of the civil rights movement. Education was and is a particularly sensitive area. Many southern universities were refusing to admit Negroes under any pretext. In September 1962 a fully qualified Negro, James Meredith, was turned away from the University of Mississippi. This was yet another case of resistance by the white majority to all forms of integration. The situation became extremely restive as the white and Negro communities faced each other in open hostility. White demonstrators taunted the Negroes, and finally blood was shed. Kennedy ordered the National Guard, under his direct authority as President, to supervise the enrolment and attendance of James Meredith at the university. The President broadcast to the nation on 30 September, asking for support and co-operation in these matters, and declaring his firm determination to act in all similar cases in the future.

Yet other cases did occur and in 1963 another series of incidents began at the University of Alabama. White segregationists there attempted to prevent the admission of qualified Negro students. Kennedy again gave orders to National Guardsmen to prevent molestation of the Negro students, and to accompany their enrolment at the university. He then broadcast to the nation once more. This was his most important speech on this vital issue, and the text shows the urgency of it, as well as leaving no room for doubt about his determination to use all the power and authority of his office to further the cause of civil rights for all Americans, whatever the colour of their skin.

DOCUMENT 13. RADIO AND TELEVISION REPORT TO THE AMERICAN PEOPLE ON CIVIL RIGHTS, BY PRESIDENT KENNEDY. 11 JUNE 1963.

This afternoon, following a series of threats and defiant statements, the presence of Alabama National Guardsmen was required at the University of Alabama to carry out the final and unequivocal order of the United States District Court of the Northern District of Alabama. That order called for the admission of two clearly qualified young Alabama residents who happened to have been born Negro.

That they were admitted peacefully on the campus is due in good measure to the conduct of the students of the University of Alabama, who met their responsibilities in a constructive way.

I hope that every American, regardless of where he lives, will stop and examine his conscience about this and other related incidents. This nation was founded by men of many nations and backgrounds. It was founded on the principle that all men are created equal, and that the rights of every man are diminished when the rights of one man are threatened.

Today we are committed to a world-wide struggle to promote and protect the rights of all who wish to be free. And when Americans are sent to Viet-Nam or West Berlin, we do not ask for white only. It ought to be possible, therefore, for American students of any color to attend any public institution they select without having to be backed up by troops.

It ought to be possible for American consumers of any color to receive equal service in places of public accomodation, such as hotels and restaurants and theaters and retail stores, without being forced to resort to demonstrations in the street, and it ought to be possible for American citizens of any color to register and to vote in a free election without interference or fear of reprisal.

It ought to be possible, in short, for every American to enjoy the privileges of being American without regard to his race or his color. In short, every American ought to have the right to be treated as he would wish to be treated, as one would wish his children to be treated. But this is not the case.

The Negro baby born in America today, regardless of the section of the nation in which he is born, has about one-half as much chance of completing high school as a white baby born in the same place on the same day, one-third as much chance of completing college, one-third as much chance of becoming a professional man, twice as much chance of becoming unemployed, about one-seventh as much chance of earning $10,000 a year, a life expectancy which is seven years shorter and the prospects of earning only half as much.

This is not a sectional issue. Difficulties over segregation and discrimination exist in every city, in every State of the Union, producing in many cities a rising tide of discontent that threatens the public safety. Nor is this a partisan issue. In a time of domestic crisis men of good will and generosity should be able to unite regardless of party or politics. This is not even a legal or legislative issue alone. It is better to settle these matters in the courts than on the streets, and new laws are needed at every level, but law alone cannot make men see right.

We are confronted primarily with a moral issue. It is as old as the scriptures and is as clear as the American Constitution.

The heart of the question is whether all Americans are to be afforded equal rights and equal opportunities, whether we are going to treat our fellow Americans as we want to be treated. If an American, because his skin is dark, cannot eat lunch in a restaurant open to the public; if he cannot send his children to the best public school available; if he cannot vote for the public officials who represent him, if, in short, he cannot enjoy the full and free life which all of us want, then who among us would be content to have the color of his skin changed and stand in his place? Who among us would then be content with the counsels of patience and delay?

One hundred years of delay have passed since President Lincoln freed the slaves, yet their heirs, their grandsons, are not fully free. They are not yet freed from the bonds of injustice. They are not yet freed from social and economic oppression. And this nation, for all its hopes and all its boasts, will not be fully free until all its citizens are free.

We preach freedom around the world, and we mean it, and we cherish our freedom here at home; but are we to say to the world, and much more importantly, to each other that this is a land of the free except for the Negroes; that we have no second-class citizens except Negroes; that we have no class or caste system, no ghettoes, no master race except with respect to Negroes?

Now the time has come for this nation to fulfill its promise. The events in Birmingham, Alabama, and elsewhere have so increased the cries for equality that no city or State legislative body can prudently choose to ignore them.

The fires of frustration and discord are burning in every city, North and South, where legal remedies are not at hand. Redress is sought in the streets, in demonstrations, parades, and protests which create tensions and threaten violence and threaten lives.

We face, therefore, a moral crisis as a country and as a people. It cannot be met by repressive police action. It cannot be left to increased demonstrations in the streets. It cannot be quieted by token moves or talk. It is a time to act in the Congress, in your State and local legislative body and, above all, in all of our daily lives.

It is not enough to pin the blame on others, to say this is a problem of one section of the country or another, or deplore the facts that we face. A great change is at hand, and our task, our obligation, is to make that revolution, that change, peaceful and constructive for all.

Those who do nothing are inviting shame as well as violence. Those who act boldly are recognizing right as well as reality.

Next week I shall ask the Congress of the United States to act, to make a commitment it has not fully made in this century to the proposition that race has no place in American life or law. The federal judiciary has upheld that proposition in a series of forthright cases. The Executive Branch has adopted that proposition in the conduct of its affairs, including the employment of federal personnel, the use of federal facilities, and the sale of federally financed housing.

But there are other necessary measures which only the Congress can provide, and they must be provided at this session. The old code of equity law under which we live commands for every wrong a remedy, but in too many communities, in too many parts of the country, wrongs are inflicted on Negro citizens and there are no remedies at law. Unless the Congress acts, their only remedy is in the street.

I am, therefore, asking the Congress to enact legislation giving all Americans the right to be served in facilities which are open to the public—hotels, restaurants, theaters, retail stores, and similar establishments.

This seems to be an elementary right. Its denial is an arbitrary indignity that no American in 1963 should have to endure, but many do.

I have recently met with scores of business leaders urging them to take voluntary action to end this discrimination and I have been encouraged by their response, and in the last two weeks over seventy-five cities have seen progress made in desegregating these kinds of facilities. But many are unwilling to act alone, and for this reason, nation-wide legislation is needed if we are to move this problem from the streets to the courts.

I am also asking Congress to authorize the federal government to participate more fully in lawsuits designed to end segregation in public education. We have succeeded in persuading many districts to desegregate voluntarily. Dozens have admitted Negroes without violence. Today a Negro is attending a State-supported institution in every one of our fifty States, but the pace is very slow.

Too many Negro children entering segregated grade schools at the time of the Supreme Court's decision nine years ago will enter segregated high schools this fall, having suffered a loss which can never be restored. The lack of an adequate education denies the Negro a chance to get a decent job.

The orderly implementation of the Supreme Court decision, therefore, cannot be left solely to those who may not have the economic resources to carry the legal action or who may be subject to harassment.

Other features will also be requested, including greater protection for the right to vote. But legislation, I repeat, cannot solve this problem alone. It must be solved in the homes of every American in every community across our country.

In this respect, I want to pay tribute to those citizens North and South who have been working in their communities to make life better for all. They are acting not out of a sense of legal duty but out of a sense of human decency.

Like our soldiers and sailors in all parts of the world they are meeting freedom's challenge on the firing line, and I salute them for their honor and their courage.

My fellow Americans, this is a problem which faces us all— in every city of the North as well as the South. Today there are Negroes unemployed, two or three times as many compared to whites, inadequate in education, moving into the large cities, unable to find work; young people particularly out of work without hope, denied equal rights, denied the opportunity to eat at a restaurant or lunch counter or go to a movie theater, denied the right to a decent education, denied almost today the right to attend a State university even though qualified. It seems to me that these are matters which concern us all, not merely Presidents or Congressmen or Governors, but every citizen of the United States.

This is one country. It has become one country because all of us and all the people who came here had an equal chance to develop their talents.

We cannot say to ten per cent of the population that you

can't have that right; that your children can't have the chance to develop whatever talents they have; that the only way that they are going to get their rights is to go into the streets and demonstrate. I think we owe them and we owe ourselves a better country than that.

Therefore, I am asking for your help in making it easier for us to move ahead and to provide the kind of equality of treatment which we would want ourselves; to give a chance for every child to be educated to the limit of his talents.

As I have said before, not every child has an equal talent or an equal ability ... but they should have the equal right to develop their talent and their ability ... to make something of themselves.

We have a right to expect that the Negro community will be responsible, will uphold the law, but they have a right to expect that the law will be fair, that the Constitution will be color blind, as Justice Harlan [of the Supreme Court] said at the turn of the century.

This is what we are talking about and this is a matter which concerns this country and what it stands for, and in meeting it I ask the support of all our citizens.

CIVIL RIGHTS LEGISLATION: PREPARING THE GROUND

Although President Kennedy's speech of 11 June 1963 on civil rights (see p. 99) was his most dramatic pronouncement on the subject, the American people demand more of their President than speeches. They require positive action from the President in his role as chief legislator.

On 19 June 1963, only eight days after his nation-wide speech, President Kennedy sent to Congress one of the most extensive civil rights bills ever placed before the federal legislature. The bill proposed to outlaw all forms of discrimination by colour or race in all places of public accommodation. Hotels, restaurants, theatres, shops and all public institutions would come under the terms of the bill. The bill also proposed a ban on all forms of segregated education in schools and colleges. Further proposals were expressly designed to protect the voting rights of Negroes in the southern states and to encourage Negroes to participate in electoral processes.

The President's bill encountered protracted opposition in both houses of Congress. In committee, southern Democrats, and other conservative elements attempted to emasculate and delay the bill. The bill finally emerged from Congress in 1964 and was enacted into law more than six months after President Kennedy's death. The Civil Rights Act of 1964 stands as a monument to President Kennedy's commitment on this vital issue.

Of course President Kennedy was fully aware of the opposition his bill would meet in Congress. Accordingly, he was attempting to prepare the ground months before he formally introduced the measure. The following Special Message to Congress, delivered in February 1963, illustrates the point. It will be seen how many of the observations it contains bear on the proposals the President planned to submit to Congress in his bill a few months later.

DOCUMENT 14. SPECIAL MESSAGE TO CONGRESS FROM PRESIDENT KENNEDY. WASHINGTON, D.C., 29 FEBRUARY 1963.

'Our Constitution is color-blind,' wrote Mr. Justice Harlan before the turn of the century, 'and neither knows nor tolerates classes among citizens.' But the practices of the country do not always conform to the principles of the Constitution. And this message is intended to examine how far we have come in achieving first-class citizenship for all citizens regardless of color, how far we have yet to go, and what further tasks remain to be carried out—by the Executive and Legislative Branches of the federal government, as well as by state and local governments and private citizens and organizations. One hundred years ago the Emancipation Proclamation was signed by a President who believed in the equal worth and opportunity of every human being. That Proclamation was only a first step, a step which its author unhappily did not live to follow up, a step which some of its critics dismissed as an action which 'frees the slave but ignores the Negro'. Through these long one hundred years, while slavery has vanished, progress for the Negro has been too often blocked and delayed. Equality before the law has not always meant equal treatment and opportunity. And the harmful, wasteful and wrongful results of racial discrimination and segregation still appear in virtually every aspect of national life, in virtually every part of the nation. . . .

The right to vote in a free American election is the most powerful and precious right in the world, and it must not be denied on the ground of race or color. It is a potent key to achieving other rights of citizens. For American history, both recent and past, clearly reveals that the power of the ballot has enabled those who achieve it to win other achievements as well, to gain a full voice in the affairs of their state and nation, and to see their interests represented in the governmental bodies which affect their future. In a free society those with the power to govern are necessarily responsive to those with the right to vote.

In enacting the 1957 and the 1960 Civil Rights Acts, Congress provided the Department of Justice with basic tools for protecting the right to vote, and this administration has not hesitated to use those tools. Legal action is brought only after voluntary efforts fail; and, in scores of instances, local officials, at the request of the Department of Justice, have voluntarily made voting records available or abandoned discriminatory registration, discriminatory voting practices or segregated balloting.

Where voluntary local compliance has not been forthcoming, the Department of Justice has approximately quadrupled the previous level of its legal effort—investigating coercion, inspecting records, initiating lawsuits, enjoining intimidation and taking whatever follow-up action is necessary to forbid further interference or discrimination. As a result, thousands of Negro citizens are registering and voting for the first time, many of them in counties where no Negro had ever voted before. The Department of Justice will continue to take whatever action is required to secure the right to vote for all Americans.

Experience has shown, however, that these highly useful acts of the Eighty-fifth and Eighty-sixth Congresses suffer from two major defects. One is the usual long and difficult delay which occurs between the filing of a lawsuit and its ultimate conclusion. In one recent case, for example, nineteen months elapsed between the filing of the suit and the judgment of the court. In another, an action brought in July 1961 has not yet come to trial. The legal maxim 'Justice delayed is justice denied' is dramatically applicable in these cases.

Too often those who attempt to assert their constitutional rights are intimidated. Prospective registrants are fired. Registration workers are arrested. In some instances, churches in which registration meetings are held have been burned. In one case where Negro tenant farmers chose to exercise their right to vote, it was necessary for the Justice Department to seek injunctions to halt their eviction and for the Department of Agriculture to help feed them from surplus stocks. Under these circumstances, continued delay in the granting of the franchise, particularly in counties where there is mass racial disfranchisement, permits the intent of the Congress to be openly flouted.

Federal executive action in such cases, no matter how speedy and how drastic, can never fully correct such abuses of power. It is necessary instead, to free the forces of our democratic system within these areas by promptly insuring the franchise to all citizens, making it possible for their elected officials to be truly responsive to all their constituents.

The second and somewhat overlapping gap in these statutes is their failure to deal specifically with the most common forms of abuse of discretion on the part of local election officials who do not treat all applicants uniformly.

Objections were raised last year to the proposed literacy test bill, which attempted to speed up the enforcement of the right to vote by removing one important area of discretion from registration officials who used that discretion to exclude Negroes. Preventing that bill from coming to a vote did not make any less real the prevalence in many counties of the use of literacy and other voter qualification tests to discriminate against prospective Negro voters, contrary to the requirements of the Fourteenth and Fifteenth Amendments [to the American Constitution] and adding to the delays and difficulties encountered in securing the franchise for those denied it.

An indication of the magnitude of the over-all problem, as well as the need for speedy action, is a recent five-state survey disclosing over two hundred counties in which fewer than 15 per cent of the Negroes of voting age are registered to vote. This cannot continue. I am, therefore, recommending legislation to deal with this problem of judicial delay and administrative abuse. . . .

Nearly nine years have elapsed since the Supreme Court ruled that state laws requiring or permitting segregated schools violate the Constitution. That decision represented both good law and good judgment; it was both legally and morally right. Since that time it has become increasingly clear that neither violence nor legalistic evasions will be tolerated as a means of thwarting court-ordered desegregation, that closed schools are not an answer, and that responsible communities are able to handle the desegregation process in a calm and sensible manner. This is as it should be, for, as I stated to the nation at the time of the Mississippi violence last September:

'Our nation is founded on the principle that observance of the law is the eternal safeguard of liberty and defiance of the law is the surest road to tyranny. The law which we obey includes the final rulings of the courts, as well as the enactments of our legislative bodies. Even among law-abiding men few laws are universally loved, but they are uniformly respected and not resisted.

'Americans are free to disagree with the law, but not to disobey it. For in a government of laws and not of men, no man, however prominent and powerful, and no mob, however unruly or boisterous, is entitled to defy a court of law. If this country should ever reach the point where any man or group of men by force or threat of force could long defy the commands of our court and our Constitution, then no law would stand free from doubt, no judge would be sure of his writ, and no citizen would be safe from his neighbors.'

The shameful violence which accompanied but did not prevent the end of segregation at the University of Mississippi was an exception. State supported universities in Georgia and South Carolina met this test in recent years with calm and maturity, as did the state-supported universities of Virginia, North Carolina, Florida, Texas, Louisiana, Tennessee, Arkansas and Kentucky in earlier years. In addition, progress toward the desegregation of education at all levels has made other notable and peaceful strides, including the following forward moves in the last two years alone:

Desegregation plans have been put into effect peacefully in

the public schools of Atlanta, Dallas, New Orleans, Memphis and elsewhere, with over sixty school districts desegregated last year, frequently with the help of federal persuasion and consultation, and in every case without incident or disorder.

Teacher training institutes financed under the National Defense Education Act are no longer held in colleges which refuse to accept students without regard to race, and this has resulted in a number of institutions opening their doors to Negro applicants voluntarily. I recommend, therefore, a program of federal technical and financial assistance to aid school districts in the process of desegregation in compliance with the Constitution. . . .

The Commission on Civil Rights, established by the Civil Rights Act of 1957, has been in operation for more than five years, and is scheduled to expire on 30 November 1963. . . . The Commission's reports and recommendations have provided the basis for remedial action both by Congress and the Executive Branch. . . . But the Commission is now in a position to provide even more useful service to the nation. As more communities evidence a willingness to face frankly their problems of racial discrimination, there is an increasing need for expert guidance and assistance in devising workable programs for civil rights progress. . . .

I recommend, therefore, that the Congress authorize the Civil Rights Commission to serve as a national civil rights clearing house providing information, advice and technical assistance to any requesting agency, private or public; that in order to fulfill these new responsibilities, the Commission be authorized to concentrate its activities upon those problems within the scope of its statute which most need attention; and that the life of the Commission be extended for a term of at least four more years.[1]

Racial discrimination in employment is especially injurious both to its victims and to the national economy. It results in a great waste of human resources and creates serious community problems. It is, moreover, inconsistent with the democratic principle that no man should be denied employment commensurate with his abilities because of his race or creed or ancestry.

The President's Committee on Equal Employment Opportunity, reconstituted by Executive Order in early 1961, has, under the leadership of the Vice-President, taken significant steps to eliminate racial discrimination by those who do business with the government. Hundreds of companies, covering seventeen million jobs, have agreed to stringent non-discriminatory provisions now standard in all government contracts. One hundred and four industrial concerns, including the nation's major employers, have in addition signed agreements calling for an affirmative attack on discrimination in employment; and 117 labor unions, representing about 85 per cent of the membership of the AFL–CIO,[2] have signed similar agreements with the Committee.

Comprehensive compliance machinery has been instituted to enforce these agreements. The Committee has received over thirteen hundred complaints in two years, more than in the entire seven and one-half years of the Committee's prior existence, and has achieved corrective action on 72 per cent. of the cases handled—a heartening and unprecedented record. Significant results have been achieved in placing Negroes with contractors who previously employed whites only, and in the elevation of Negroes to a far higher proportion of professional, technical and supervisory jobs. Let me repeat my assurances that these provisions in government contracts and the voluntary non-discrimination agreements will be carefully monitored and strictly enforced. . . .

No act is more contrary to the spirit of our democracy and Constitution, or more rightfully resented by a Negro citizen who seeks only equal treatment, than the barring of that citizen from restaurants, hotels, theaters, recreational areas and other public accommodations and facilities.

Wherever possible, this administration has dealt sternly with such acts. In 1961 the Justice Department and the Interstate Commerce Commission successfully took action to bring an end to discrimination in rail and bus facilities. In 1962 the fifteen airports still maintaining segregated facilities were persuaded to change their practices, thirteen voluntarily and two others after the Department of Justice brought legal action. As a result of these steps, systematic segregation in interstate transportation has virtually ceased to exist. No doubt isolated instances of discrimination in transportation terminals, restaurants, rest rooms and other facilities will continue to crop up, but any such discrimination will be dealt with promptly.

In addition, restaurants and public facilities in buildings leased by the federal government have been opened up to all federal employees in areas where previously they had been segregated. The General Services Administration no longer contracts for the lease of space in office buildings unless such facilities are available to all federal employees without regard to race. This move has taken place without fanfare and practically without incident; and full equality of facilities will continue to be made available to all federal employees in every state.

National parks, forests and other recreation areas, and the [government-financed] District of Columbia Stadium are open to all without regard to race. Meetings sponsored by the federal government or addressed by federal appointees are held in hotels and halls which do not practice discrimination or segregation. The Department of Justice has asked the Supreme Court to reverse the convictions of Negroes arrested for seeking to use public accommodations and took action both through the courts and the use of federal marshals to protect those who were testing the desegregation of transportation facilities.

In these and other ways, the federal government will continue to encourage and support action by state and local communities, and by private entrepreneurs, to assure all members of the public equal access to all public accommodations. . . .

NOTES

(1) Commission on Civil Rights. A bi-partisan Commission set up in 1957 for a proposed limited period, but backed by the full powers of the federal courts and the President of the United States. Its purpose is to investigate fully any charges of the denial of civil rights to any American or group of Americans. The Commission continued in being and is now an agency of the federal government with a permanent staff of more than one hundred persons.

(2) The American Federation of Labor and Congress of Industrial Organizations. Formed in 1955 by a merger of the two largest labour organization in the United States. Equivalent to the Trades Union Congress in Britain.

PART V

Foreign Policy and the Cold War

The most intractable problems for a newly-elected President of the United States are those connected with foreign policy. As leading nation of the western democracies in the cold war era, and with global responsibilities, the United States is almost inevitably drawn in to every major problem or crisis, wherever it occurs. This places immense burdens on the President of the United States, who has special responsibility for making prompt decisions when these are called for.

Whilst it is true that American leaders recognize and accept American commitments around the world, there has been a strong tradition of isolationism in American history. This tradition argues that it is not in the best interests of the United States to maintain 'entangling' alliances with foreign powers, and that wars between, for instance, European states, are not the concern of the United States. There are powerful voices in America which still argue for a return to that tradition.

Recognizing this, Kennedy made an important, policy-making speech in July 1962 in which he attempted, by implication if not by the letter of the word, to bury the old tradition of isolationism. He argued that the balance of power in the world today, in an age of inter-continental missiles, makes the old tradition of American independence and non-involvement unrealistic. Just how radical a departure this was from many firmly held American beliefs is indicated in the extract from an article in the London *Observer* at the time. This extract provides a useful introduction to the text of the President's speech which follows.

It is also worth noting that President Kennedy gave this important address on a special date, in a special place, and before an unusual audience. July 4 is of course the most famous date in the American historical calendar, for on that date in 1776 the American Declaration of Independence was signed in the State House (later named Independence Hall) at Philadelphia. President Kennedy's audience on 4 July 1962 contained the assembled governors of the fifty United States of America.

DOCUMENT 15. EXTRACT FROM 'KENNEDY'S NEW TESTAMENT', BY GODFREY HODGSON (FROM *The Observer*, LONDON, 7 JULY 1962).

It is hard for non-Americans, unfamiliar with the holy writ of Americanism, to understand how far—how *blasphemously* far —President Kennedy went in his Independence Day speech in Philadelphia.

This is a matter not only of what he said, but of the language in which he chose to clothe his grand design of an Atlantic Partnership.

Standing in front of Independence Hall, on the most sacred soil of American political tradition, he plunged both his hands in the splendid phraseology of the Founding Fathers—not simply to dress himself in their rhetoric, but to drive home to Americans their changed situation in the world.

Again and again, beyond the possibility of coincidence, he used the language of the Founding Fathers in a way no American could miss. But he was talking not about American independence and the American Union, but about inter-dependence and union between America and foreigners.

He took Alexander Hamilton's injunction to think continent-ally and superseded it: 'Today Americans should think inter-continentally'. He contrasted—a still novel and shocking thought for most Americans—the new Europe with 'the old American Union'. He went step by step through the sonorous and familiar clauses of the preamble to the Constitution and cast them aside as inadequate.

'By ourselves we cannot,' he dared to say, 'establish justice, insure domestic tranquillity, provide for common defense, promote the general welfare, or secure the blessings of peace to ourselves and our posterity. But joined with other free nations, we can do all this and more.'

With a supreme touch of iconoclasm he even spoke of 'a more perfect union ... with our European friends'.

These were, to American ears, the most telling circumstances and the most telling language in which to call the old world to bear its share of the white man's burden. It would be wrong not to recognize the grandeur and generosity of the President's vision of an Atlantic Partnership as the first step on the way to an 'eventual union of all free men'. . . .

DOCUMENT 16. SPEECH BY PRESIDENT KENNEDY TO THE STATE GOVERNORS, INDEPENDENCE HALL, PHILADELPHIA, PENNSYLVANIA, 4 JULY 1962.

It is a high honor for any citizen of the great Republic to speak at this Hall of Independence on this day of Independence. To speak as President of United States, to the chief executives of our fifty states, is both an opportunity and an obligation. The necessity for comity between the national government and the several states is an indelible lesson of our history.

Because our system is designed to encourage both differences and dissent, because its checks and balances are designed to preserve the rights of the individual and the locality against pre-eminent central authority, you and I both recognize how dependent we are, one upon the other, for the successful operation of our unique and happy form of government. Our system and our freedom permit the legislative to be pitted upon occasions against the executive, the state against the federal government, the city against the countryside, party against party, interest against interest, all in competition or in contention one with another. Our task—your task in the State House and my task in the White House—is to weave from all these tangled threads a fabric of law and progress. Others may confine themselves to debate, discussion and that ultimate luxury, free advice. Our responsibility is one of decision, for to govern is to choose.

Thus in a very real sense you and I are the executors of the testament handed down by those who gathered in this historic hall 186 years ago today. For they gathered to affix their names to a document which was above all else a document not of rhetoric, but of bold decision. It was, it is true, a document of protest, but protests had been made before. It set forth their grievances with eloquence, but such eloquence had been heard before. But what distinguished this paper from all the others was the final irrevocable decision that it took to assert the independence of free states in place of colonies and to commit to that goal their lives, their fortunes and their sacred honor.

Today, 186 years later, that Declaration, whose yellowing parchment and fading, almost illegible lines I saw in the past week in the National Archives in Washington, is still a revolutionary document. To read it today is to hear a trumpet call. For that Declaration unleashed not merely a revolution against the British, but a revolution in human affairs. Its authors were highly conscious of its world-wide implications, and George Washington declared that liberty and self-government were, in his words, 'finally staked on the experiment entrusted to the hands of the American people'.

This prophecy has been borne out for 186 years. This doctrine of national independence has shaken the globe, and it remains the most powerful force anywhere in the world today. There are those struggling to eke out a bare existence in a barren land who have never heard of free enterprise, but who cherish the idea of independence. There are those who are grappling with overpowering problems of illiteracy and ill health, and who are ill-equipped to hold free elections, but they are determined to hold fast to their national independence in those newly emerging areas whose troubles some hope to exploit.

The theory of independence, as old as man himself, was not invented in this hall, but it was in this hall that the theory became a practice, that the word went out to all the world that 'the God who gave us life gave us liberty at the same time'.

And today this nation, conceived in revolution, nurtured in liberty, matured in independence, has no intention of abdicating its leadership in that world-wide movement for independence to any nation or society committed to systematic human suppression.

As apt and applicable as this historic Declaration of Independence is today, we would do well to honor that other historic document drafted in this hall, the Constitution of the United States, for it stressed not independence but interdependence, not the individual liberty of one but the indivisible liberty of all.

In most of the old colonial world the struggle for independence is coming to an end. Even in areas behind the [Iron] Curtain, that which Jefferson called 'the disease of liberty' still appears to be infectious. With the passing of ancient empires, today less than two per cent. of the world's population lives in territories officially termed 'dependent'. As this effort for independence, inspired by the spirit of the American Declaration of Independence, now approaches a successful close, a great new effort for independence is transforming the world about us. And the spirit of that new effort is the same spirit which gave birth to the American Constitution.

That spirit is today most clearly seen across the Atlantic Ocean. The nations of Western Europe, long divided by feuds more bitter than any which existed among the thirteen colonies, are joining together, seeking, as our forefathers sought, to find freedom in diversity and unity in strength.

The United States looks on this vast new enterprise with hope and admiration. We do not regard a strong and united Europe as a rival but as a partner. To aid its progress has been the basic objective of our foreign policy for seventeen years. We believe that a united Europe will be capable of playing a greater role in the common defense, of responding more generously to the needs of poorer nations, of joining with the United States and others in lowering trade barriers, resolving problems of currency and commodities and developing co-ordinated policies in all other economic diplomatic and political areas. We see in such a Europe a partner with whom we could deal on a basis of full equality in all the great and burdensome tasks of building and defending a community of free nations.

It would be premature at this time to do more than to indicate the high regard with which we view the formation of this partnership. The first order of business is for our European friends to go forward in forming the more perfect union which will some-day make this partnership possible.

A great new edifice is not built overnight. It was eleven years from the Declaration of Independence to the writing of the Constitution. The construction of workable federal institutions required still another generation. The greatest works of our nation's founders lay not in documents and declarations, but in creative, determined action. The building of the new house of Europe has followed this same practical and purposeful course. Building the Atlantic Partnership will not be cheaply or easily finished.

But I will say here and now on this day of Independence, that the United States will be ready for a Declaration of Interdependence, that we will be prepared to discuss with a United Europe the ways and means of forming a concrete Atlantic Partnership, a mutually beneficial partnership between the new union now emerging in Europe and the old American Union founded here 175 years ago.

All this will not be completed in a year, but let the world know it is our goal.

In urging the adoption of the United States Constitution, Alexander Hamilton told his fellow New Yorkers to 'think continentally'. Today Americans must learn to think intercontinentally.

Acting on our own by ourselves, we cannot establish justice throughout the world. We cannot insure its domestic tranquillity, or provide for its common defense, or promote its general welfare, or secure the blessings of liberty to ourselves and our posterity. But joined with other free nations, we can do all this and more. We can assist the developing nations to throw off the yoke of poverty. We can balance our world-wide trade and payments at the highest possible level of growth. We can mount a deterrent powerful enough to deter any aggression, and ultimately we can help achieve a world of law and free choice, beginning the world of war and coercion.

For the Atlantic Partnership of which I speak would not look inward only, pre-occupied with its own welfare and advancement. It must look outward to co-operate with all nations in meeting their common concern. It would serve as a nucleus for the eventual union of all free men, those who are now free and those who are avowing that some-day they will be free.

On Washington's birthday in 1861, President-Elect Abraham Lincoln spoke at this hall on his way to the nation's capital. And he paid a brief and eloquent tribute to the men who wrote, and fought for, and who died for, the Declaration of Independence. Its essence, he said, was its promise not only of liberty 'to the people of this country, but hope to the world.

... [hope] that in due time the weights should be lifted from the shoulders of all men, and that *all* should have an equal chance'.

On this fourth day of July 1962, we who are gathered at this same hall, entrusted with the fate and future of our states and nation, declare now our vow to do our part to lift the weights from the shoulders of all, to join other men and nations in preserving both peace and freedom, and to regard any threat to the peace or freedom of one as a threat to the peace and freedom of all. 'And for the support of this Declaration, with a firm reliance on the Protection of Divine Providence, we mutually pledge to each other our lives, our Fortunes, and our sacred Honor.'[1]

NOTE

(1) From the concluding sentence of the American Declaration of Independence adopted on 4 July 1776.

THE PEACE CORPS PROPOSAL

One of many new ideas introduced in the early months of the Kennedy Administration was for a 'Peace Corps'. This was to consist of carefully selected and rigorously trained men and women who would voluntarily live in developing countries and seek to help the new nations in various ways. They were to take with them special skills developed in their training. Medical skills, or perhaps a knowledge of horticulture for particular climates and conditions, or engineering skills, were typical examples. Their mission was thus a peaceful one, and the personal rewards would be slim: those selected, it was made clear, would receive only small, subsistence salaries, and would undertake to accept the standard of living they found in the country to which they were accredited, rather than the normal comforts of an American standard of living. Selection procedures were carefully designed to winnow out all but the most resilient.

Many thousands of volunteers immediately came forward. Special training, including language instruction, followed and after completing this, the selected volunteers were sent abroad to assist the people they had elected to serve.

Undoubtedly some mistakes were made, and some recruits

later proved to be failures. But there is little doubt that the Peace Corps proved to be a successful venture, and gave to many young Americans a sense of purpose and the opportunity to give real service to the world community.

DOCUMENT 17. MESSAGE FROM PRESIDENT KENNEDY TO CONGRESS ON THE PEACE CORPS PROPOSAL, 1 MARCH 1961.

To the Congress of the United States:
I recommend to the Congress the establishment of a permanent Peace Corps—*a pool of trained American men and women sent overseas by the U.S. Government or through private organizations and institutions to help foreign countries meet their urgent needs for skilled manpower.*

I have today signed an Executive Order establishing a Peace Corps on a temporary pilot basis.

The temporary Peace Corps will be a source of information and experience to aid us in formulating more effective plans for a permanent organization. In addition, by starting the Peace Corps now we will be able to begin training young men and women for overseas duty this summer with the objective of placing them in overseas positions by late fall [autumn]. This temporary Peace Corps is being established under existing authority in the Mutual Security Act and will be located in the Department of State. Its initial expenses will be paid from appropriations currently available for our foreign aid program.

Throughout the world the people of the newly developing nations are struggling for economic and social progress which reflects their deepest desires. Our own freedom, and the future of freedom around the world, depend, in a very real sense, on their ability to build growing and independent nations where men can live in dignity, liberated from the bonds of hunger, ignorance and poverty.

One of the greatest obstacles to the achievement of this goal is the lack of trained men and women with the skill to teach the young and assist in the operation of development projects —men and women with the capacity to cope with the demands of swiftly evolving economies, and with the dedication to put that capacity to work in the villages, the mountains, the towns and the factories of dozens of struggling nations.

The vast task of economic development urgently requires

skilled people to do the work of the society—to help teach in the schools, construct development projects, demonstrate modern methods of sanitation in the villages, and perform a hundred other tasks calling for training and advanced knowledge.

To meet this urgent need for skilled manpower we are proposing the establishment of a Peace Corps—an organization which will recruit and train American volunteers, sending them abroad to work with the people of other nations.

This organization will differ from existing assistance programs in that its members will supplement technical advisers by offering the specific skills needed by developing nations if they are to put technical advice to work. They will help provide the skilled manpower necessary to carry out the development projects planned by the host governments, acting at a working level and serving at great personal sacrifice. There is little doubt that the number of those who wish to serve will be far greater than our capacity to absorb them.

The Peace Corps or some similar approach has been strongly advocated by Senator Humphrey, Representative Reuss and others in the Congress. It has received strong support from universities, voluntary agencies, student groups, labor unions and business and professional organizations.

Last session, the Congress authorized a study of these possibilities. Preliminary reports of this study show that the Peace Corps is feasible, needed, and wanted by many foreign countries.

Most heartening of all, the initial reaction to this proposal has been an enthusiastic response by student groups, professional organizations and private citizens everywhere—a convincing demonstration that we have in this country an immense reservoir of dedicated men and women willing to devote their energies and time and toil to the cause of world peace and human progress.

Among the specific programs to which Peace Corps members can contribute are: teaching in primary and secondary schools, especially as part of national English-language-teaching programs; participation in the world-wide program of malaria eradication; instruction and operation of public health and sanitation projects; aiding in village development through school construction and other programs; increasing rural agricultural productivity by assisting local farmers to use modern implements and techniques. The initial emphasis of these programs will be on teaching. Thus the Peace Corps members will be an effective means of implementing the development programs of the host countries—programs which our technical operations have helped to formulate.

The Peace Corps will not be limited to the young, or to college graduates. All Americans who are qualified will be welcome to join this effort. But undoubtedly the Corps will be made up primarily of young people as they complete their formal education.

Because one of the greatest resources of a free society is the strength and diversity of its private organizations and institutions, much of the Peace Corps program will be carried out by these groups, financially assisted by the Federal Government.

Peace Corps personnel will be made available to developing nations in the following ways:

1. Through private voluntary agencies carrying on international assistance programs.
2. Through overseas programs of colleges and universities.
3. Through assistance programs of international agencies.
4. Through assistance programs of the United States government.
5. Through new programs which the Peace Corps itself directly administers.

In the majority of cases the Peace Corps will assume the entire responsibility for recruitment, training and the development of overseas projects. In other cases it will make available a pool of trained applicants to private groups who are carrying out projects approved by the Peace Corps.

In the case of Peace Corps programs conducted through voluntary agencies and universities, these private institutions will have the option of using the national recruitment system —the central pool of trained manpower—or developing recruitment systems of their own.

In all cases men and women recruited as a result of Federal assistance will be members of the Peace Corps and enrolled in the central organization. All private recruitment and training programs will adhere to Peace Corps standards as a condition of Federal assistance.

In all instances the men and women of the Peace Corps will go only to those countries where their services and skills are genuinely needed and desired. U.S. Operations Missions, supplemented where necessary by special Peace Corps teams, will consult with leaders in foreign countries in order to determine where Peace Corpsmen are needed, the types of job they can best fill, and the number of people who can be usefully employed. The Peace Corps will not supply personnel for marginal undertakings without a sound economic or social justification. In furnishing assistance through the Peace Corps careful regard will be given to the particular country's development priorities.

Membership in the Peace Corps will be open to all Americans and applications will be available shortly. Where application is made directly to the Peace Corps—the vast majority of cases—they will be carefully screened to make sure that those who are selected can contribute to Peace Corps programs, and have the personal qualities which will enable them to represent the United States abroad with honor and dignity. In those cases where application is made directly to a private group, the same basic standards will be maintained. Each new recruit will receive a training and orientation period varying from six weeks to six months. This training will include courses in the culture and language of the country to which they are being sent and specialized training designed to increase the work skills of recruits. In some cases training will be conducted by participant agencies and universities in approved training programs. Other training programs will be conducted by the Peace Corps staff.

Length of service in the Corps will vary depending on the kind of project and the country, generally ranging from two to three years. Peace Corps members will often serve under conditions of physical hardship, living under primitive conditions among the people of developing nations. For every Peace Corps member, service will mean a great financial sacrifice. They will receive no salary. Instead they will be given an allowance which will only be sufficient to meet their basic needs and maintain health.

It is essential that Peace Corpsmen and women live simply and unostentatiously among the people they have come to assist. At the conclusion of their tours, members of the Peace Corps will receive a small sum in the form of severance pay based on length of service abroad, to assist them during their first weeks back in the United States. Service with the Peace Corps will not exempt volunteers from Selective Service.

The United States will assume responsibility for supplying medical services to Peace Corps members and ensuring supplies and drugs necessary to good health.

I have asked the temporary Peace Corps to begin plans and make arrangements for pilot programs. A minimum of several hundred volunteers could be selected, trained and at work abroad by the end of this calendar year. It is hoped that within a few years several thousand Peace Corps members will be working in foreign lands.

It is important to remember that this program must, in its early stages, be experimental in nature. This is a new dimension in our overseas program and only the most careful planning and negotiation can ensure its success.

The benefits of the Peace Corps will not be limited to the countries in which it serves. Our own young men and women will be enriched by the experience of living and working in foreign lands. They will have acquired new skills and experience which will aid them in their future careers and add to our own country's supply of trained personnel and teachers. They will return better able to assume the responsibilities of American citizenship and with greater understanding of our global responsibilities.

Although this is an American Peace Corps, the problem of world development is not just an American problem. Let us hope that other nations will mobilize the spirit and energies and skill of their people in some form of Peace Corps—making our own effort only one step in a major international effort to increase the welfare of all men and improve understanding among nations.

THE CUBAN PROBLEM

Events in Cuba provided the most crucial test of President Kennedy's leadership. A President is always heir to some of the policies of his predecessor in office. During the last years of the Eisenhower regime, the Castro revolution in Cuba presented to the President and the State Department (concerned with foreign policy formulation) many acute problems. The friendship which rapidly developed between Premier Castro's left-wing revolutionary government and Soviet Russian leaders alarmed many Americans. Various solutions were proposed in order to meet the problem of an unfriendly —though a very small—state so close to American soil in the Caribbean. These proposals extended from limited economic sanctions all the way to invasion by the armed forces of the United States.

There was no agreed solution, however, and when Kennedy became President in January 1961, it was the duty of President Eisenhower and of advisers in the State Department and the Central Intelligence Agency to brief the new President fully on any plans and proposals under consideration. This was done even earlier than January when Eisenhower passed important information to Kennedy soon after the election of November 1960.

In April 1961 an abortive raid was made on Cuba, launched from American soil, ostensibly by loyalists of the regime ousted by the Castro revolution. The United States could claim formally that it had no part in the raid, which ended in complete failure. But there was some evidence that the State Department and the Central Intelligence Agency of the United States were involved in the plans to attack Cuba. Premier Castro, together with the Soviet leaders and their representatives at the United Nations, did not hesitate to charge that the United States—and thus President Kennedy personally—had connived at the raid. The complete failure of the raid was extremely damaging to the United States before world opinion, and also to President Kennedy personally. Whether he was fully informed about the nature of the operation before it went into effect, or how reliable was the information he received from his advisers on conditions in Cuba is still conjectural. But as President he could not escape responsibility for the operation once it had been put into effect. As the first major test of his leadership and competence, the fiasco of the Cuban landing was damaging to President Kennedy's reputation at home and abroad.

It was possibly this damage to Kennedy's—and to America's —prestige which encouraged the Soviet Union to respond to Castro's urgent requests for Soviet weapons on Cuban soil. Accordingly, after secret negotiations, the Russians began to construct a series of missile sites on the island to receive Soviet nuclear missiles.

American intelligence sources, assisted by aerial reconnaissance, noted the sites, and by the summer of 1962 there was unmistakable evidence that the construction of the missile launching pads was proceeding with great speed. Once these were completed and the missiles assembled, almost every major city and centre of population in the United States would become vulnerable to attack. President Kennedy was thus confronted with another, but much worse crisis in the second year of his Presidency. The situation was extremely delicate. The presence of Soviet engineers and military experts at the sites was confirmed by aerial photographs and intelligence reports. An air strike on Cuba would undoubtedly be regarded as an act of war by a large and powerful nation on a tiny island which relied on the support of another nuclear power. In the likely event that Russian lives were lost in an American air strike, the world would certainly be on the brink of nuclear war. Yet if the construction of the missile sites continued, they would be completed within a matter of weeks, and it might then be too late to take action.

President Kennedy was thus confronted with a grave and urgent situation. Public opinion in the United States would never tolerate nuclear missiles pointing at the heartland of America from the small island just south of Florida. Prompt and effective action was vital. But what action to take? Kennedy's action during this major crisis provides a fascinating study on the uses of power, of nuclear power-politics, and also of leadership in a time of crisis.

After making absolutely certain (by careful checking and cross-checking), that the information from Cuba was reliable beyond all doubt, Kennedy held urgent, secret discussions with his advisers and experts from the Department of Defense, the three services, and the State Department. He conferred with the National Security Council. Various proposals came forward. These varied from an all-out invasion and air strike, to some form of embargo or quarantine of the island, using American naval superiority in the area. Kennedy weighed each proposal carefully, and then took his decision. He announced this in a nationwide address on television and radio. What he decided is given in the text of that address which follows here. It was a moment of crisis in world affairs, for unless the Russians accepted what Kennedy proposed to do, war between the two nations might be unavoidable.

After an ominous silence from Moscow, when it seemed to government officials and observers everywhere that nuclear war was imminent, the silence was broken, and Premier Khrushchev announced that Russia was prepared to dismantle the sites, have the missiles crated and then ship them back to Russia under United Nations supervision.

Kennedy's conduct of this crisis earned high praise. It was noted that he deliberately left room for manoeuvre to the Russians, so that they would not be compelled to regard all-out war as the only alternative to an intolerable loss of face. It was also noted that when the crisis was over, Kennedy made no attempt to capitalize on his diplomatic victory by taunts to the Soviet leaders. It seems likely that a new respect for Kennedy dated from this period, a respect which led to a gradual, yet definite rapprochement between the Soviet Union and the United States.

The text of President Kennedy's address to the American nation should be studied for the careful appeals it includes to world opinion; for his studied appeal to the spirit of international law; and for his final appeal to Premier Khrushchev to join in a constructive and historic effort to end the arms race and thus 'transform the history of man'.

DOCUMENT 18. RADIO AND TELEVISION ADDRESS TO THE NATION BY PRESIDENT KENNEDY ON SOVIET MISSILES IN CUBA. 22 OCTOBER 1962.

My fellow-citizens—

This Government, as promised, has maintained the closest surveillance of the Soviet military build-up on the island of Cuba. Within the past week, unmistakable evidence has established the fact that a series of offensive missile sites is now in preparation on that imprisoned island. The purpose of these bases can be none other than to provide a nuclear strike capability against the Western hemisphere.

Upon receiving the first preliminary hard information of this nature last Tuesday morning at 9 a.m., I directed that our surveillance be stepped up. And having now confirmed and completed our evaluation of the evidence and our decision on a course of action, this Government feels obliged to report this new crisis to you in full detail.

The characteristics of these new missile sites indicate two distinct types of installations. Several of them include medium-range ballistic missiles, capable of carrying a nuclear warhead for a distance of more than 1,000 nautical miles. Each of these missiles, in short, is capable of striking Washington, D.C., the Panama Canal, Cape Canaveral, Mexico City, or any other city in the Eastern part of the United States, in Central America or in the Caribbean area.

Additional sites not yet completed appear to be designed for intermediate-range ballistic missiles—capable of travelling more than twice as far—and thus capable of striking most of the major cities in the Western hemisphere, ranging as far North as Hudson's Bay, Canada, and as far South as Lima, Peru. In addition, jet bombers, capable of carrying nuclear weapons, are now being uncrated and assembled on Cuba, while the necessary air bases are being prepared.

This urgent transformation of Cuba into an important strategic base—by the presence of these large, long-range and clearly offensive weapons of sudden mass destruction—constitutes an explicit threat to the peace and security of all the Americas, in flagrant and deliberate defiance of the Rio Pact of 1947, the traditions of this nation and hemisphere, the joint resolution of the 87th Congress, the Charter of the United Nations and my own public warnings to the Soviets on 4 and 13 September. This action also contradicts the repeated assurances of Soviet spokesmen, both publicly and privately delivered, that the arms build-up in Cuba would retain its original defensive character, and that the Soviet Union had no need or desire to station strategic missiles on the territory of any other nation.

The size of this undertaking makes clear that it had been

planned some months ago. Yet only last month, after I had made clear the distinction between any introduction of ground-to-ground missiles and the existence of defensive anti-aircraft missiles, the Soviet Government publicly stated on 11 September that 'the armaments and military equipment sent to Cuba are designed exclusively for defensive purposes', that 'there is no need for the Soviet Union to shift its weapons ... for a retaliatory blow to any other country, for instance Cuba', and that 'the Soviet Union has so powerful rockets to carry these nuclear warheads that there is no need to search for sites for them beyond the boundaries of the Soviet Union'. That statement was false.

Only last Thursday, as evidence of this rapid offensive build-up was already in my hand, Soviet Foreign Minister Gromyko told me in my office that he was instructed to make it clear once again, as he said his Government had already done, that Soviet assistance to Cuba 'pursued solely the purpose of contributing to the defense capabilities of Cuba', that 'training by Soviet specialists of Cuban nationals in handling defensive armaments was by no means offensive', and that 'if it were otherwise, the Soviet Government would never become involved in rendering such assistance'. That statement also was false.

Neither the United States of America nor the world community of nations can tolerate deliberate deception and offensive threats on the part of any nation, large or small. We no longer live in a world where only the actual firing of weapons represents a sufficient challenge to a nation's security to constitute a maximum peril. Nuclear weapons are so destructive, and ballistic missiles are so swift, that any substantially increased possibility of their use or any sudden change in their deployment may well be regarded as a definite threat to the peace.

For many years, both the Soviet Union and the United States—recognizing this fact—have deployed strategic nuclear weapons with great care, never upsetting the precarious *status quo* which ensured that these weapons would not be used in the absence of some vital challenge. Our own strategic missiles have never been transferred to the territory of any other nation under a cloak of secrecy and deception; and our history—unlike that of the Soviets since World War II—demonstrates that we have no desire to dominate or conquer any other nation or impose our system upon its people.

Nevertheless, American citizens have become adjusted to living daily on the bull's eye of Soviet missiles located inside the USSR or in submarines. In that sense, missiles in Cuba add to an already clear and present danger—although, it should be noted, the nations of Latin America have never previously been subjected to a potential nuclear threat.

But this secret, swift and extraordinary build-up of Communist missiles—in an area well-known to have a special and historical relationship to the United States and the nations of the Western hemisphere, in violation of Soviet assurances, and in defiance of American and hemispheric policy—this sudden decision to station strategic weapons for the first time outside of Soviet soil—is a deliberately provocative and unjustified change in the *status quo* which cannot be accepted by this country, if our courage and our commitments are ever to be trusted again by either friend or foe.

The 1930's taught us a clear lesson: aggressive conduct, if allowed to grow unchecked and unchallenged, ultimately leads to war. This nation is opposed to war. We are also true to our word. Our unswerving objective, therefore, must be to prevent the use of these missiles against this or any other country, and to secure their withdrawal or elimination from the Western hemisphere.

Our policy has been one of patience and restraint, as befits a peaceful and powerful nation which leads a world-wide alliance. We have been determined not to be diverted from our central concerns by mere irritants and fanatics. But now further action is required—and it is under way; and these actions may only be the beginning. We will not prematurely or unnecessarily risk the costs of world-wide nuclear war in which even the fruits of victory would be ashes in our mouth —but neither will we shrink from that risk at any time it must be faced.

Acting, therefore, in the defense of our own security and that of the entire Western hemisphere, and under the authority entrusted to me by the Constitution as endorsed by the resolution of the Congress, I have directed that the following initial steps be taken immediately:

First: to halt this offensive build-up, a strict quarantine on all offensive military equipment under shipment to Cuba is being initiated. All ships of any kind bound for Cuba, from whatever nation or port, will, if found to contain cargoes of offensive weapons, be turned back. This quarantine will be extended, if needed, to other types of cargo and carriers. We are not at this time, however, denying the necessities of life as the Soviets attempted to do in their Berlin blockade of 1948.

Second: I have directed the continued and increased close surveillance of Cuba and its military build-up. The Foreign Ministers of the OAS in their communique of 6 October rejected secrecy on such matters in this hemisphere.[1] Should these offensive military preparations continue, thus increasing the threat to the hemisphere, further action will be justified. I have directed the Armed Forces to prepare for any eventualities; and I trust that, in the interest of both the Cuban people and the Soviet technicians at these sites, the hazards to all concerned of continuing this threat will be recognized.

Third: It shall be the policy of this nation to regard any nuclear missile launched from Cuba against any nation in the Western hemisphere as an attack by the Soviet Union on the United States requiring a full retaliatory response upon the Soviet Union.

Fourth: As a necessary military precaution, I have reinforced our base at Guantanamo, evacuated today the dependents of our personnel there and ordered additional military units to be on a stand-by alert basis.

Fifth: We are calling tonight for an immediate meeting of the Organ of Consultation under the Organisation of American States, to consider this threat to hemispheric security and to invoke Articles 6 and 8 of the Rio Treaty in support of all necessary action. The United Nations Charter allows for regional security arrangements, and the nations of this hemisphere decided long ago against the military presence of outside powers. Our other Allies around the world have also been alerted.

Sixth: Under the Charter of the United Nations, we are asking tonight that an emergency meeting of the Security Council be convoked without delay to take action against this latest Soviet threat to world peace. Our resolution will call for the prompt dismantling and withdrawal of all offensive weapons in Cuba, under the supervision of U.N. observers, before the quarantine can be lifted.

Seventh, and finally: I call upon Chairman Khrushchev to halt and eliminate this clandestine, reckless and provocative threat to world peace and to stable relations between our two nations. I call upon him further to abandon this course of world domination, and to join in an historic effort to end the perilous arms race and transform the history of man. He has an opportunity now to move the world back from the abyss of destruction—by returning to his Government's own words that it had no need to station missiles outside its own territory, and withdrawing these weapons from Cuba—by refraining from any action which will widen or deepen the present crisis—and then by participating in a search for peaceful and permanent solutions.

This nation is prepared to present its case against this Soviet threat to peace, and our own proposals for a peaceful world, at any time and in any forum—in the OAS, in the United Nations, or in any other meeting that could be useful—without limiting our freedom of action. We have in the past made strenuous efforts to limit the spread of nuclear weapons. We have proposed the elimination of all arms and military bases in a fair and effective disarmament treaty. We are prepared to discuss new proposals for the removal of tensions on both sides —including the possibilities of a genuinely independent Cuba, free to determine its own destiny. We have no wish to war with the Soviet Union—for we are a peaceful people who desire to live in peace with all other peoples.

But it is difficult to settle or even discuss these problems in an atmosphere of intimidation. That is why this latest Soviet threat—or any other threat which is made either independently or in response to our actions this week—must and will be met with determination. Any hostile move anywhere in the world against the safety and freedom of peoples to whom we are committed—including in particular the brave people of West Berlin—will be met by whatever action is needed.

Finally, I want to say a few words to the captive people of Cuba, to whom this speech is being directly carried by special radio facilities. I speak to you as a friend, as one who knows of your deep attachment to your fatherland, as one who shares your aspirations for liberty and justice for all. And I have watched with deep sorrow how your nationalist revolution was betrayed and how your fatherland fell under foreign domination. Now your leaders are no longer Cuban leaders inspired by Cuban ideals. They are puppets and agents of an international conspiracy which has turned Cuba against your friends and neighbors in the Americas—and turned it into the first Latin-American country to become a target for nuclear war—the first Latin-American country to have these weapons on its soil.

These new weapons are not in your interest. They contribute nothing to your peace and well-being. They can only undermine it. But this country has no wish to cause you to suffer or to impose any system upon you. We know your lives and land are being used as pawns by those who deny your freedom.

Many times in the past, the Cuban people have risen to throw out tyrants who destroyed their liberty. And I have no doubt that most Cubans today look forward to the time when they will be truly free—free from foreign domination, free to choose their own leaders, free to select their own system, free to own their own land, free to speak and write and worship without fear or degradation. And then shall Cuba be welcomed back to the society of free nations and to the associations of this hemisphere.

My fellow citizens: let no one doubt that this is a difficult and dangerous effort on which we have set out. No one can foresee precisely what course it will take or what costs or casualties will be incurred. Many months of sacrifice and self-discipline lie ahead—months in which both our will and our patience will be tested—months in which many threats and denunciations will keep us aware of our danger. But the greatest danger of all would be to do nothing.

The path we have chosen for the present is full of hazards, as all paths are—but it is the one most consistent with our character and courage as a nation and our commitments around the world. The cost of freedom is always high—but Americans have always paid it. And one path we shall never choose is the path of surrender or submission.

Our goal is not the victory of might but the vindication of

right; not peace at the expense of freedom, but both peace and freedom, here in this hemisphere, and, we hope, around the world. God willing, that goal will be achieved.

NOTE

(1) OAS. The Organisation of American States. Formed at Bogota, Colombia, in 1948 between the United States and the Latin-American countries. A pact to preserve hemisphere interests, chiefly economic and strategic. Cuba was originally a member but on 31 January 1962 a vote in the OAS council excluded Cuba 'from participation in the American system' (though without formally depriving Cuba of OAS membership) because of Cuba's 'alignment with the Communist bloc'.

THE SOVIET WITHDRAWAL

At his news conference on 20 November 1962, President Kennedy announced that the Russians had carried out the major part of their undertaking to withdraw missiles and bombers from Cuba, though some combat units remained. Kennedy insisted that the promise be carried out fully, but went on to give an assurance in turn that the United States, for her part, would respect the territorial integrity of Cuba, and that no invasion would be launched on the island by American forces. This statement was an important contribution to reducing tension in a sensitive area where the two major nuclear powers had narrowly averted a head-on collision. President Kennedy's statement may also be read as an early document in the 'dialogue' which now developed between the United States and Soviet Russia. In that dialogue, evidence mounted that both sides genuinely sought to ease the tensions of the cold war and reach some form of agreement for co-existence. In the following document, President Kennedy is clearly addressing the Soviet leaders as much as the journalists assembled at his news conference in Washington.

DOCUMENT 19. STATEMENT ON THE WITHDRAWAL OF SOVIET BOMBERS FROM CUBA. PRESIDENT KENNEDY'S NEWS CONFERENCE, WASHINGTON, D.C., 20 NOVEMBER 1962.

I have today been informed by Chairman Khrushchev that all of the Il-28 bombers now in Cuba will be withdrawn in thirty days. He also agrees that these planes can be observed and counted as they leave. Inasmuch as this goes a long way toward reducing the danger which faced this hemisphere four weeks ago, I have this afternoon instructed the Secretary of Defense to lift our naval quarantine.

In view of this action, I want to take this opportunity to bring the American people up to date on the Cuban crisis and to review the progress made thus far in fulfilling the understandings between Soviet Chairman Khrushchev and myself....

Chairman Khrushchev, it will be recalled, agreed to remove from Cuba all weapons systems capable of offensive use, to halt the further introduction of such weapons into Cuba, and to permit appropriate United Nations observation and supervision to insure the carrying out and continuation of these commitments. We on our part agreed that once these adequate arrangements for verification had been established, we would remove our naval quarantine and give assurances against invasion of Cuba.

The evidence to date indicates that all known offensive missile sites in Cuba have been dismantled. The missiles and their associated equipment have been loaded on Soviet ships. And our inspection at sea of these departing ships has confirmed that the number of missiles reported by the Soviet Union as having been brought into Cuba, which closely corresponded to our own information, has now been removed. In addition, the Soviet Government has stated that all nuclear weapons have been withdrawn from Cuba and no offensive weapons will be re-introduced.

Nevertheless, important parts of the understanding of 27 and 28 October remain to be carried out. The Cuban Government has not yet permitted the United Nations to verify whether all offensive weapons have been removed, and no lasting safeguards have yet been established against the future introduction of offensive weapons back into Cuba.

Consequently, if the Western Hemisphere is to continue to be protected against offensive weapons, this government has no choice but to pursue its own means of checking on military activities in Cuba. The importance of our continued vigilance is underlined by our identification in recent days of a number of Soviet ground combat units in Cuba, although we are informed that these and other Soviet units were associated with the protection of offensive weapons systems, and will also be withdrawn in due course.

I repeat, we would like nothing better than adequate international arrangements for the task of inspection and verification in Cuba, and we are prepared to continue our efforts to achieve such arrangements. Until that is done, difficult problems remain. As for our part, if all offensive weapons systems are removed from Cuba and kept out of the hemisphere in the future, under adequate verification and safeguards, and if Cuba is not used for the export of aggressive Communist purposes, there will be peace in the Caribbean. And as I said in September, 'we shall neither initiate nor permit aggression in this hemisphere'.

We will not, of course, abandon the political, economic and other efforts of this hemisphere to halt subversion from Cuba nor our purpose and hope that the Cuban people shall someday be truly free. But these policies are very different from any intent to launch a military invasion of the island.

May I add this final thought: There is much for which we can be grateful as we look back to where we stood only four weeks ago. The unity of this hemisphere, the support of our allies and the calm determination of the American people—these qualities may be tested many more times in this decade, but we have increased reason to be confident that they will continue to serve the cause of freedom with distinction in the years to come.

A THAW IN THE COLD WAR

President Kennedy deliberately gave many of his most important speeches before university audiences. In this way, he could deal at some length with subjects of great importance, in a manner befitting the occasion as well as the subject. In the summer of 1963, he gave one of his most outstanding speeches before American University in Washington, D.C.

The speech was a careful attempt to install a new spirit of peaceful negotiation between the Western democracies and the Communist nations. However there is no woolly sentiment in the speech; it is hard-headed and realistic. As such, it had the maximum chance of achieving positive results. Among the various points and proposals it contained, there was a concrete undertaking that the United States would immediately cease to carry out nuclear tests in the atmosphere, provided other nations followed suit.

The successful negotiations which followed, and the signing of a comprehensive test ban treaty by ninety-nine nations—including the Soviet Union and the United States—within four months of this speech, undoubtedly owed something to the careful appeal President Kennedy made on 10 June 1963.

DOCUMENT 20. THE COMMENCEMENT ADDRESS AT AMERICAN UNIVERSITY BY PRESIDENT KENNEDY, WASHINGTON, 10 JUNE 1963.

'There are few earthly things more beautiful than a university,' wrote John Masefield, in his tribute to English universities—and his words are equally true today. He did not refer to spires and towers, to campus greens and ivied walls. He admired the splendid beauty of the university, he said, because it was 'a place where those who hate ignorance may strive to know, where those who perceive truth may strive to make others see'.

I have, therefore, chosen this time and this place to discuss a topic on which ignorance too often abounds and the truth is too rarely perceived—yet it is the most important topic on earth: world peace.

What kind of peace do I mean? What kind of peace do we seek? Not a *Pax Americana* enforced on the world by American weapons of war. Not the peace of the grave or the security of the slave. I am talking about genuine peace, the kind of peace that makes life on earth worth living, the kind that enables men and nations to grow and to hope and to build a better life for their children—not merely peace for Americans but peace for all men and women—not merely peace in our time but peace for all time.

I speak of peace because of the new face of war. Total war makes no sense in an age when great powers can maintain large and relatively invulnerable nuclear forces and refuse to surrender without resort to those forces. It makes no sense in an age when a single nuclear weapon contains almost ten times the explosive force delivered by all of the allied air forces in the Second World War. It makes no sense in an age when the deadly poisons produced by a nuclear exchange would be carried by wind and water and soil and seed to the far corners of the globe and to generations yet unborn.

Today the expenditure of billions of dollars every year on weapons acquired for the purpose of making sure we never need to use them is essential to keeping the peace. But surely the acquisition of such idle stockpiles—which can only destroy and never create—is not the only, much less the most efficient, means of assuring peace.

I speak of peace, therefore, as the necessary rational end of rational men. I realize that the pursuit of peace is not as dramatic as the pursuit of war—and frequently the words of the pursuer fall on deaf ears. But we have no more urgent task.

Some say that it is useless to speak of world peace or world law or world disarmament—and that it will be useless until the leaders of the Soviet Union adopt a more enlightened attitude. I hope they do. I believe we can help them do it. But I also believe that we must re-examine our own attitude—as individuals and as a Nation—for our attitude is as essential as theirs. And every graduate of this school, every thoughtful citizen who despairs of war and wishes to bring peace, should begin by looking inward—by examining his own attitude toward the possibilities of peace, toward the Soviet Union, toward the course of the cold war and toward freedom and peace here at home.

First: Let us examine our attitude toward peace itself. Too many of us think it is impossible. Too many think it unreal. But that is a dangerous, defeatist belief. It leads to the conclusion that war is inevitable—that mankind is doomed—that we are gripped by forces we cannot control.

We need not accept that view. Our problems are man-made —therefore, they can be solved by man. And man can be as big as he wants. No problem of human destiny is beyond human beings. Man's reason and spirit have often solved the seemingly unsolvable—and we believe they can do it again.

I am not referring to the absolute, infinite concept of universal peace and good will of which some fantasts and fanatics dream. I do not deny the value of hopes and dreams, but we merely invite discouragement and incredulity by making that our only and immediate goal.

Let us focus instead on a more practical, more attainable peace, based not on a sudden revolution in human nature but on a gradual evolution in human institutions—on a series of concrete actions and effective agreements which are in the interest of all concerned. There is no single, simple key to this peace—no grand or magic formula to be adopted by one or two powers. Genuine peace must be the product of many nations, the sum of many acts. It must be dynamic, not static, changing to meet the challenge of each new generation. For peace is a process—a way of solving problems.

With such a peace, there will still be quarrels and conflicting interests, as there are within families and nations. World peace, like community peace, does not require that each man love his neighbor—it requires only that they live together in mutual tolerance, submitting their disputes to a just and peaceful settlement. And history teaches us that enmities between nations, as between individuals, do not last forever. However fixed our likes and dislikes may seem, the tide of time and events will often bring surprising changes in the relations between nations and neighbors.

So let us persevere. Peace need not be impracticable, and war need not be inevitable. By defining our goal more clearly, by making it seem more manageable and less remote, we can help all peoples to see it, to draw hope from it, and to move irresistibly toward it.

Second: Let us re-examine our attitude toward the Soviet Union. It is discouraging to think that their leaders may actually believe what their propagandists write. It is discouraging to read a recent authoritative Soviet text on Military Strategy and find, on page after page, wholly baseless and incredible claims—such as the allegation that 'American imperialist circles are preparing to unleash different types of wars ... that there is a very real threat of a preventive war being unleashed by American imperialists against the Soviet Union ... [and that] the political aims of the American imperialists are to enslave economically and politically the European and other capitalist countries. ... [and] to achieve world domination. ... by means of aggressive wars'.

Truly, as it was written long ago: 'The wicked flee when no man pursueth'. Yet it is sad to read these Soviet statements—

to realize the extent of the gulf between us. But it is also a warning—a warning to the American people not to fall into the same trap as the Soviets, not to see only a distorted and desperate view of the other side, not to see conflict as inevitable, accommodation as impossible, and communication as nothing more than an exchange of threats.

No government or social system is so evil that its people must be considered as lacking in virtue. As Americans, we find Communism profoundly repugnant as a negation of personal freedom and dignity. But we can still hail the Russian people for their many achievements—in science and space, in economic and industrial growth, in culture and in acts of courage.

Among the many traits the peoples of our two countries have in common, none is stronger than our mutual abhorrence of war. Almost unique among the major world powers, we have never been at war with each other. And no nation in the history of battle ever suffered more than the Soviet Union suffered in the course of the Second World War. At least 20 million lost their lives. Countless millions of homes and farms were burned or sacked. A third of the nation's territory, including nearly two-thirds of its industrial base, was turned into a wasteland—a loss equivalent to the devastation of this country East of Chicago.

Today, should total war ever break out again—no matter how—our two countries would become the primary targets. It is an ironic but accurate fact that the two strongest powers are the two in the most danger of devastation. All we have built, all we have worked for, would be destroyed in the first twenty-four hours. And even in the cold war, which brings burdens and dangers to so many countries, including this Nation's closest allies—our two countries bear the heaviest burdens. For we are both devoting massive sums of money to weapons that could be better devoted to combating ignorance, poverty, and disease. We are both caught up in a vicious and dangerous cycle in which suspicion on one side breeds suspicion on the other, and new weapons beget counter-weapons.

In short, both the United States and its allies, and the Soviet Union and its allies, have a mutually deep interest in a just and genuine peace and in halting the arms race. Agreements to this end are in the interests of the Soviet Union as well as ours—and even the most hostile nations can be relied upon to accept and keep those treaty obligations, and only those treaty obligations, which are in their own interest.

So, let us not be blind to our differences—but let us also direct attention to our common interests and to the means by which those differences can be resolved. And if we cannot end now our differences, at least we can help make the world safe for diversity. For in the final analysis, our most basic common link is that we all inhabit this small planet. We all breathe the same air. We all cherish our children's future. And we are all mortal.

Third: Let us re-examine our attitude toward the cold war, remembering that we are not engaged in a debate, seeking to pile up debating points. We are not here distributing blame or pointing the finger of judgment. We must deal with the world as it is, and not as it might have been had the history of the last eighteen years been different.

We must, therefore, persevere in the search for peace in the hope that constructive changes within the Communist bloc might bring within reach solutions which now seem beyond us. We must conduct our affairs in such a way that it becomes in the Communists' interest to agree on a genuine peace. Above all, while defending our own vital interests, nuclear powers must avert those confrontations which bring an adversary to a choice of either a humiliating retreat or a nuclear war. To adopt that kind of course in the nuclear age would be evidence only of the bankruptcy of our policy—or of a collective death-wish for the world.

To secure these ends, America's weapons are non-provocative, carefully controlled, designed to deter, and capable of selective use. Our military forces are committed to peace and disciplined in self-restraint. Our diplomats are instructed to avoid unnecessary irritants and purely rhetorical hostility.

For we can seek a relaxation of tensions without relaxing our guard. And, for our part, we do not need to use threats to prove that we are resolute. We do not need to jam foreign broadcasts out of fear our faith will be eroded. We are unwilling to impose our system on any unwilling people—but we are willing and able to engage in peaceful competition with any people on earth.

Meanwhile, we seek to strengthen the United Nations, to help solve its financial problems, to make it a more effective instrument for peace, to develop it into a genuine world security system—a system capable of resolving disputes on the basis of law, of insuring the security of the large and the small, and of creating conditions under which arms can finally be abolished.

At the same time we seek to keep peace inside the non-Communist world, where many nations, all of them our friends, are divided over issues which weaken Western unity, which invite Communist intervention, or which threaten to erupt into war. Our efforts in West New Guinea, in the Congo, in the Middle East, and in the Indian sub-continent, have been persistent and patient despite criticism from both sides. We have also tried to set an example for others—by seeking to adjust small but significant differences with our closest neighbors in Mexico and in Canada.

Speaking of other nations, I wish to make one point clear. We are bound to many nations by alliances. Those alliances exist because our concerns and theirs substantially overlap. Our commitment to defend Western Europe and West Berlin, for example, stands undiminished because of the identity of our vital interests. The United States will make no deal with the Soviet Union at the expense of other nations and other peoples, not merely because they are our partners, but also because their interests and ours converge.

Our interests converge, however, not only in defending the frontiers of freedom, but in pursuing the paths of peace. It is our hope—and the purpose of allied policies—to convince the Soviet Union that she, too, should let each nation choose its own future, so long as that choice does not interfere with the choices of others. The Communist drive to impose their political and economic system on others is the primary cause of world tension today. For there can be no doubt that, if all nations could refrain from interfering in the self-determination of others, the peace would be much more assured.

This will require a new effort to achieve world law—a new context for world discussions. It will require increased understanding between the Soviets and ourselves. And increased understanding will require increased contact and communication. One step in this direction is the proposed arrangement for a direct line between Moscow and Washington, to avoid on each side the dangerous delays, misunderstandings, and mis-readings of the other's actions which might occur at a time of crisis.

We have also been talking in Geneva about other first-step measures of arms control, designed to limit the intensity of the arms race and to reduce the risks of accidental war. Our primary long-range interest in Geneva, however, is general and complete disarmament—designed to take place by stages, permitting parallel political developments to build the new institutions of peace which would take the place of arms. The pursuit of disarmament has been an effort of this Government since the 1920s. It has been urgently sought by the past three administrations. And however dim the prospects may be today, we intend to continue this effort—to continue it in order that all countries, including our own, can better grasp what the problems and possibilities of disarmament are.

The one major area of these negotiations where the end is in sight, yet where a fresh start is badly needed, is in a treaty to outlaw nuclear tests. The conclusion of such a treaty, so near and yet so far, would check the spiraling arms race in one of its most dangerous areas. It would place the nuclear powers in a position to deal more effectively with one of the greatest hazards which man faces in 1963, the further spread of nuclear arms. It would increase our security—it would decrease the prospects of war. Surely this goal is sufficiently important to require our steady pursuit, yielding neither to the temptation to give up the whole effort nor the temptation to give up our insistence on vital and responsible safeguards.

I am taking this opportunity, therefore, to announce two important decisions in this regard.

First: Chairman Khrushchev, Prime Minister Macmillan, and I have agreed that high-level discussions will shortly begin in Moscow looking toward early agreement on a comprehensive test ban treaty. Our hopes must be tempered with the caution of history—but with our hopes go the hopes of all mankind.

Second: To make clear our good faith and solemn convictions on the matter, I now declare that the United States does not propose to conduct nuclear tests in the atmosphere so long as other states do not do so. We will not be the first to resume. Such a declaration is no substitute for a formal binding treaty, but I hope it will help us achieve one. Nor would such a treaty be a substitute for disarmament, but I hope it will help us achieve it.

Finally, my fellow Americans, let us examine our attitude toward peace and freedom here at home. The quality and spirit of our own society must justify and support our efforts abroad. We must show it in the dedication of our own lives— as many of you who are graduating today will have a unique opportunity to do, by serving without pay in the Peace Corps abroad or in the proposed National Service Corps here at home.

But wherever we are, we must all, in our daily lives, live up to the age-old faith that peace and freedom walk together. In too many of our cities today, the peace is not secure because freedom is incomplete.

It is the responsibility of the executive branch at all levels of government—local, State, and National—to provide and protect that freedom for all of our citizens by all means within their authority. It is the responsibility of the legislative branch at all levels, wherever that authority is not now adequate, to make it adequate. And it is the responsibility of all citizens in all sections of this country to respect the rights of all others and to respect the law of the land.

All this is not unrelated to world peace. 'When a man's ways please the Lord,' the Scriptures tell us, 'he maketh even his enemies to be at peace with him.' And is not peace, in the last analysis, basically a matter of human rights—the right to live out our lives without fear of devastation—the right to breathe air as nature provided it—the right of future generations to a healthy existence?

While we proceed to safeguard our national interests, let us also safeguard human interests. And the elimination of war and arms is clearly in the interest of both. No treaty, however much it may be to the advantage of all, however tightly it may be worded, can provide absolute security against the risks of deception and evasion. But it can—if it is sufficiently effective in its enforcement and if it is sufficiently in the interests of its signers—offer far more security and far fewer risks than an unabated, unpredictable arms race.

The United States, as the world knows, will never start a war. We do not want a war. We do not now expect a war. This generation of Americans has already had enough—more than enough—of war and hate and oppression. We shall be prepared if others wish it. We shall be alert to try to stop it. But we shall also do our part to build a world of peace where the weak are safe and the strong are just. We are not helpless before that task or hopeless of its success. Confident and unafraid, we labor on—not toward a strategy of annihilation but toward a strategy of peace.

TWO SPEECHES ON THE NUCLEAR TEST BAN TREATY

Only six weeks after his 10 June 1963 speech at the American University, President Kennedy announced a treaty with Soviet Russia for banning nuclear tests in the atmosphere, in outer space and under water. The treaty was signed in Moscow on 5 August, and when the United States Senate voted approval by 80 votes to 19 on 24 September, President Kennedy signed it on 7 October.

This treaty was welcomed as a hopeful and significant sign of a definite 'thaw' in Soviet–American relations. Two days after signing the treaty, President Kennedy announced the sale of $250 million worth of American wheat to the U.S.S.R.

DOCUMENT 21. TWO SPEECHES BY PRESIDENT KENNEDY ON THE NUCLEAR TEST BAN TREATY: I. TELEVISION ADDRESS TO THE PEOPLE, THE WHITE HOUSE, WASHINGTON, D.C., 26 JULY 1963.

I speak to you tonight in a spirit of hope. Eighteen years ago the advent of nuclear weapons changed the course of the world as well as the war. Since that time, all mankind has been struggling to escape from the darkening prospect of mass destruction on earth. In an age when both sides have come to possess enough nuclear power to destroy the human race several times over, the world of Communism and the world of free choice have been caught up in a vicious circle of conflicting ideology and interest. Each increase of tension has produced an increase of arms; each increase of arms has produced an increase of tension.

In these years the United States and the Soviet Union have frequently communicated suspicion and warnings to each other, but very rarely hope. Our representatives have met at the summit and at the brink; they have met in Washington and in Moscow, in Geneva and at the United Nations. But too often these meetings have produced only darkness, discord or disillusion.

Yesterday a shaft of light cut into the darkness. Negotiations were concluded in Moscow on a treaty to ban all nuclear tests in the atmosphere, in outer space and under water. For the first time, an agreement has been reached on bringing the forces of nuclear destruction under international control. . . .

That plan and many subsequent disarmament plans, large and small, have all been blocked by those opposed to international inspection. A ban on nuclear tests, however, requires on-the-spot inspection only for underground tests. This nation now possesses a variety of techniques to detect the nuclear tests of other nations which are conducted in the air or under water. For such tests produce unmistakable signs which our modern instruments can pick up.

The treaty initialed yesterday, therefore, is a limited treaty which permits continued underground testing and prohibits only those tests that we ourselves can police. It requires no control posts, no on-site inspection, no international body.

We should also understand that it has other limits as well. Any nation which signs the treaty will have an opportunity to withdraw if it finds that extraordinary events related to the subject matter of the treaty have jeopardized its supreme interests; and no nation's right of self-defense will in any way be impaired. Nor does this treaty mean an end to the threat of nuclear war. It will not reduce nuclear stockpiles; it will not halt the production of nuclear weapons; it will not restrict their use in time of war.

Nevertheless, this limited treaty will radically reduce the nuclear testing which would otherwise be conducted on both sides; it will prohibit the United States, the United Kingdom, the Soviet Union and all others who sign it from engaging in the atmospheric tests which have so alarmed mankind; and it offers to all the world a welcome sign of hope.

For this is not a unilateral moratorium, but a specific and

solemn legal obligation. While it will not prevent this nation from testing underground, or from being ready to conduct atmospheric tests if the acts of others so require, it gives us a concrete opportunity to extend its coverage to other nations and later to other forms of nuclear tests.

This treaty is in part the product of Western patience and vigilance. We have made clear, most recently in Berlin and Cuba, our deep resolve to protect our security and our freedom against any form of aggression. We have also made clear our steadfast determination to limit the arms race. In three administrations our soldiers and diplomats have worked together to this end, always supported by Great Britain. Prime Minister Macmillan joined with President Eisenhower in proposing a limited test ban in 1959, and again with me in 1961 and 1962.

But the achievement of this goal is not a victory for one side; it is a victory for mankind. It reflects no concessions either to or by the Soviet Union. It reflects simply our common recognition of the dangers in further testing.

This treaty is not the millennium. It will not resolve all conflicts, or cause the Communists to forgo their ambitions, or eliminate the danger of war. It will not reduce our need for arms or allies or programs of assistance to others. But it is an important first step—a step toward peace, a step toward reason, a step away from war. . . .

II. SPEECH FROM THE TREATY ROOM, THE WHITE HOUSE, WASHINGTON, D.C., 7 OCTOBER 1963.

In its first two decades, the Age of Nuclear Energy has been full of fear, yet never empty of hope. Today the fear is a little less and the hope a little greater. For the first time we have been able to reach an agreement which can limit the dangers of this age.

The agreement itself is limited, but its message of hope has been heard and understood not only by the peoples of the three originating nations, but by the peoples and governments of the hundred other countries that have signed. This treaty is the first fruit of labors in which multitudes have shared—citizens, legislators, statesmen, diplomats and soldiers, too.

Soberly and unremittingly this nation, but never this nation alone, has sought the doorway to effective disarmament into a world where peace is secure. Today we have a beginning, and it is right for us to acknowledge all whose work across the years has helped make this beginning possible.

What the future will bring, no one of us can know. This first fruit of hope may or may not be followed by larger harvests. Even this limited treaty, great as it is with promise, can survive only if it has from others the determined support in letter and in spirit which I hereby pledge on behalf of the United States.

If this treaty fails, it will not be our doing, and even if it fails, we shall not regret that we have made this clear and honorable national commitment to the cause of man's survival. For under this treaty we can and must still keep our vigil in defense of freedom.

But this treaty need not fail. This small step towards safety can be followed by others longer and less limited, if also harder in the taking. With our courage and understanding enlarged by this achievement, let us press onward in quest of man's essential desire for peace.

As President of the United States and with the advice and consent of the Senate, I now sign the instruments of ratification of this treaty.

PART VI

The Presidential Office

The documents and articles in this section deal with the office of President of the United States. In this context, 'office' does not of course mean simply the oval room in the White House where the President spends much of his working day. It means the vastly expanded Executive Office which a modern President must maintain in order to run the nation's affairs.

One of the features of the Executive Office is that although the President is surrounded by scores of advisers, specialists and consultants, he is nevertheless a lonely figure in the office which President Kennedy called a 'mysterious institution'. The passages included in this section illustrate this. The section concludes with two articles on the Presidency by independent observers.

The passage immediately following is taken from the account of President Kennedy's years in the White House by Arthur Schlesinger Jr. in his book *A Thousand Days*. Arthur Schlesinger was in a special position (see pp. 85–6) to observe President Kennedy's daily routine. Again, as the historian of the New Deal and the Presidency of Franklin Roosevelt, Schlesinger is able to compare and contrast the methods of the two men in carrying out the responsibilities of the office.

DOCUMENT 22. EXTRACTS FROM 'KENNEDY IN THE PRESIDENTIAL OFFICE', BY ARTHUR M. SCHLESINGER, JR., FROM *A Thousand Days: John F. Kennedy in the White House* (ANDRE DEUTSCH and HOUGHTON MIFFLIN, 1965). (PP. 671–685.)

In the office

It has been traditional for Presidents to curse the Presidency. Washington said he felt like 'a culprit, who is going to the place of his execution'. Jefferson called the Presidency a 'splendid misery', Buchanan 'a crown of thorns'; for Truman the White House was 'the finest prison in the country'. Such melodramatic lamentations never escaped the lips of John F. Kennedy. He had wanted to become President, he loved being President and at times he could hardly remember that he had ever been anything else. He never complained about the 'terrible loneliness' of the office or its 'awesome burdens'. I do not think he felt terribly lonely; as he once remarked to William Manchester, 'In many ways I see and hear more than anyone else'. . . .

He had to an exceptional degree the talent for concentration. When he put on his always surprising horn-rimmed glasses and read a document, it was with total intentness; in a moment he would have seized its essence and returned to the world he had left. He was for the same reason a superb listener. 'Whoever he's with,' someone said, 'he's with them completely.' He would lean forward, his eyes protruding slightly, concerned with using the occasion not to expound his own thoughts but to drag out of the talker whatever could be of use to him. Isaiah Berlin was reminded of a remark made about Lenin: that he could exhaust people by listening to them. In this way he ventilated problems in great detail without revealing his own position and without making his visitors conscious that he was holding back. . . .

He came to the Presidency almost without break of stride. Yet the Presidency, as he once put it, is a 'mysterious institution'. 'There is no experience you can get,' he said at the end of 1962, 'that can possibly prepare you adequately for the Presidency.' He himself came to feel the mystique of the Presidency strongly enough to doubt whether the quality of the presidential experience could be understood by those who had not shared it. My father, who had asked a panel of historians and political scientists in 1948 to rate the Presidents in categories from 'great' to 'failure', repeated the poll in early 1962 and sent a ballot to the historian who had written *Profiles in Courage* and *A Nation of Immigrants*.[1] Kennedy started to fill in the ballot but, as he thought about it, came to the conclusion that the exercise was unprofitable. 'A year ago,' he wrote my father, 'I would have responded with confidence . . . but now I am not so sure. After being in the office for a year I feel that

a good deal more study is required to make my judgment sufficiently informed. There is a tendency to mark the obvious names. I would like to subject those not so well known to a long scrutiny after I have left this office.' He said to me later, 'How the hell can you tell? Only the President himself can know what his real pressures and his real alternatives are. If you don't know that, how can you judge performance?' Some of his greatest predecessors, he would sometimes say, were given credit for doing things when they could do nothing else; only the most detailed study could disclose what difference a President had made by his own individual effort. War, he pointed out, made it easier for a President to achieve greatness. But would Lincoln have been judged so great a President if he had lived long enough to face the almost insoluble problem of Reconstruction?
. . .

In the Executive branch

. . . In order to get the country moving again, he had to get the government moving. He came to the White House at a time when the ability of the President to do this had suffered steady constriction. The clichés about the 'most powerful office on earth' had concealed the extent to which the mid-century Presidents had much less freedom of action than, say, Jackson or Lincoln or even Franklin Roosevelt. No doubt the mid-century Presidents could blow up the world, but at the same time they were increasingly hemmed in by the growing power of the executive bureaucracy and of Congress—and at a time when crisis at home and abroad made clear decision and swift action more imperative than ever before. The President understood this. 'Before my term has ended,' he said in his first State of the Union address, 'we shall have to test anew whether a nation organized and governed such as ours can endure. The outcome is by no means certain.'

Kennedy was fully sensitive—perhaps oversensitive—to the limitations imposed by Congress on the presidential freedom of maneuver. But, though he was well aware of the problem within the executive domain, I do not think he had entirely appreciated its magnitude. The textbooks had talked of three coordinate branches of government: the executive, the legislative, the judiciary. But with an activist President it became apparent that there was a fourth branch: the Presidency itself. And, in pursuing his purposes, the President was likely to encounter almost as much resistance from the executive branch as from the others. By 1961 the tension between the permanent government and the presidential government was deep in our system.

The Eisenhower administration in the end met the problem of the permanent government by accepting the trend toward routinization and extending it to the Presidency itself. This was congenial both to President Eisenhower, accustomed all his life to the military staff system, and to the needs of a regime more concerned with consolidation than with innovation. The result was an effort to institutionalize the Presidency, making it as nearly automatic in its operations and as little dependent on particular individuals as possible. It was a perfectly serious experiment; but in the end it was defeated, both by the inextinguishably personal character of the Presidency, which broke out from time to time even in the case of one so well disciplined to the staff system as Eisenhower, and also by the fact that even the Eisenhower administration was occasionally forced to do new things in order to meet new challenges.

Kennedy, who had been critical of the Eisenhower effort to institutionalize the Presidency, was determined to restore the personal character of the office and recover presidential control over the sprawling feudalism of government. This became a central theme of his administration and, in some respects, a central frustration. The presidential government, coming to Washington aglow with new ideas and a euphoric sense that it could not go wrong, promptly collided with the feudal barons of the permanent government, entrenched in their domains and fortified by their sense of proprietorship; and the permanent government, confronted by this invasion, began almost to function (with, of course, many notable individual exceptions) as a resistance movement, scattering to the *maquis* in order to pick off the intruders. This was especially true in foreign affairs. . . .

In the long run, the problem of the permanent government could no doubt be solved by permeation and attrition. 'Getting the bureaucracy to accept new ideas,' as Chester Bowles once said, 'is like carrying a double mattress up a very narrow and winding stairway. It is a terrible job, and you exhaust yourself when you try it. But once you get the mattress up it is awfully hard for anyone else to get it down.' But it also required day-to-day direction and control. This was Kennedy's preferred method: hence his unceasing flow of suggestions, inquiries, phone calls directly to the operating desks and so on. This approach enabled him to imbue government with a sense of his own desires and purposes. A Foreign Service officer once remarked on the feeling that 'we were all reading the cables together'—the man at the desk, the Secretary of State and the White House. Nothing was more invigorating and inspiring, especially for the imaginative official, than personal contact with the President. . . .

He considered results more important than routine. 'My experience in government,' he once said, 'is that when things are noncontroversial, beautifully coordinated, and all the rest, it must be that not much is going on.' He was not, like Roosevelt, a deliberate inciter of bureaucratic disorder; he found no pleasure in playing off one subordinate against another. But his total self-reliance, his confidence in his own priorities and his own memory, freed him from dependence on orderly administrative arrangements. In any case, the Constitution made it clear where the buck stopped. 'The President,' he once said, 'bears the burden of the responsibility. . . . The advisers may move on to new advice.' The White House, of course, could not do everything, but it could do something. 'The President can't administer a department,' he said drily on one occasion, 'but at least he can be a stimulant.' This Kennedy certainly was, but on occasion he almost administered departments too.

His determination was to pull issues out of the bureaucratic ruck in time to defend his own right to decision and his own freedom of innovation. One devoted student of his methods, Prime Minister Harold Wilson, later spoke of the importance of getting in on emerging questions 'by holding meetings of all relevant ministers at an early stage before the problem gets out of hand. That's one of the techniques the world owes to Kennedy'. . . .

NOTE

(1) Arthur Schlesinger Senior (died 1965) was one of the foremost American historians of our time.
A Nation of Immigrants. A short book by John F. Kennedy (see p. 223).

THE POWERS OF THE PRESIDENCY

As Special Counsel to the President (see pp. 76–7), Theodore Sorensen was also in a special position to observe President Kennedy in the Executive Office. The following is taken from his book *Kennedy* and brings out further aspects of Kennedy's approach to his Presidential responsibilities.

DOCUMENT 23. 'THE POWERS OF THE PRESIDENCY', FROM *Kennedy*, BY THEODORE SORENSEN (New York, 1965). (CHAP. XV, PP. 389–392.)

One of John Kennedy's most important contributions to the human spirit was his concept of the office of the Presidency. His philosophy of government was keyed to power, not as a matter of personal ambition but of national obligation: the primacy of the White House within the Executive Branch and of the Executive Branch within the Federal Government, the leadership of the Federal Government within the United States and of the United States within the community of nations.

And yet he almost never spoke of 'power'. Power was not a goal he sought for its own sake. It was there, in the White House, to be used, without any sense of guilt or greed, as a means of getting things done. He felt neither uplifted nor weighed down by power. He enjoyed the Presidency, thinking not of its power but its opportunities, and he was sobered by the Presidency, thinking not of its power but its obligations. He was a strong President primarily because he was a strong person.

He was slightly annoyed by all the newspaper fuss during the transition over the fact that he enjoyed reading Dick Neustadt's *Presidential Power* [see p. 222] with its emphasis on 'personal power and its politics; what it is, how to get it, how to keep it, how to use it'. For Neustadt would be the first to agree that John Fitzgerald Kennedy, a third-generation practitioner of political power, already knew its nature without being obsessed by either its burdens or its glories.

As a Senator he had supported more power and discretion for the President in foreign aid, trade, item vetoes and national emergency disputes, and opposed curbs on the President's treaty-making power and electoral base. As an author and historian he had praised the independent Presidency and the men who stretched its limits and preserved its prerogatives. As a candidate he both launched and closed his campaign with addresses focused upon Presidential responsibility as the No. 1 issue. And as President he both expanded and exerted the full power of that office, the informal as well as the formal, 'all that are specified and some that are not'. In my judgment, few features of the Kennedy Presidency were as distinctive as his concept and conduct of the office itself.

Any affront to his office—whether it came from Congress. . . . Khrushchev on Cuba, 'Big Steel' on prices,[1] or his own church on education—was resisted. What he could not accomplish through legislation—to fight recession, inflation, race discrimination and other problems—he sought to accomplish through Executive Orders, proclamations, contingency funds, inherent powers, unused statutes, transfers of appropriations, reorganization plans, patronage, procurement, pardons, Presidential memos, public speeches and private pressures.

Example: In the summer of 1963, unable to obtain passage of his education bill and concerned about growing youth unemployment, he used his Presidential 'emergency fund' to distribute $250,000 for guidance counselors in a drive against school dropouts.

Example: His first Executive Order, improving surplus food distribution to the needy, had been previously held up by his predecessor for lack of clear statutory authority. Kennedy issued it immediately, drawing upon his constitutional powers and on revenues available from customs fees.

'The Constitution has served us extremely well,' he explained to a group of students in the White House flower garden, 'but . . . all its clauses had to be interpreted by men and had to be made to work by men, and it has to be made to work today in an entirely different world from the day in which it was written.'

Within the Executive Branch he accepted responsibility for every major decision, delegating work but never responsibility to Cabinet, National Security Council, Joint Chiefs of Staff, White House aides or other advisers. He did not wait for unanimity among them or permit them to disregard his instructions. In reporting on executive actions to the Congress, he deliberately worded his messages to read 'I have directed the Secretary . . .' rather than 'I have requested . . .'

He had no intention of using his staff, he said, 'to get a pre-arranged agreement which is only confirmed at the President's desk. That I don't agree with.' He wanted no one shielding him from anticipating problems and seeking to initiate solutions. Told in one conference by a sub-Cabinet member that the issue at hand involved the biggest decision he would ever have to make, he replied drily: 'We get one of those every week.'

He was very clear about the distinct roles of advisers and Presidents. The Joint Chiefs of Staff, he said, 'advise you the way a man advises another one about whether he should marry a girl. He doesn't have to live with her.' And in the three-network television interview of December 1962 [see p. 157] which contained his remarkably candid views on the Presidency, he stated:

> There is such a difference between those who advise or speak or legislate and . . . the man who must . . . finally make the judgment. . . . Advisers are frequently divided. If you take the wrong course, and on occasion I have, the President bears the burden of the responsibility quite rightly. The advisers may move on—to new advice.

He deliberately had many advisers of varying points of view. Some outsiders mistook their clash of ideas for confusion, and assumed that a multiplicity could only produce uncertainty. Because they could not tell whether Dillon or Heller was in charge of tax planning, or whether Acheson or Rusk was in charge of Berlin planning, they assumed the President was either equally confused or compromising two views. Actually, he was in charge and liked hearing alternatives and assumptions challenged before he made up his mind.

His decisions were not fixed by any 'grand design' for the future. He started his term with basic convictions and broad goals just as a scientist begins with faith in his hypothesis, but each new discovery and experience would broaden his perspective and recast his strategy. Because he had a shrewd judgment of the possible, he did not exhaust his energies or hopes on the impossible. Asked what kind of world he hoped to leave his successor in 1969, he replied in mid-1961, 'I haven't had time to think about that yet'.

Yet ever since his youth he had possessed an unusual ability to take the long view. 'I sometimes think,' he said, 'we are too much impressed by the clamor of daily events. Newspaper headlines and the television screens give us a short view. . . . Yet it is the . . . great movements of history, and not the passing excitements, that will shape our future.' Despite his fascination with the past, he oriented his policies to the future. His speeches were increasingly addressed to the next generation as well as his own, and he wanted to make sure there would be one. 'Each President,' he wrote, 'is the President not only of all who live, but, in a very real sense, of all those who have yet to live.' To help the next generation, he was always fashioning, not grand designs, but single steps—toward disarmament and space discoveries and salt water conversion and an end to illiteracy and disease. He talked of laying the groundwork now for foreign policy beyond the cold war—of preparing now for coming water shortages, doctor shortages, classroom shortages, power and timber and park and playground shortages—of an Alliance for Progress a decade from now and an Atlantic Partnership a generation from now and wilderness preserves a century from now. Maintaining our forest lands is a 'challenge to our foresight", he said, because 'trees planted today will not reach the minimum sizes needed for lumber until the year 2000'.

In fact, one of his favorite stories, which he repeated again on 15 November, 1963, related how French Marshal Lyautey's gardener sought to put off the persistent Marshal by reminding him that the trees which he wanted planted would not flower for a hundred years. 'In that case,' the Marshal had said, 'plant it this afternoon'. John Kennedy believed in planting trees this afternoon.

As his months in office increased, however, he talked more and more about the limitations of power.

'Every President,' he wrote in the Foreword to my book on *Decision Making in the White House* [see p. 222] 'must endure a gap between what he would like and what is possible.' And he quoted Roosevelt's statement that 'Lincoln was a sad man because he couldn't get it all at once. And nobody can'.

His strategy in the Presidency, as in politics, was to keep moving, looking for openings, hoping to make the breaks fall his way. He was wise enough to know that in a nation of consent, not command, Presidential words alone cannot always produce results.

Near the end of November 1963, he wrote a letter to Professor Clinton Rossiter, whose work on *The American Presidency* [see p. 222] he greatly admired. Rossiter had dedicated his book with a line from Shakespeare's *Macbeth*: 'Methought I heard a voice cry, "Sleep no more!"' Kennedy, who could sleep with his perils but not always waken others to them, suggested in his letter as 'more appropriate' the exchange between Glendower and Hotspur in Part I of Shakespeare's *Henry IV*:

GLENDOWER: I can call spirits from the vasty deep.
HOTSPUR: Why, so can I, or so can any man;
But will they come when you do call for them?

NOTES

(1) 'Big Steel.' The major steel corporations of the United States. One of the sternest tests of President Kennedy's authority came in 1962 when the giant steel corporations of the United States announced increases in the price of steel. Kennedy was strongly opposed to this because of the inflationary pressure it would generate in the economy through other price increases which were bound to follow. Kennedy used the full powers of his office—including threats to cancel and transfer large government contracts from firms who increased their prices. He finally compelled the big corporations to cancel the increases.
Full accounts are given in the books by Arthur Schlesinger Jr. and Theodore Sorensen (see p. 222) and see also Grant McConnell, *Steel and the Presidency* (New York, 1962).

PRESIDENT KENNEDY DISCUSSES THE PRESIDENCY

On 16 December 1962 President Kennedy agreed to discuss the Presidency on radio and television with three experienced commentators. They were William Lawrence, George Herman and Sander Vanocur, representing the three major television networks in the United States. The following extracts are taken from the transcript of the discussion. With due allowance for the unrehearsed nature of the President's remarks, the extracts reveal some of his reflections after two years in office.

DOCUMENT 24. EXTRACTS FROM A RADIO AND TELEVISION DISCUSSION ON THE PRESIDENCY BETWEEN PRESIDENT KENNEDY AND COMMENTATORS. 16 DECEMBER 1962. [Note: the transcript has been edited slightly to give unity to the extracts.]

Lawrence: As you look back upon your first two years in office, sir, has your experience in the office matched your expectations? You had studied a good deal the power of the Presidency, the methods of its operations. How has this worked out as you saw it in advance?

The President: Well, I think in the first place the problems are more difficult than I had imagined they were. Secondly, there is a limitation upon the ability of the United States to solve these problems. We are involved now in the Congo in a very difficult situation. We have been unable to secure an implementation of the policy which we have supported. We are involved in a good many other areas. We are trying to see if a solution can be found to the struggle between Pakistan and India, with whom we want to maintain friendly relations. Yet they are unable to come to an agreement. There is a limitation, in other words, upon the power of the United States to bring about solutions.

I think our people get awfully impatient and maybe fatigued and tired, and saying 'We have been carrying this burden for 17 years; can we lay it down?' We can't lay it down, and I don't see how we are going to lay it down in this century.

So that I would say that the problems are more difficult than I had imagined them to be. The responsibilities placed on the United States are greater than I imagined them to be, and there are greater limitations upon our ability to bring about a favorable result than I had imagined them to be. And I think that is probably true of anyone who becomes President, because there is such a difference between those who advise or speak or legislate, and between the man who must select from the various alternatives proposed and say that this shall be the policy of the United States. It is much easier to make the speeches than it is to finally make the judgments, because unfortunately your advisers are frequently divided. If you take the wrong course, and on occasion I have, the President bears the burden of the responsibility quite rightly. The advisers may move on to new advice.

Lawrence: Well, Mr. President, that brings up a point that has always interested me. How does a President go about making a decision, like Cuba, for example?

The President: The most recent one was hammered out really on policy and decision over a period of five or six days. During that period, the 15 people more or less who were directly consulted frequently changed their view, because whatever action we took had so many disadvantages to it, and each action we took raised the prospect that it might escalate with the Soviet Union into a nuclear war. Finally, however, I think a general consensus developed, and certainly seemed after all alternatives were examined, that the course of action that we finally adopted was the right one.

Herman: I would like to go back to the question of the consensus and your relationship to the consensus. You have said and the Constitution says that the decision can be made only by the President.

The President: Well, you know that old story about Abraham Lincoln and the Cabinet. He says, 'All in favor, say "aye",' and the whole cabinet voted 'aye', and then 'All opposed, no,' and Lincoln voted 'No', and he said, 'The vote is no.' So that naturally the Constitution places the responsibility on the President. There was some disagreement with the course we finally adopted, but the course we finally adopted had the advantage of permitting other steps if this one was unsuccessful. In other words, we were starting in a sense at a minimum place. Then if that were unsuccessful, we could have gradually stepped it up until we had gone into a much more massive action, which might have become necessary if the first step had been unsuccessful. I would think that the majority finally came to accept that, though at the beginning there was a much sharper division. And after all, this was very valuable, because the people who were involved had particular responsibilities of their own; Mr. McNamara, Secretary of Defense, therefore had to advise me on the military capacity of the United States in that area, the Secretary of State, who had to advise on the attitude of the OAS and NATO. So that in my opinion, the majority came to accept the course we finally took. It made it much easier. In Cuba of 1961, the advice of those who were brought in on the Executive Branch was also unanimous, and the advice was wrong. And I was responsible. So that finally it comes down that no matter how many advisers you have, frequently they are divided, and the President must finally choose.

The other point is something that President Eisenhower said to me on 19 January. He said 'There are no easy matters that will ever come to you as President. If they are easy, they will be settled at a lower level.' So that the matters that come to you as President are always the difficult matters, and matters that carry with them large implications. So this contributes to some of the burdens of the office of the Presidency, which other Presidents have commented on.

Vanocur: Is it true that during your first year, sir, you would get on the phone personally to the State Department and try to get a response to some inquiry that had been made?

The President: Yes, I still do that when I can, because I think there is a great tendency in government to have papers stay on desks too long, and it seems to me that is really one function. After all, the President can't administer a department, but at least he can be a stimulant.

Vanocur: Do you recall any response that you received from somebody who was not suspecting a phone call in the State Department, any specific response somebody made to you?

The President: No, they always respond. They always say 'Yes'. It takes a little while to get it. You know, after I met Mr. Khrushchev in Vienna and they gave us an *aide memoir*, it took me many weeks to get our answer out through the State Department coordinated with the British, the French and the Germans. It took much too long. Now, it seems to me we have been able to speed it up, but this is a constant problem in various departments. There are so many interests that are involved in any decision. No matter whether the decision is about Africa or Asia, it involves the desk, it involves the desk of the place, it involves the Defense Department, it might involve the CIA, it frequently involves the Treasury, it might involve the World Bank, it involves the United Nations Delegation. So it seems to me that one of the functions of the President is to try to have it move with more speed. Otherwise you can wait while the world collapses.

Vanocur: You once said that you were reading more and enjoying it less. Are you still as avid a newspaper reader, magazine—I remember those of us who traveled with you on the campaign, a magazine wasn't safe around you.

The President: Oh, yes. No, no, I think it is invaluable, even though it may cause you—it is never pleasant to be reading things that are not agreeable news, but I would say that it is an invaluable arm of the Presidency, to check really on what is going on in the Administration, and more things come to my attention that cause me concern or give me information. So I would think that Mr. Khrushchev operating a totalitarian system which has many advantages as far as being able to move in secret, and all the rest, there is a terrific disadvantage not having the abrasive quality of the Press applied to you daily, to an administration even though we never like it, and even though we wish they didn't write it, and even though we disapprove, there isn't any doubt that we could not do the job at all in a free society without a very, very active Press.

Now, on the other hand, the Press has the responsibility not to distort things for political purposes, not to just take some news in order to prove a political point. It seems to me their obligation is to be as tough as they can on the Administration but do it in a way which is directed towards getting as close to the truth as they can get and not merely because of some political motivation.

Lawrence: As a young Congressman, sir, you voted to impose a two-term limitation on Presidents. Now that you have held the office for a while, and also observed its effect on President Eisenhower's second term, would you repeat that vote, even if the amendment did not apply to yourself?

The President: Yes, I would. I think eight years is enough, and I am not sure that a President, in my case if I were re-elected, is at such a disadvantage. . . .

But I have no reason to believe that a President with the powers of this office and the responsibilities placed on it, if he has a judgment that some things need to be done, I think he can do it just as well the second time as the first, depending, of course, on the make-up of the Congress. The fact is, I think, the Congress looks more powerful sitting here than it did when I was there in the Congress. But that is because when you are in the Congress you are one of a hundred in the Senate or one of 435 in the House. So that the power is so divided. But from here I look at a Congress, and I look at the collective power of the Congress, particularly the bloc action, and it is a substantial power.

Vanocur: Do you think we could turn for a moment to this subject of the President's responsibility in foreign affairs? Now, when some Congressman disagreed with your course of action over Cuba, the responsibility you have by the Constitution in this is very clear, but in domestic matters, the responsibility is divided. How do you use the Presidency in Theodore Roosevelt's phrase, 'the bully pulpit', to move these men who really are kind of barons and sovereigns in their own right up there on Capitol Hill? Have you any way to move them toward a course of action which you think is imperative?

The President: Well, the Constitution and the development of the Congress all give advantage to delay. It is very easy to defeat a bill in the Congress. It is much more difficult to pass one. To go through a committee, say the Ways and Means Committee of the House, subcommittee, and get a majority vote, the full committee and get a majority vote, go to the Rules Committee and get a rule, go to the Floor of the House and get a majority, start over again in the Senate, subcommittee and full committee, (and in the Senate there is unlimited debate), so you can never bring a matter to a vote if there is enough determination on the part of the opponents, even if they are a minority, to go through the Senate with the bill. And then unanimously get a conference between the House and Senate to adjust the bill, or if one member objects, to have it go back through the Rules Committee, back through the Congress, and have this done on a controversial piece of legislation where powerful groups are opposing it, that is an extremely difficult task. So that the struggle of a President who has a program to move it through the Congress, particularly when the seniority system may place particular individuals in key positions who may be wholly unsympathetic to your program, and may be, even though they are members of your own party, in political opposition to the President, this is a struggle which every President who has tried to get a program through has had to deal with. After all, Franklin Roosevelt was elected by the largest majority in history in 1936, and he got his worst defeat a few months afterwards in the Supreme Court bill.

So that they are two separate offices and two separate powers, the Congress and the Presidency. There is bound to be conflict, but they must cooperate to the degree that is possible. But that is why no President's program is ever put in. The only time a President's program is put in quickly and easily is when the program is insignificant. But if it is significant and affects important interests and is controversial, then there is a fight, and the President is never wholly successful.

Vanocur: Mr. President, which is the better part of wisdom, to take a bill which is completely emasculated, that you had great interest in and accept it, or accept its defeat in the hope of building up public support for it at a later time?

The President: Well, I would say given the conditions you described, I think it would be better to accept the defeat, but usually what has happened, and what has happened to us in the last two years, a good many of our bills passed in reasonable position, not the way we sent them up, but after all, the Congress has its own will and its own feelings and its own judgment, and they are close to the people. The whole House of Representatives has just been elected. So that it is quite natural that they will have a different perspective than I may have. So I would say what we ought to do is to do the best we can. But if it is completely emasculated, then there is no sense in having a shadow of success and not the substance.

Lawrence: Mr. President, you spoke the other day of the dangers and difficulties of slow communications between here and the Soviet Union, as it exhibited itself during the Cuban crisis. I suppose this would be an even greater problem if your radar screen were to pick up missiles or at least what appeared to be missiles in any substantial number?

The President: Yes. Well, there is—one of the arguments for the continuation of the airplane is that if you picked up missiles coming toward you, you could have your planes take off and be in the air. Then if it proved to be a false alarm, then you could call them back. For missiles, you can't do that, and the President might have to make a judgment in a 15-minute period, and the information would be incomplete. You recall that incident where the moon came up, and it appeared to be a whole variety of missiles coming in. Of course, it was picked up several years ago. I think that is oversimplified. The fact of the matter is that the United States could wait quite long because we have missiles in hardened sites, and those missiles, even if there was a missile attack on the United States, those missiles could still be fired and destroy the Soviet Union, and so could the Polaris submarine missiles. So that I don't think there is a danger that we would fire based on incomplete and inaccurate information, because we were only given five or six minutes to make a judgment. I think the Polaris alone permits us to wait to make sure that we are going to have sufficient in hand that he knows that we could destroy the Soviet Union. Actually that is the purpose of the deterrent. Once he fires his missiles, it is all over anyway, because we are going to have sufficient resources to fire back at him to destroy the Soviet Union. When that day comes, and there is a massive exchange, then that is the end, because you are talking about Western Europe, the Soviet Union, the United States, of 150 million fatalities in the first 18 hours. Now, you could go on, if everybody aimed at cities in order to have as many killed as possible in all these communities with all the weapons you could fire, you could kill, and you might be having more fire. So that the nuclear age is a very dangerous period, and that is why I frequently read these speeches about how we must do this and that. But I think they ought to just look at what we are talking about.

Lawrence: How urgent is this need for quicker communication between here and the Soviet Union?

The President: It is desirable. It is not—if he fires his missiles at us, it is not going to do any good for us to have a telephone at the Kremlin and ask him whether it is really true. But I do think it is better that we should be quicker than we now are. It took us some hours in the Cuban matter, and I think that communication is important. In addition to the communications with the Kremlin, we have very poor communications to a good deal of Latin America, and we don't know what is going on there very frequently. So we are trying to improve our communications all around the world, because that knowledge is so vital to an effective decision.

Vanocur: Mr. President, back before you were elected, your father used to have a favorite story he told reporters. He asked you once why do you want the job, and he cited the reasons why you shouldn't want it, and you apparently gave him an answer —I don't know whether it satisfied him, but apparently you satisfied yourself. Would you give him the same answer today after serving in this office for two years?

The President: Oh, you mean that somebody is going to do it?

Vanocur: Yes, Sir.

The President: Yes. I think that there are a lot of satisfactions to the Presidency, particularly, as I say, we are all concerned as citizens and as parents and all the rest, with all the problems we have been talking about tonight. They are all the problems which if I was not the President, I would be concerned about as a father or a citizen. So at least you have an opportunity to do something about them. And if what you do is useful and successful, then of course that is a great satisfaction. When as a result of a decision of yours, failure comes, or you are unsuccessful, then of course that is a great setback. But I must say after being here for two years, and having the experience of the Presidency, and there is no experience you can get that can possibly prepare you adequately for the Presidency, I must say that I have a good deal of hope for the United States. Just because I think that this country, which, as I say, criticizes itself and is criticized around the world, 180 million people, for 17 years, really for more than that, for almost 20 years, have been the great means of defending first the world against the Nazi threat, and since then against the Communist threat, and if it were not for us, the Communists would be dominant in the world today, and because of us, we are in a strong position. Now, I think that is a pretty good record for a country with 6 per cent of the world's population, which is very reluctant to take on these burdens. I think we ought to be rather pleased with ourselves this Christmas.

HOW POWERFUL IS THE PRESIDENCY?

In the following article an American political scientist examines the popular assumption that the Presidency carries enormous reserves of power. He is critical of this assumption and uses several examples drawn from recent experiences of Presidential performance to present an alternative view.

DOCUMENT 25. 'HOW POWERFUL IS THE PRESIDENCY?' BY SIDNEY WARREN (FROM *The Saturday Review*, 21 JULY 1962).

For years we have been hearing that the powers of the American Presidency have been increasing. We have come to look to the White House for an immediate answer to any major problem that arises. We have had warnings about the danger of too much centralization of power in the executive branch of government.

Yet it is doubtful whether anywhere in the world today is executive leadership more hemmed in, more effectively limited by political considerations, more vulnerable to debilitating pressures from within and without, than in the United States. Pressures from the opposing party and from within the President's own party; pressures from Congress, with its power to enact or block Presidential programs; pressures from strongly established departments of government, like the Defense Department and the Atomic Energy Commission; pressures from the press and various agencies of public opinion—all these make the President's job the most difficult and complicated balancing act in the world.

That the Founding Fathers intended to make the Presidency 'the vital place of action in the American system', as Woodrow Wilson expressed it, is apparent from a reading of the Constitution. In this office they combined the duties of chief executive, commander-in-chief of the armed forces, director of the nation's foreign relations, and initiator of legislation. John Adams regarded it as of such eminence that he wrote:

The duration of our President is neither perpetual nor for life; it is only for four years; but his power during those four years is much greater than that of an avoyer, a consul, a podesta, a doge, a stadholder. I know of no first magistrate in any Republican government, except England and Neuchâtel [a Swiss canton], who possesses a constitutional dignity, authority, and power comparable to his.

While this was an exaggeration of the President's stature at the time, considering the size and influence of the new nation, subsequent national development, the growth of governmental responsibilities, and the influence of the men who have since occupied the office have all enlarged the Presidency to an extent that could not even have been imagined by the makers of the Constitution. To the duties prescribed by the law of the land have been added such roles as party chief, custodian of the economy, and world leader.

At the same time, the world has leaped into an era so complex and in such violent contrast to either the near or distant past that it has become increasingly difficult for the President to stay 'on top of events'. The fact is that the chief executive of the Sixties must lead his nation through global agitations that are beyond his capacity to subdue; he can only try to control them and prevent disastrous eruptions. President Kennedy was not indulging in mere rhetoric when he declared in his inaugural address: 'The great work of the nation will not be finished in the first thousand days, nor in the life of this administration, nor even perhaps in our lifetime on this planet.'

By contrast, within the nineteenth century, the United States was able without too much stress to achieve its national objective of preserving independence, developing its resources, expanding the continental limits, and increasing the nation's influence as a member of the international community. And the means employed was simply disengagement from the politics of European power.

Disengagement did not imply passive withdrawal from the affairs of the world. On the contrary, our Presidents were diligent and active in exploiting any circumstances that would strengthen the nation's security and increase its opportunities to develop. Jefferson's purchase of the Louisiana Territory, Monroe's Doctrine, and Polk's war with Mexico are a few examples. Contributing to the Presidential ability to act were our defensive moats, the Atlantic and Pacific Oceans; the preoccupation of the European powers with their own involved affairs; and our community of interests with Great Britain.

Even in our own century, as recently as the time of Theodore Roosevelt, America was still free to decide its own course. Convinced that national security would be strengthened by an Isthmian canal, Roosevelt assisted willing Panamanians to foment a revolution, thus making construction of the canal possible. Or he brandished his big stick at designing creditor nations across the Atlantic who desired to penetrate the Caribbean area, and the warning sufficed. By Presidential fiat we assumed the role of policeman of the Caribbean, allocating to ourselves the right to intervene when our interests seemed to require protection.

The Cuban fiasco of 1961 offers an illustration of how infinitely more complicated was the situation which confronted President Kennedy. Communist penetration into Latin America made some response by the United States appear to be necessary and desirable. Yet the President had to consider the American-Soviet power relationship, the impact of Cuba's social revolution upon the peoples of Central and South America, and the views and reactions of the other sovereign members of the Organization of American States.

Compounding the dilemma of statesmanship was the competing and contradictory advice offered the President. One group advocated an all-out invasion backed by American military forces; the other urged no action at all. The former course, even if successful, would have won us the battle but might have lost us the war; the latter had its own risks. As it turned out, the President's solution, a middle course, proved to be the most futile of all. But, considering the possibly unhappy consequences of any action, how much power did the President have to control the situation?

Traditionally, the United States has pursued an independent course in dealing with international problems, preferring unilateralism to collaboration, freedom of action to binding commitments. The requirements of America's new leadership in world affairs, however, have necessitated a growing emphasis upon cooperation and coalition. Franklin D. Roosevelt learned how difficult it was to lead an alliance of nations even when engaged in a common military cause. His successors have discovered that in peacetime, although exercising a commanding influence over an international community, they have been subject to still greater restrictions.

At home the President has always been responsible to several constituencies: the government bureaucracy, the party, the national electorate. He has always had to balance the national interest or welfare against sectional and local interests of one kind or another. Now vast international constituencies with competing and conflicting needs have been made part of the equation.

The series of military alliances with which the United States is linked, the reemergence of Western Europe as a vital political and economic force, the commitment of the Afro-Asian nations to a policy of nonalignment, the independent position of the Latin American republics—each factor in its own way circumscribes the President's authority. He is frequently impelled to consult with one or more nations before deciding on some issues, and yet must sometimes refrain from acting after consulting; with other nations he must collaborate even more completely.

These new constituencies far beyond our borders are influential determinants of America's power status; and since American leadership depends upon the support that its friends are willing to give and the respect that its enemies are compelled to acknowledge, the President's range of free choice is narrowed. He must compromise in view of the opposing positions among friends or the intentions or actions of rivals.

Finally, there is the United Nations: the world's security structure, its forum, the bar of world public opinion. A President who exercises sound and wise leadership can utilize it as an instrument for reaching and influencing peoples all over the world. The representation which he or his ambassador makes to this body has a direct effect on the prestige of the nation abroad. Today, when popular reactions are a significant element in international power, when the result of the rivalry between Communist and democratic ideologies for the allegiances of the underdeveloped nations may be crucial, the American image is of cardinal importance.

The obligations undertaken by the United States in subscribing to the United Nations charter require not only joint undertakings with other member states in a variety of political and humanitarian endeavors, but also bind us to the decisions that are made. To win support from the many constituent members in a particular situation involves us in a continual process of negotiation and accommodation. In other words, the kind of unilateral action President Polk could take in 1846, in sending troops to occupy Mexican territory during a dispute with that country, or William McKinley half a century later, in taking the country into war with Spain, is no longer possible.

Today the President possesses terrifying military power—the right to order the use of the nuclear bomb. Ironically, however, the existence of the ultimate weapon limits his power to well under that of his prenuclear-age predecessors. For the first time in history the President of the United States must consider the safety not only of his nation but of the entire world. The nature of military technology and the entangled web of international life have drastically altered his perspective. There are no longer any simple panaceas, nor can there be any easy or decisive victories as were possible in the past.

When in 1917 'a little group of wilful men' in the United States Senate filibustered to death a White House proposal to arm merchant vessels, Wilson went ahead and had them armed by executive order. And though he agonized over the possibility of war with Germany, he risked involvement because he was determined to resist the assault on the nation's neutral rights. Franklin D. Roosevelt's conviction that the survival of Great Britain was essential to American security led him to assist her even to the point of war. By executive agreement he effected an exchange of destroyers for British bases and obtained from Congress wide latitude under the terms of the Lend-Lease Act.

Today President Kennedy, in attempting to strengthen the nation's security and its diplomatic position, cannot readily consider force to promote these interests. As an illustration, the direct physical confrontation between Americans and Russians in Berlin prevents the President from risking military action. He can only continue to negotiate.

That the President cannot absolutely control the Berlin situation or other international events is frustrating to the American people, whose history has taught them to regard their nation as invincible. Their inability to accept fully the fact that we live in a revolutionary age of continuing crises and that the times demand a revamping of traditional views cannot help but hamper the President's leadership. To jolt the people out of their conventional views, to make them aware of what Walter Lippmann calls 'the intangible realities of international power' is far more onerous than it was for any previous President.

After he had left office Theodore Roosevelt once remarked: 'People always used to say of me that I was an astonishingly good politician and divined what the people were going to think. This really was not an accurate way of stating the case. I did not 'divine' how the people were going to think; I simply made up my mind what they ought to think, and then did my best to get them to think it.' The issues of his time, however, were immediate, readily comprehensible, and within a familiar frame of reference.

President Kennedy must create an awareness of the new and

bewildering fact that the dichotomy between foreign and domestic policy has been all but obliterated in the postwar world. In the past, the nature of our economy was considered to be purely an internal affair, but now our economic health has direct repercussions on our ability to maintain leadership in a world where the race goes to the strongest. Full employment, gross national product, and our international trade balance directly affect our position in the world arena.

Education, which at one time was entirely a matter of local concern, is now very much the President's affair. The present competition with the Soviet Union requires an acceleration in quality and quantity of professional and technical personnel, of higher educational standards for the training of intellectual leaders.

Civil rights for our minorities have similarly become involved with our world position, and here we are perhaps most vulnerable. In the past, the wide gulf between the profession of equal rights and the performance, especially as regards the Negro citizen, may have deeply troubled thoughtful Americans and embarrassed them when they were abroad, but it did not impinge on foreign policy. Today, this internal matter is a crucial factor in our relationship with the millions of Afro-Asians whose friendship and support we must have.

The President's maneuverability is also circumscribed by the ideological conflict. The cold war has created issues that involve passionately held doctrinal convictions, and years of suspended peace have exacted a toll. Irrationalities born of fear and frustration have infected segments of the population. Individuals and groups have resorted to the shorthand of slogans and shibboleths—'soft on communism', 'better dead than red', 'appeasement'—as a substitute for sober discussion and calm analysis. To a considerable extent rigid views and inflexible positions have stifled free inquiry into alternative solutions to certain international problems. Assuming, for instance, that a fundamental change in our China policy would be advantageous to the national interest at this point, could President Kennedy feel politically free to advocate it? Would he not be pilloried by members of both parties in Congress, to say nothing of a large section of the population, and risk the loss of his political leadership if he did so?

To guide public opinion in our time requires the gift of a Pericles, of whom Thucydides said: 'Certainly when he saw that they were going too far in a mood of overconfidence, he would bring back to them a sense of their dangers; and when they were discouraged for no good reason, he would restore their confidence.' The irony of the President's situation is that while he has instruments of mass communication at his disposal that early leaders would have envied, the task of persuading the people is far greater than it was in their time.

If we live in an age of ideologies, we also live in an age dominated by science. The new military and space technology have made the government heavily dependent on the scientific experts. President Eisenhower formally acknowledged this development when he appointed a scientific advisor to the chief executive. Many of the problems which are within the purview of governmental responsibility are so technical in nature that the layman, even the layman occupying the high office of the Presidency, must bow to the judgment of the professionals.

In this sense he is far less autonomous in arriving at a policy than his pre-World War II predecessors, while at the same time his power is unprecedented. The President of today cannot escape reliance upon experts, yet he alone remains solely responsible for the great decisions of national destiny.

Since World War II the decision-making process has been further complicated by the vast institutional apparatus which was created by Congress to assist the President in discharging his duties. Even before the many agencies, commissions, and councils began to proliferate in Washington, Harold Laski, a careful observer of the American Presidency, commented on the problems arising out of the inevitable expansion of the office.

One of the fundamental qualities a President should possess, Laski stated, is the ability to coordinate. He must also be able to delegate and put his trust in those whom he has appointed. since, for the most part, he can be concerned only with outlines, 'The details of the picture must be filled in by subordinates'. Professor Laski continued:

Here certainly an art is required which must operate upon a scale quite different from any with which a Prime Minister is concerned. For the dignity of cabinet colleagues and the relative certainty with which he can control the House of Commons means that he is free, once policy in the large is settled, to leave its implementation alone. But a President may lose a bill in Congress if his subordinates proceed untactfully. . . . Every delegation of power is therefore a risk to be taken, and this makes his judgment of men a matter of supreme importance. He must know that the men he uses will see things through his eyes. . . . He must delegate, too, knowing that at best he is bound to make mistakes, both in men and in things. This is, above all, the case in matters of foreign policy.

The problem of coordination is indeed prodigious, and the President can never be certain that the policies which he has initiated will be implemented in a way that will insure their success.

The significant place occupied today by such groups as the Joint Chiefs of Staff, the Council of Economic Advisors, the Atomic Energy Commission, the Central Intelligence Agency, the National Security Council, etc., does not detract from the President's preeminent position, but it places a premium upon his ability to work out flexible formulas and to remain in control of the situation. Each President uses the approach he considers most suitable to his own ideas of leadership. Kennedy, for example, prefers to place less formal reliance on the National Security Council than did Eisenhower. Nevertheless, the massive institution of which the President is the center will continue to restrict even as it assists.

The nation has traveled a longer distance than that represented by actual time from the point when Theodore Roosevelt kept his State Department in complete ignorance for several weeks of the delicate negotiations he was carrying on with Japan and Russia. Or when Woodrow Wilson composed on his own typewriter diplomatic protests to the German government which were of the greatest significance to both nations.

We return, then, to the paradox of Presidential power. The Constitution and the force of custom have made the chief executive the most powerful figure on the domestic scene; the status of the nation has made him the most influential man in the world. But the circumstances of our age have subjected his leadership both domestically and internationally to many limitations. While he remains the pivotal figure in the affairs of mankind, he is circumscribed by the nature of the nuclear age in ways that were unknown to Presidents of simpler eras who had less power.

The American people have a right to expect leadership from the White House, leadership that is wise, imaginative, humanitarian, courageous. They can hope for a President with the capacity to perceive the direction of our time and to move the nation in that direction. But they cannot expect the Presidents of our day to surmount what has become insurmountable.

PART VII

The Kennedy Regime : Three Appraisals

If the journalist's main task is to record and interpret events as they occur, the scholar's is to gather all the available evidence at a later date and attempt a considered appraisal of those events. His duty is to be dispassionate in weighing the evidence, though of course any appraisal which lacks opinions, convictions, or a point of view is bound to be arid, even if it was possible.

To date, the Presidency of John F. Kennedy has presented special problems for scholarly appraisal. The shock and anger generated by his assassination naturally affected all thinking men. A natural tendency would be to extol the performance in office of one whose death was mourned throughout the world. Again, we are still too close to many of the events of the Kennedy years for their final significance to be assessed.

In this section three articles from scholarly journals are included. Each of them attempts to appraise Kennedy's Presidential performance from different perspectives. The first is by the political scientist Richard Neustadt, who has written a scholarly work on the Presidency (see p. 222). In 1960 and 1961 Professor Neustadt advised President Kennedy on the complex problem of organizing the transition of the government from President Eisenhower's Administration to the newly formed Kennedy Administration.

As Professor Neustadt points out, 1964 was too early a date on which to attempt an appraisal of Kennedy in the Presidency, but in response to a special request he attempted to do so. In the course of his article he also makes suggestive observations of a more general nature for students of the American Presidency.

DOCUMENT 26. 'KENNEDY IN THE PRESIDENCY: A PREMATURE APPRAISAL', BY RICHARD E. NEUSTADT (FROM *Political Science Quarterly*, VOL. LXXIX, NO. 3, SEPTEMBER 1964, PP. 321–334).

There are many ways to look at the performance of a president of the United States. One way—not the only one—is to assess his operational effectiveness as man in office, a single individual amidst a vast machine. This has been my own approach in previous writings on past presidents. Regarding our most recent President, John F. Kennedy, it is foolhardy to attempt appraisal in these terms. He died too soon and it is too soon after his death. Still, the POLITICAL SCIENCE QUARTERLY has asked me to attempt it. And assuming that my readers will indulge the folly, I shall try.

I

In appraising the personal performance of a president it is useful to ask four questions. First, what were his purposes and did these run with or against the grain of history; how relevant were they to what would happen in his time? Second, what was his 'feel,' his human understanding, for the nature of his power in the circumstances of his time, and how close did he come in this respect to the realities around him (a matter again of relevance)? Third, what was his stance under pressure in office, what sustained him as a person against the frustrations native to the place, and how did his peace-making with himself affect the style and content of his own decision-making? This becomes especially important now that nuclear technology has equipped both Americans and Russians with an intercontinental capability; stresses on the presidency grow apace. Fourth, what was his legacy? What imprint did he leave upon the office, its character and public standing; where did he leave his party and the other party nationally; what remained by way of public policies adopted or in controversy; what remained as issues in American society, insofar as his own stance may have affected them; and what was the American position in the world insofar as his diplomacy may have affected it?

With respect to each of these four questions, the outside observer looks for certain clues in seeking answers.

First, regarding purpose, clues are found in irreversible

commitments to defined courses of action. By 'purpose' I mean nothing so particular as an endorsement for, say, 'medicare,' or anything so general as a pledge to 'peace'. (All presidents desire peace.) By 'course of action' I mean something broader than the one but more definable than the other: Harry S. Truman's commitment to 'containment,' so called, or Dwight D. Eisenhower's to what he called 'fiscal responsibility'. By 'commitment' I mean personal involvement, in terms of what the man himself is seen to say and do, so plain and so direct that politics—and history—will not let him turn back: Truman on civil rights, or Eisenhower on the Army budget.

Second, regarding feel for office, sensitivity to power, clues are drawn from signs of pattern in the man's own operating style as he encounters concrete cases, cases of decision and of following through in every sphere of action, legislative and executive, public and partisan, foreign and domestic—Truman seeking above all to be decisive; Eisenhower reaching for a place above the struggle.

Third, regarding pressure and its consequences, clues are to be drawn again from cases; here one examines crisis situations, seeking signs of pattern in the man's response—Truman at the time of the Korean outbreak, or of Chinese intervention; Eisenhower at the time of Hungary and Suez, or of Little Rock— times like these compared with others just as tough in terms of stress.

And fourth, regarding the man's legacy, one seeks clues in the conduct of the *next* administration. Roosevelt's first New Deal in 1933 tells us a lot about the Hoover presidency. Truman's troubled turnabout in postwar foreign policy casts shadows on the later Roosevelt presidency. And Kennedy's complaint at Yale two years ago about the 'myths' retarding economic management is testimony to one part of Eisenhower's legacy: that part identified with his redoubtable Secretary of the Treasury, George Humphrey.

To list these sources of the wherewithal for answers is to indicate the folly of pursuing my four questions when the object of the exercise is Kennedy-in-office. He was President for two years and ten months. Were one to assess Franklin Roosevelt on the basis of performance before January 1936, or Harry Truman on his accomplishments before enactment of the

Marshall Plan, or Eisenhower had he not survived his heart attack—or Lincoln, for that matter, had he been assassinated six months after Gettysburg—one would be most unlikely to reach judgments about any of these men resembling current judgments drawn from the full record of their terms. We cannot know what Kennedy's full record would have been had he escaped assassination. Still more important, we can never know precisely how to weigh events in his truncated term.

Truman's seven years and Eisenhower's eight suggest a certain rhythm in the modern presidency. The first twelve to eighteen months become a learning time for the new president who has to learn—or unlearn—many things about his job. No matter what his prior training, nothing he has done will have prepared him for all facets of that job. Some aspects of the learning process will persist beyond the first year-and-a-half. Most presidents will go on making new discoveries as long as they hold office (until at last they learn the bitterness of leaving office). But the intensive learning time comes at the start and dominates the first two years. A president's behavior in those years is an uncertain source of clues to what will follow after, unreliable in indicating what will be the patterns of performance 'on the job' once learning has been done. Yet the fourth year is also unreliable; traditionally it brings a period of pause, dominated by a special test requiring special effort—the test of re-election. The way that test is taken tells us much about a president, but less about his conduct on the job in other years. The seventh year is the beginning of the end—now guaranteed by constitutional amendment—as all eyes turn toward the coming nominations and the *next* administration.

So in the search for signs of pattern, clues to conduct, the key years are the third, the fifth, the sixth. Kennedy had only one of these.

Moreover, in this presidential cycle, retrospect is an essential aid for sorting evidence. What a man does in his later years sheds light on the significance of what he did in early years, distinguishing the actions which conform to lasting patterns from the aspects of behavior which were transient. The man's early performance will include a host of clues to what is typical throughout his term of office. But it also will include assorted actions which turn out to be unrepresentative. Looking back from later years these become easy to distinguish. But in the second or the third year it is hard indeed to say, 'This action, this behavior will be dominant throughout.' That is the sort of statement best reserved for retrospect. Kennedy's case leaves no room for retrospect; he was cut off too early in the cycle. (And when it comes to sorting out the legacy he left, Lyndon Johnson has not yet been long enough in office.)

No scholar, therefore, should have the temerity to undertake what follows.

II

Turning to appraise this President in office, I come to my first question, the question of purpose. This is not a matter of initial 'ideology,' fixed intent; far from it. Franklin Roosevelt did not enter office bent upon becoming 'traitor to his class'. Truman did not swear the oath with any notion that he was to take this country into the cold war. Lincoln certainly did not assume the presidency to gain the title of 'Great Emancipator'. The purposes of presidents are not to be confused with their intentions at the start; they are a matter, rather, of responses to events. Nor should they be confused with signs of temperament, with 'passion.' Whether Kennedy was 'passionate' or not is scarcely relevant. Truman certainly deserves to have the cause of civil rights cited among his purposes, but were he to be judged in temperamental terms according to the standards of, say, Eastern liberals, he scarcely could be called a man of passion on the point. And FDR goes down historically as 'Labor's friend', although his coolness toward the greatest show of that friendship in his time, the Wagner Act, remained until he sensed that it was sure to be enacted. What counts here is not 'passion', but the words and acts that lead to irreversible *commitment*.

In his three years of office, what were Kennedy's commitments? Never mind his private thoughts at twenty, or at forty; never mind his preferences for one thing or another; never mind his distaste for a passionate display—taking the real world as he found it, what attracted his commitment in the sense that he identified himself beyond recall?

The record will, I think, disclose at least three purposes so understood: First, above all others, most compelling, most

179

intense, was a commitment to reduce the risk of holocaust by *mutual* miscalculation, to 'get the nuclear genie back in the bottle', to render statecraft manageable by statesmen, tolerable for the rest of us. He did not aim at anything so trite (or unachievable) as 'victory' in the cold war. His aim, apparently, was to outlast it with American society intact and nuclear risks in check. Nothing, I think, mattered more to Kennedy than bottling that genie. This, I know, was deeply in his mind. It also was made manifest in words, among them his address at American University on June 10 1963. That speech is seal and symbol of this purpose. But other signs are found in acts, as well, and in more private words accompanying action: from his Vienna interview with Khrushchev, through the Berlin crisis during 1961, to the Cuban missile crisis and thereafter—this commitment evidently deepened with experience as Kennedy responded to events.

Another speech in June of 1963 stands for a second purpose: the speech on civil rights, June 11, and the message to Congress eight days later launched Kennedy's campaign for what became the Civil Rights Act of 1964. Thereby he undertook an irreversible commitment to Negro integration in American society, aiming once again to get us through the effort with society intact. He evidently came to see the risks of social alienation as plainly as he saw the risks of nuclear escalation, and he sought to steer a course toward integration which could hold inside our social order both impatient Negroes and reactive whites—as tough a task of politics as any we have known, and one he faced no sooner than he had to. But he faced it. What Vienna, Berlin, Cuba were to his first purpose, Oxford and then Birmingham were to this second purpose: events which shaped his personal commitment.

A third speech is indicative of still another purpose, a speech less known and a commitment less apparent, though as definite, I think, as both of the others: Kennedy's commencement speech at Yale on June 11, 1962, soon after his short war with Roger Blough. He spoke of making our complex economy, our somewhat *sui generis* economy, function effectively for meaningful growth, and as the means he urged an end-of-ideology in problem-solving. His speech affirmed the notion that the key problems of economic growth are technical, not ideological, to

be met not by passion but by intellect, and that the greatest
barriers to growth are the ideas in people's heads—'myths' as
he called them—standing in the way of reasoned diagnosis and
response. Kennedy, I think, was well aware (indeed he was
made painfully aware) that only on our one-time Left is
ideology defunct. Elsewhere it flourishes, clamping a lid upon
applied intelligence, withholding brainpower from rational
engagement in the novel problems of our economic management. He evidently wanted most of all to lift that lid.

Failing a response to his Yale lecture, Kennedy retreated to
the easier task of teaching one simple economic lesson, the
lesson of the recent tax reductions: well-timed budget deficits can
lead to balanced budgets. This, evidently, was the most that he
thought he could manage in contesting 'myths', at least before
election. But his ambition, I believe, was to assault a lot more
myths than this, when and as he could. That ambition measures
his commitment to effective growth in the economy.

Stemming from this third commitment (and the second) one
discerns a corollary which perhaps would have become a
fourth: what Kennedy's successor now has named 'the war
against poverty'. During the course of 1963, Kennedy became
active in promoting plans for an attack on chronic poverty. His
prospective timing no doubt had political utility, but it also had
social utility which evidently mattered quite as much. Historically, the 'war' is Lyndon Johnson's. All we know of Kennedy is that he meant to make one. Still, for either of these men
the effort, if sustained, would lead to irreversible commitment.

Each purpose I have outlined meant commitment to a course
of action which engaged the man—his reputation, *amour propre*,
and sense of self in history—beyond recall. The question then
becomes: how relevant were these, historically? How relevant
to Kennedy's own years of actual (and of prospective) office?
Here I can only make a judgment, tentative of course, devoid
of long perspective. These purposes seem to me entirely relevant.
In short perspective, they seem precisely right as the pre-
eminent concerns for the first half of this decade.

III

So much for Kennedy as man-of-purpose. What about the
man-of-power?

He strikes me as a senator who learned very fast from his confrontation with the executive establishment, particularly after the abortive Cuban invasion which taught him a great deal. On action-issues of particular concern to him he rapidly evolved an operating style which he maintained consistently (and sharpened at the edges) through his years of office. If one looks at Berlin, or Oxford, Mississippi, or the Cuban missile crisis, or at half a dozen other issues of the sort, one finds a pattern: the personal command post, deliberate reaching down for the details, hard questioning of the alternatives, a drive to protect options from foreclosure by sheer urgency or by *ex parte* advocacy, finally a close watch on follow-through. Even on the issues which were secondary to the President and left, perforce, primarily to others, Kennedy was constantly in search of means and men to duplicate at one remove this personalized pattern with its stress on open options and on close control. Numbers of outsiders—Hans Morgenthau and Joseph Alsop for two—sometimes viewed the pattern with alarm and saw this man as 'indecisive'. But that was to consult *their* preferences, not his performance. Kennedy seemed always keen to single out the necessary from the merely possible. He then decided with alacrity.

Not everything was always done effectively, of course, and even the successes produced side effects of bureaucratic bafflement, frustration, irritation which were not without their costs. Even so, the pattern testifies to an extraordinary feel for the distinction between president and presidency, an extraordinary urge to master the machine. This took him quite a way toward mastery in two years and ten months. We shall not know how far he might have got.

Kennedy's feel for his own executive position carried over into that of fellow rulers everywhere. He evidently had great curiosity and real concern about the politics of rulership where-ever he encountered it. His feel for fine distinctions among fellow 'kings' was rare, comparable to the feel of Senate-Leader Johnson for the fine distinctions among fellow senators. And with this Kennedy apparently absorbed in his short time a lesson Franklin Roosevelt never learned about the Russians (or de Gaulle): that in another country an *effective* politician can have motives very *different* from his own. What an advantageous lesson to have learned in two years time! It would have served him well. Indeed, while he still lived I think it did.

The cardinal test of Kennedy as an executive in his own right and also as a student of executives abroad was certainly the confrontation of October 1962, the Cuban missile crisis with Khrushchev. For almost the first time in our foreign relations, the President displayed on that occasion both concern for the psychology of his opponent and insistence on a limited objective. Contrast the Korean War, where we positively courted Chinese intervention by relying on Douglas MacArthur as psychologist and by enlarging our objective after each success. 'There is no substitute for victory,' MacArthur wrote, but at that time we virtually had a nuclear monopoly and even then our government hastened to find a substitute. Now, with mutual capability, the whole traditional meaning has been taken out of 'victory'. In nuclear confrontations there is room for no such thing. Kennedy quite evidently knew it. He also knew, as his performance demonstrates, that risks of escalation lurk in high-level misjudgments *and* in low-level momentum. Washington assuredly was capable of both; so, probably, was Moscow. Accordingly, the President outstripped all previous efforts to guard options and assure control. His operating style was tested then as not before or after. It got him what he wanted.

In confrontations with Congress, quite another world than the executive, the key to Kennedy's congressional relations lay outside his feel for power, beyond reach of technique; he won the presidency by a hair, while in the House of Representatives his party lost some twenty of the seats gained two years earlier. The Democrats *retained* a sizeable majority as they had done in earlier years, no thanks to him. With this beginning, Kennedy's own record of accomplishment in Congress looks enormous, indeterminate, or small, depending on one's willingness to give him credit for enactment of the most divisive, innovative bills he espoused: the tax and civil rights bills passed in Johnson's presidency. Certainly it can be said that Kennedy prepared the way, negotiating a bipartisan approach, and also that he took the heat, stalling his whole program in the process. Equally, it can be said that with his death—or by it—the White House gained advantages which he could not have mustered. Johnson made the most of these. How well would Kennedy have done without them? My own guess is that in the end, with rancor and delay, both bills would have been passed. But it is a moot point. Accordingly, so is the Kennedy record.

Whatever his accomplishment, does it appear the most he could have managed in his years? Granting the limits set by his election, granting the divisiveness injected after Birmingham with his decisive move on civil rights, did he use to the fullest his advantages of office? The answer may well be 'not quite'. Perhaps a better answer is, 'This man could do no more'. For Kennedy, it seems, was not a man enamored of the legislative way of life and legislators knew it. He was wry about it. He had spent fourteen years in Congress and he understood its business, but he never was a 'member of the family' on the Hill. 'Downtown' had always seemed his native habitat; he was a natural executive. They knew that, too. Besides, he was a young man, very young by Senate standards, and his presence in the White House with still younger men around him was a constant irritant to seniors. Moreover, he was not a 'mixer' socially, not, anyway, with most members of Congress and their wives. His manners were impeccable, his charm impelling, but he kept his social life distinct from his official life and congressmen were rarely in his social circle. To know how Congress works but to disdain its joys is an acquired taste for most ex-congressmen downtown, produced by hard experience. Kennedy, however, brought it with him. Many of the difficulties he was to encounter in his day-by-day congressional relations stemmed from that.

But even had he been a man who dearly loved the Congress, even had that feeling been reciprocated, nothing could have rendered their relationship sweetness-and-light in his last year, so long as he persisted with his legislative program. As an innovative President confronting a reluctant Congress, he was heir to Truman, and to Roosevelt after 1936. Kennedy's own manner may have hurt him on the Hill, but these were scratches. Deeper scars had more substantial sources and he knew it.

In confrontations with the larger public outside Washington (again a different world), Kennedy made a brilliant beginning, matched only by the start in different circumstances of his own successor. The 'public relations' of transition into office were superb. In three months after his election, Kennedy transformed himself from 'pushy', 'young', 'Catholic', into President-of-all-the-people, widening and deepening acceptance of his presidency out of all proportion to the election returns. The Bay of Pigs was a severe check, but his handling of the aftermath displayed again superb feel for the imagery befitting an incumbent of the White House, heir to FDR *and* Eisenhower. That feel he always had. I think it never failed him.

What he also had was a distaste for preaching, really for the preachiness of politics, backed by genuine mistrust of mass emotion as a tool in politics. These attitudes are rare among American politicians; with Kennedy their roots ran deep into recesses of experience and character where I, as an outsider, cannot follow. But they assuredly were rooted in this man and they had visible effects upon his public style. He delighted in the play of minds, not of emotions. He doted on Press conferences, not set performances. He feared 'over-exposure'; he dreaded over-reaction. Obviously he enjoyed responsive crowds, and was himself responsive to a sea of cheering faces, but I think he rarely looked at their reaction—or his own—without a twinge of apprehension. He never seems to have displayed much fondness for the 'fireside chat', a form of crowd appeal without the crowd; television talks in evening hours evidently struck him more as duty than as opportunity, and dangerous at that; some words on air-raid shelters in a talk about Berlin could set off mass hysteria—and did. At the moment when he had his largest, most attentive audience, on the climactic Sunday of the Cuban missile crisis, he turned it away (and turned attention off) with a two-minutes announcement, spare and dry.

Yet we know now, after his death, what none of us knew before: that with a minimum of preaching, of emotional appeal, or of self-justification, even explanation, he had managed to touch millions in their private lives, not only at home but emphatically abroad. Perhaps his very coolness helped him do it. Perhaps his very vigor, family, fortune, sense of fun, his manners, taste, and sportsmanship, his evident enjoyment of his life and of the job made him the heart's desire of all sorts of people everywhere, not least among the young. At any rate, we know now that he managed in his years to make enormous impact on a world-wide audience, building an extraordinary base of public interest and affection (interspersed, of course, with doubters and detractors). What he might have made of this or done with it in later years, nobody knows.

IV

So much for power; what of pressure? What sustained this man in his decisions, his frustrations, and with what effect on his approach to being President? For an answer one turns to the evidence of crises, those already mentioned among others, and the *surface* signs are clear. In all such situations it appears that Kennedy was cool, collected, courteous, and terse. This does not mean that he was unemotional. By temperament I think he was a man of mood and passion. But he had schooled his temperament. He kept his own emotions under tight control. He did not lose his temper inadvertently, and never lost it long. He was observer and participant combined; he saw himself as coolly as all others—and with humor. He always was a witty man, dry with a bit of bite and a touch of self-deprecation. He could laugh at himself, and did. Often he used humor to break tension. And in tight places he displayed a keen awareness of the human situation, human limits, his included, but it did not slow his work.

Readers over forty may recognize this portrait as 'the stance of junior officers in the Second World War'; Elspeth Rostow coined that phrase and, superficially at least, she is quite right. This was the Kennedy stance and his self-confidence, his shield against frustration, must have owed a lot to his young manhood in that war.

This tells us a good deal but not nearly enough. At his very first encounter with a crisis in the presidency, Kennedy's self-confidence seems to have been severely strained. The Bay of Pigs fiasco shook him deeply, shook his confidence in methods and associates. Yet he went on governing without a break, no change in manner, or in temper, or in humor. What sustained him? Surely much that went beyond experience of war.

What else? I cannot answer. I can only conjecture. His family life and rearing have some part to play, no doubt. His political successes also: in 1952 he bucked the Eisenhower tide to reach the Senate; in 1960 he broke barriers of youth and of religion which had always held before; on each occasion the Conventional Wisdom was against him: 'can't be done.'

Beyond these things, this man had been exceptionally close to death, not only in the war but ten years after. And in his presidential years his back was almost constantly a source of pain; he never talked about it but he lived with it. All this is of a piece with his behavior in a crisis. His control, his objectivity, his humor, and his sense of human limits, these were but expressions of his confidence; its sources must lie somewhere in this ground.

Whatever the sources, the results were rewarding for this President's performance on the job. In the most critical, nerve-straining aspects of the office, coping with its terrible responsibility for use of force, Kennedy's own image of himself impelled him neither to lash out nor run for cover. Rather, it released him for engagement and decision as a reasonable man. In some of the less awesome aspects of the presidency, his own values restrained him, kept him off the pulpit, trimmed his guest list, made him shy away from the hyperbole of politics. But as a chief *executive*, confronting action-issues for decision and control, his duty and his confidence in doing it were nicely matched. So the world discovered in October 1962.

v

Now for my last question. What did he leave behind him? What was the legacy of his short years? At the very least he left a myth: the vibrant, youthful leader cut down senselessly before his time. What this may come to signify as the years pass, I cannot tell. He left a glamorous moment, an engaging, youthful time, but how we shall remember it depends on what becomes of Lyndon Johnson. He left a broken promise, that 'the torch has been passed to a new generation', and the youngsters who identified with him felt cheated as the promise, like the glamor, disappeared. What do their feelings matter? We shall have to wait and see.

May this be all that history is likely to record? Perhaps, but I doubt it. My guess is that when the observers can appraise the work of Kennedy's successors, they will find some things of substance in his legacy. Rashly, let me record what I think these are.

To begin with, our first Catholic President chose and paved the way for our first Southern President since the Civil War.

(Woodrow Wilson was no Southerner *politically*; he came to the White House from the State House of New Jersey.) While Texas may be suspect now in Southern eyes, it certainly is of the South in Northern eyes, as Johnson found so painfully in 1960. Kennedy made him President. How free was the choice of Johnson as vice-presidential candidate is subject to some argument. But what appears beyond dispute is that once chosen, Johnson was so treated by his rival for the White House as to ease his way enormously when he took over there. Johnson may have suffered great frustration as Vice-President, but his public standing and his knowledge of affairs were nurtured in those years. From this he gained a running start. The credit goes in no small part to Kennedy.

Moreover, Kennedy bequeathed to Johnson widened options in the sphere of foreign relations: a military posture far more flexible and useable than he himself inherited; a diplomatic posture more sophisticated in its whole approach to neutralists and Leftists, markedly more mindful of distinctions in the world, even among allies.

On the domestic side, Kennedy left a large inheritance of controversies, opened by a youthful, Catholic urbanite from the North-east, which his South-western, Protestant successor might have had more trouble stirring at the start, but now can ride and maybe even 'heal'. This may turn out to have been a productive division of labor.

However it turns out, Kennedy lived long enough to keep at least one promise. He got the country 'moving again'. For in our politics, the *sine qua non* of innovative policy is controversy. By 1963 we were engaged in controversy with an openness which would have been unthinkable, or at least 'un-American', during the later Eisenhower years. Events, of course, have more to do with stirring controversy than a President. No man can make an issue on his own. But presidents will help to shape the meaning of events, the terms of discourse, the attention paid, the noise-level. Eisenhower's years were marked by a pervasive fog of self-congratulation, muffling noise. The fog-machine was centered in the White House. Perhaps there had been need for this after the divisive Truman years. By the late nineteen-fifties, though, it fuzzed our chance to innovate in time. Kennedy broke out of it.

Finally, this President set a new standard of performance on the job, suitable to a new state of presidential being, a state he was the first to face throughout his term of office: the state of substantial, deliverable, nuclear capability in other hands than ours. Whatever else historians may make of Kennedy, I think them likely to begin with this. There can be little doubt that his successors have a lighter task because *he* pioneered in handling nuclear confrontations. During the Cuban missile crisis and thereafter, he did something which had not been done before, did it well, and got it publicly accepted. His innovation happened to be timely, since the need for innovation was upon us; technology had put it there. But also, in his reach for information and control, his balancing of firmness with caution, his sense of limits, he displayed and dramatized what presidents must do to minimize the risk of war through mutual miscalculation. This may well be the cardinal risk confronting his successors. If so, he made a major contribution to the presidency.

KENNEDY AND CONGRESS

The writer gives a critical assessment of President Kennedy's legislative performance between 1961 and early 1963. The article was written before President Kennedy's death and therefore does not take into account subsequent action in the Congress to legislate parts of President Kennedy's programme.

DOCUMENT 27. 'THE KENNEDY STYLE AND CONGRESS', BY CARROLL KILPATRICK (FROM *The Virginia Quarterly Review*, VOL. 39, NO. 1, 1963, PP. 1–11).

John F. Kennedy campaigned for the Presidency at a time when congressional leadership was strong. He promised that if elected he would be a forceful executive, a leader of his party, the center of a vibrant, imaginative Administration eager to meet and to deal with the nation's challenging domestic and foreign problems.

To a degree which only historians will be able to define he has provided leadership in many fields. But Congress has forced him to be more pragmatic than his pragmatic philosophy would dictate and to leaven his promise to be a forceful executive with a large dash of compromise and adjustment.

The record of President Kennedy's first two years with Congress was not without notable successes. But there were notable failures as well, and the amount of energy he expended in gaining as much as he did was enormous. The President's power struggle with Congress was almost equal to that of his struggle with the Communist leaders abroad. And Congress was under the control of Democrats. Although the President was 'heartened', as he said, by the results of the November election, and can look forward to slightly improved relations with the new Congress, he faces essentially the same institutional problems. The struggle will be continued in the 88th Congress.

Indeed, it will begin on the opening day in the House of Representatives just as it began there immediately after Mr. Kennedy's inauguration nearly two years ago. By a vote of 217 to 212, the House in early 1961 increased the size of its Rules Committee from twelve to fifteen members to break the controlling power of the Republican-conservative Democratic coalition. In January 1963, the size of the committee will revert to twelve, and conservatives now are confident that they will dominate it once again. If they are successful, they will be in a position to keep almost any bill they wish off the House floor. Another victory over the Rules Committee is a vital necessity for the President if he is to win important victories in the next two years.

The significance of this power struggle between the President and Congress is that there is nothing new about it, nor is there any easy or permanent solution in sight; but on its outcome hangs the success or failure of the Kennedy Administration. Throughout our history the legislative and executive branches have been less co-ordinate than rival instruments of government. From the days of the first President there has been a struggle for supremacy except when weak Presidents accepted congressional leadership.

Having called for the invigoration of the executive power, Mr. Kennedy will be judged in large part by the success with which he leads his party in Congress. He learned early in his Administration that his fundamental weakness as leader is that he heads a party which is not united behind him. It resists his leadership. He has neither the machinery, in congressional organization, patronage, or party discipline, to impose his will on his party nor the necessary popular support to win against a well-organized opposition.

That is why he campaigned in September and October more than any President has done before him for the election of a more sympathetic Congress. He said at one point during the campaign that whenever he sent a proposal on domestic affairs to Congress he knew it would be opposed by seven-eighths of the Republicans and about a fourth of the Democrats.

'We have a party which covers all parts of the country,' he explained. 'We include in it Wayne Morse and Strom Thurmond and Harry Byrd, men who don't agree on a good many things, particularly on domestic matters. So I usually figure that we are going to lose one-fourth of the Democrats.'

In the 87th Congress, which is the one the President was talking about, Democrats controlled the Senate by 64 to 36 and the House by 262 to 174 (one vacancy). Yet with those top-heavy majorities the Administration's omnibus farm bill was lost in the House by 10 votes and the medical care bill was lost in the Senate by five votes. 'We passed an agricultural bill (not the omnibus bill that was killed) the other day by one vote in the House, lost it by one vote in the Senate,' the President commented during the campaign.

When Congress adjourned in October, the Administration was able to boast of winning a major new foreign trade bill, a modified tax revision bill, a communication satellite measure, a strong drug labeling law, a much-modified farm bill, a new public works measure, an increase in postal rates and Federal pay, and other significant measures.

But in nearly every instance the President gave ground. He made important concessions to the textile industry to win support of his trade bill, the most far-reaching achievement of the 87th Congress. He obtained far less than half a loaf in the tax revision bill Congress finally passed. He accepted amendments to the communication satellite and drug labeling law and to the postal rate and pay increase bills.

Some of these compromises may have resulted in improvements, some may have been no more than the normal give-and-take expected in a free society. But all represented retreat on the President's part.

The President's losses in the 87th Congress included medical care for the aged under social security, a bill to create a Department of Urban Affairs, a farm bill with controls on feed grains, the proposal to withhold taxes on dividends and interest, the request for authority to make limited Federal income tax adjustments in accordance with changing economic conditions, Federal aid for public schools, Federal aid for higher education, sharp cuts in foreign aid appropriations, a rider withdrawing most-favored nation treatment to trade with Poland and Yugoslavia, the Justice Department's new proposals to control wire-tapping, a mass transportation bill, and other measures.

History may record that the most important defeat was one which was lost without a vote ever having been taken or a bill introduced. During the summer, there was strong pressure for a tax cut to bolster the economy. The President himself and the majority of his economic advisers concluded that a cut was desirable. But rather than risk an impossible battle in Congress the President decided against making the request.

That decision, in fact, was made for the President by Chairman Wilbur D. Mills of the House Ways and Means Committee. In that intra-party battle Mills exercized more power than the President, recalling Harold Laski's comment that influential members of Congress have more power than any private members of any other legislative assembly in the world.

There is no abler man in the House than Mills. But his loyalty is primarily to the voters of his rural Arkansas district, however different their interests, prejudices, and information may be from those of a majority of the American people. Mill's great power derives, of course, not from his constituents but from the system that elevates him to the Ways and Means chairmanship solely on the basis of seniority.

Students of the problem of congressional vs. presidential power have proposed many reforms. Some have been tried in the past, such as the caucus system, and proved to be temporarily successful. Others are desirable and urgently needed today. But the President's problem, as he interprets it, is to work with what he has, much as other Presidents have done, in attempting to impose his program on a Congress jealous of its rights and endowed by the Constitution with extraordinary powers. Those who propose the most drastic reforms of Congress forget that they really are proposing a reform of the American constitutional system. Logic and right may be on their side, but logic and right, when they go against tradition in politics, are exceedingly difficult to impose.

A reform of the seniority system, which could be made without violating anything but tradition and which is urgently needed, is a case in point. There would be no constitutional barrier to such a reform, yet it would be almost as easy to transport Vermont's snows to Florida as to change this system that on occasion gives men like Mills or Chairman Harry F. Byrd of the Senate Finance Committee virtual veto power over a Chief Executive.

Mr. Kennedy, like his predecessors, has decided to pursue the art of the possible with the tools at hand. He may be criticized for that, but that was his decision. He knows that the Constitution-makers intended Congress to have great power. Influenced as they were by the English Whigs, by Locke's doctrine of legislative supremacy, and by Montesquieu's warning that power must be checked by power, the framers of the Constitution instituted a government of divided powers and of checks and balances that has ever made a President's burdens onerous.

When Mr. Kennedy was elected in 1960 by the narrowest of margins and with the loss of twenty Democratic seats in the House he knew that he faced a formidable challenge in his relations with Congress. Some of his advisers told him that the only way he could succeed was to take his case to the people, to use public opinion to compel Congress to do his bidding. 'The Presidency is pre-eminently the people's office,' said Grover Cleveland, to which Woodrow Wilson added: 'He has no means of compelling Congress except through public opinion.'

The President, however, followed his own inclination and the advice of the late Speaker Sam Rayburn and of Vice-President Lyndon B. Johnson when he chose to work with Congress and to try to woo its recalcitrant members by favors, pork, patronage, and charm. He never appealed over the heads of Congressmen to the people except once last summer—and that was after the event—when the Senate defeated his medical care program.

In the first session of the 87th Congress, in an attempt to woo its members, the President met privately at the White House with every committee chairman. He had coffee hours with small groups from time to time. He held briefing sessions on important bills with Democratic members as well as foreign policy briefings for bi-partisan groups.

These were important and made for more cordial relations. But members of Congress have a habit of listening more attentively to the dominant pressure groups from their districts than to the President. The President's brother, Edward M. Kennedy, made this clear during his campaign for the Senate in Massachusetts. He said that he would not support the President in all matters. The President's loyalty, he explained, was to the voters of fifty states whereas the loyalty of the Senator from Massachusetts was to the voters of Massachusetts. The younger Kennedy said that he expected the President to fight for tariff cuts but that he himself would do all he could to assure that there would be no tariff cuts affecting Massachusetts industries. However understandable all this may be in a representative assembly, it hardly makes for responsible party government.

'I have a very strong feeling,' Theodore Roosevelt once said while still in the White House, 'that it is a President's duty to get on with Congress if he possibly can, and that it is a reflection upon him if he and Congress come to a complete break.' Later, he told how he had tried repeatedly to work with the congressional leaders. 'We succeeded in working together, although with increasing friction, for some years, I pushing forward and they hanging back,' he wrote in his 'Autobiography'. 'Gradually, however, I was forced to abandon the effort to persuade them to come my way, and then I achieved results only by appealing over the heads of the Senate and House leaders to the people, who were the masters of both of us. I continued in this way to get results until almost the close of my term.'

Each successful President has worked out his own methods of dealing with Congress. Jefferson, although leader of a party which called for a stronger legislative than executive power, worked quietly to establish his leadership. As Wilfred E. Binkley has said in his excellent 'President and Congress,' when the House of Representatives was organized in Jefferson's first term, 'it was apparent to the discerning that lieutenants of the President occupied every key position'. If as much could be said for President Kennedy his troubles would be cut in half. Jefferson, as well as Wilson later, effectively used the caucus to bind the party members in advance of a vote so that they would be united on the floor. Jefferson himself is said to have presided at some meetings of the caucus.

A few days after Woodrow Wilson's inauguration he summoned Postmaster-General Albert S. Burleson, his patronage chief and an experienced politician, to the White House, and said: 'Now, Burleson, I want to say to you that my Administration is going to be a progressive Administration. I am not going to advise with reactionary or standpat Senators or Representatives in making these appointments. I am going to appoint forward-looking men, and I am going to satisfy myself that they are honest and capable. I am not going to consult the standpatters in our party'.

Burleson expressed astonishment. He replied that if the President followed such a course 'your Administration is going to be a failure. It means the defeat of the measures of reform that you have next to your heart'.

Burleson left the White House not knowing whether his argument had had any effect on the stubborn Presbyterian occupant. But Burleson had made an impression, as events were to demonstrate. Wilson made many compromises with the conservatives in his party to win approval of his domestic programs. He worked closely, for example, with conservatives like Representative Oscar W. Underwood, chairman of the Ways and Means Committee, who had opposed Wilson's nomination. Wilson appointed men whom his supporters cried out against as reactionaries, because that was one way to win recalcitrant Democrats in Congress.

Wilson also used other tools to persuade Congress—his skill as an orator, a much tighter party organization on Capitol Hill than exists today, and a Democratic and liberal Republican coalition that worked with him. Now President Kennedy faces a Republican and conservative Democratic coalition that works against him.

Wilson had another advantage. He came to the White House from the New Jersey Governor's office, where he had gained experience in exercising leadership over a legislature as well as over a bureaucracy. President Kennedy, the more experienced politician, came from the Senate, where the training is in compromise and adjustment rather than in the exercise of the executive talents. Perhaps this training helps to explain why the President appears to be quicker to compromise and less willing to use the vast powers of persuasion at his command.

In addition, in Wilson's day the Democratic caucus was a useful and important instrument of translating New Freedom proposals into reality. It is inconceivable that with the deep Democratic divisions that exist today an effective caucus could be instituted. Arthur S. Link says in his biography of Wilson that Wilson was the leader of his party 'during a time when it was consciously attempting to transform itself from a sectional, agrarian party into a truly national organization representative of all sections and classes'. President Kennedy is leader of his party during a time when it is consciously divided along sectional and ideological lines and when one wing is fighting against the establishment of a truly national organization.

Link wrote of Wilson:

It is no derogation of Wilson's contribution to emphasize the circumstances that made strong leadership possible from 1913 to 1917, for his contribution in techniques was of enormous importance.

The first of these techniques was to assert the position of the President as the spokesman of the people and to use public opinion as a spur on Congress. Theodore Roosevelt had demonstrated the usefulness of this method, but Wilson used it to the fullest advantage and made it inevitable that any future President would be powerful only in so far as he established communication with the people and spoke effectively for them.

His chief instruments in achieving a position as national spokesman were of course oratory and public messages, by means of which he gave voice to the highest aspirations, first, of the American people, and then, during the war and afterward, of the people of the world.

It is in the use of public opinion to spur Congress that President Kennedy has most disappointed some of his supporters. During the long second session of the 87th Congress, which lasted from January to October, the President made three formal radio-television reports to the American people. The first was in March when he announced the resumption of nuclear testing: the second was in August when he defensively announced that he would postpone until 1963 a request to Congress to cut income taxes; the third was in October when he spoke briefly on the desegregation crisis at the University of Mississippi. Only one of these involved the President's relations with Congress, and that was the speech on taxation delivered after Congress through Chairman Mills had in effect dictated the President's position to him.

In the congressional campaign, before the President cut short his participation because of the Cuban crisis, he had an opportunity to explain his objectives, to elucidate the issues, and to arouse the people's interest in New Frontier programs. Instead, he contented himself with trying to make the election a popularity contest. His campaigning was designed to take advantage of his high personal standing with the voters and to contrast the wickedness of backward Republicans with the generosity of forward-looking Democrats.

The President has relied heavily on the Press conference to influence opinion and to state his case against his critics in Congress. It is highly questionable whether the usefulness of the Press conference to him has been as great as he expected. He has not used it to the full extent to explain, argue, and educate. Instead, he often has been content to state a conclusion rather than to use the occasion to mobilize support with strong argument.

That the President is capable of explaining an issue and arguing for it with force was demonstrated best of all in a notable address in December 1961, before the National Association of Manufacturers. He spoke at length, in detail, and with great force on the reasons why he was asking Congress for broad new trade legislation. Carefully argued speeches like that one are worth more than a dozen offhand appeals for support on an issue that is never fully clarified.

Unlike Wilson and the two Roosevelts, President Kennedy has refused to go over the heads of his former colleagues on Capitol Hill. He has neglected his opportunities to use the forum of the Presidency as an educational institution. He has not used the many facilities at his command to build fires under the feet of hesitant legislators. Instead, he has sought to win them over by the elements of compromise and adjustment he learned so well in the Senate. That has been the Kennedy style in the first two years. He signed several bills distasteful to him, including the measure he had opposed to permit tax deductions for private pension funds, rather than alienate friends in Congress.

In the President's defense, it must be said that while he pressed for New Frontier domestic programs, his larger object-ive always was to maintain a united front on foreign affairs. Neither Wilson nor FDR had to temper his actions in his first years because of overseas crises. Even when this is said, however, it has come as a surprise to the President's early supporters to see that he has not used the Presidency in a more dramatic way to deal with his party in Congress. The rôle of the great compromiser hardly befits his own definition of the Presidency. And it neglects the fact that his power with Congress rests with the people. As all the great Presidents learned, only the people can give the Chief Executive sustenance and establish him in fact as leader of his party in Congress. Perhaps with the clearer mandate the voters gave the President in 1962, and with the confidence gained from the Cuban experience, his leadership will be firmer in the 88th Congress than it was in the 87th.

KENNEDY AND HISTORY

In the article below the writer attempts the difficult task of assessing Kennedy's performance as a President and as a world leader. The writer makes both praise and criticism in his appraisal. Despite the opening observations, one can still argue the difficulties of attempting to place Kennedy in historical perspective in 1964.

DOCUMENT 28. 'KENNEDY IN HISTORY: AN EARLY APPRAISAL',
BY WILLIAM G. CARLETON (FROM *The Antioch Review*, VOL.
XXIV, NO. 3, 1964, PP. 277–99).

I

Although John F. Kennedy has been dead less than a year, it
is not too early to assess his place in history. Judgments about
historical figures never come finally to rest. Reputations fluc-
tuate through the centuries, for they must constantly do battle
with oblivion and compete with the shifting interests and values
of subsequent generations. Even so, contemporary estimates are
sometimes not markedly changed by later ones.

The career of a public man, the key events of his life, most of
his record, the questions he confronted, the problems he tackled,
the social forces at work in his time are largely open to scrutiny
when he leaves public life. The archives and subsequently
revealed letters, memoirs, and diaries will yield important new
material, but usually these merely fill out and embellish the
already known public record.

What more frequently alters an early historical appraisal
than later revealed material is the course of events after the
hero has left the stage. For instance, should President Johnson,
during the next few years, succeed in breaking the legislative
log-jam and driving through Congress a major legislative
program, then President Kennedy's failure to do this will be
judged harshly. But should the congressional stalemate continue, then the Kennedy difficulties likely will be chalked up
not so much against him personally but against the intricacies
of the American system of separation of powers and pluralized,
divided parties. Even so, it will not be easy to defend the meager
Kennedy legislative performance.

If popular passion is running high at the time an historical
personage makes his exit, then it is difficult for a contemporary
to be relatively objective in his evaluation. (At no time is there
absolute objectivity in history.) For instance, Woodrow Wilson
left office amidst such violent misunderstanding that few con-
temporaries could do him justice, and only now, four decades
later, is he being appraised with relative fairness. With Kennedy, one collides with adoration. The uncritical bias in favor
of Kennedy derives from his winsome personality, his style and

elan, the emotional euphoria arising from his tragic death, and the sympathetic spiritual kinship with him felt by historians, political scientists, intellectuals, and writers. There is, to be sure, considerable hate-Kennedy literature, most of it written before his death and reflecting ultra right-wing biases, but few will be fooled into taking diatribes for serious history.

II

Although as President he clearly belongs to the liberal tradition of the Democratic party's twentieth-century presidents, Kennedy's pre-presidential career can scarcely be said to have been liberal. During his congressional service he refused to hew to an ideological or even a party line. Kennedy often asked: 'Just what is a liberal?' He confessed that his glands did not operate like Hubert Humphrey's.

Reviewing Kennedy's votes in House and Senate from 1947 to 1958, the AFL–CIO's Committee on Political Education gave him a pro-labor score of twenty-five out of twenty-six, which in considerable part may be explained by the large number of low-income wage-earners in his district. Kennedy usually followed the views and interests of his constituents, and this gave his congressional career its greatest measure of consistency. With respect to welfare programs which did not much concern his constituents—farm price supports, flood control, TVA, the Rural Electrification Administration—Kennedy sometimes joined the Byrd economy bloc. On occasion, Kennedy could fly in the face of New England sentiment, as when he supported reciprocal tariff laws and the St. Lawrence Seaway, and again when he publicly stated that he thought President Eisenhower, in an attempt to salvage the Paris summit conference, should apologize to Khrushchev for the U-2 incident. At such times, Kennedy displayed a disarming candor.

In foreign policy, Kennedy's early pronouncements had a right-wing flavor, especially with respect to China, but he soon developed a greater interest in foreign affairs than in domestic ones, and he moved away from right-wing attitudes to favor foreign economic aid, to rebuff the Committee of One Million devoted to keeping Red China out of the United Nations, to speak up for abandoning Quemoy and Matsu, to fight for economic help to Communist Poland, to advocate Algerian independence, and to encourage international arms-control negotiations.

In general, through the years, in both domestic and foreign policy, Kennedy moved from positions right of center or at center to positions left of center.

Since Negro rights played so important and dramatic a part in his Presidency, historians will always be interested in Kennedy's earlier stand on civil rights. Until the presidential campaign of 1960, Kennedy was not an aggressive fighter for the Negro. During his quest for the vice-presidential nomination in 1956, he wooed the Southern delegations and stressed his moderation. After 1956, he sought to keep alive the South's benevolent feeling for him, and his speeches in that region, sprinkled with unflattering references to carpetbaggers like Mississippi Governor Alcorn and praise for L. Q. C. Lamar and other Bourbon 'redeemers', had a faint ring of Claude Bowers' *Tragic Era*.[1] In 1957, during the fight in the Senate over the civil rights bill, Kennedy lined up for the O'Mahoney amendment to give trials to those held in criminal contempt of court. Civil rights militants regarded this as emasculating, since those accused of impeding Negro voting would find more leniency in Southern juries than in federal judges.

What will disturb historians most about Kennedy's pre-presidential career was his evasion of the McCarthy challenge. In his early congressional days, Kennedy himself often gave expression to the mood of frustration, especially with reference to the loss of China, out of which McCarthyism came. In a talk at Harvard in 1950, Kennedy said that 'McCarthy may have something', and he declared that not enough had been done about Communists in government.[2]

By the time McCarthyism had emerged full blow, Kennedy was caught in a maze of entanglements. His Irish-Catholic constituents were ecstatically for McCarthy, and Kennedy's own family was enmeshed. Westbrook Pegler, McCarthy's foremost journalistic supporter, was close to father Joseph P. Kennedy; the elder Kennedy entertained McCarthy at Hyannis Port and contributed to his political fund; brother Robert Kennedy became a member of McCarthy's investigating staff. John Kennedy himself not only kept mum on the

McCarthy issue but actually benefited from it. During Kennedy's senatorial campaign against Lodge, the latter was portrayed as soft on Communism, leading McCarthyite politicians and newspapers in Massachusetts backed Kennedy, and McCarthy was persuaded to stay out of Massachusetts and do nothing for Lodge there.

When McCarthyism finally climaxed in the debate and vote in the Senate over censuring the Great Inquisitor, Kennedy was absent because of an illness which nearly cost him his life. At no time did Kennedy ever announce how he would have voted on censure. He did not exercise his right to pair his vote with another absent colleague who held an opposite view. It may be that Kennedy was too ill for even that. Kennedy's subsequent private explanations—that to have opposed McCarthy would have been to commit political hara-kiri and that he was caught in a web of family entanglements—were lame and unworthy.[3]

Nevertheless, there can be no doubt that McCarthyism was a searing experience for John Kennedy. During his convalescence, as a sort of personal catharsis, he wrote his book *Profiles in Courage*, which dealt with famous senators of the past who had to choose between personal conscience and violent mass execration and political extinction. Kennedy seems to be saying: 'This is the kind of cruel dilemma I would have faced had I been present in the Senate when the vote was taken on the McCarthy censure.' *Profiles in Courage* is Kennedy's examination of his own Procrustean anguish. Such soul-searching may have helped him psychologically, but it added not a whit to the fight against McCarthy's monstrous threat to the free and open society.

Some years later, when even then Eleanor Roosevelt sought to prod Kennedy into making an *ex post facto* condemnation of McCarthyism, he wisely refused. He observed, with that candor which was his most engaging hallmark, that since he had not been in opposition during the controversy, to take a decided stand after Senator McCarthy was politically dead would make him (Kennedy) a political prostitute and poltroon.[4]

In the future, historians sympathetic to President Kennedy are likely to seriously underestimate the right-wing influences that played upon him and his brother Robert during their formative years and early life in politics. The influence of Joseph P. Kennedy was strong, and in the pre-Pearl Harbor years the Kennedy household was the center of 'America First' leaders, journalists, and ideas, and in the early 1950's of McCarthy leaders, journalists, and ideas. It is not remarkable that John and Robert reflected some right-wing attitudes in their early political careers; what is remarkable is that first John and then Robert, who is less flexible, emancipated themselves from these attitudes.

III

In all likelihood, John Kennedy would never have become President had his brother Joe lived; or had he (John) been nominated for Vice-President in 1956; or had the Paris summit of May 1960 not blown up.

All of those who have followed the Kennedy story know well that it was the eldest son of the family, Joe, Jr., and not John, who was slated for politics. If Joe, Jr., had lived, John would not have gone into politics at all. (This is not to say that Joe, Jr., would have 'made the grade' in high politics, as believers in the Kennedy magic now assume. Joe, Jr., was an extrovert; he was obviously the political 'type'. John's mind was more penetrating and dispassionate, and he did not fit the stereotype of the politician, particularly the Irish politician. What endeared John to the status-seeking minorities was that he appeared more the scion of an old aristocratic Yankee family than the authentic scions themselves. Had Joe, Jr., lived, the Kennedy family in all probability would never have had a President at all. (In part, this evaluation of Joe, Jr., and John is derived from personal observation. I recall vividly an evening, April 4, 1941, when I was a guest at the Kennedy home in Palm Beach. Following dinner, the entire family, including the younger children, assembled in the drawing-room for a discussion of public affairs. Ambassador Kennedy was particularly interested in canvassing our views about the content of commencement addresses he was to deliver later that spring at Oglethorpe University and at Notre Dame University, but the discussion ranged widely over world politics and foreign policy. Mr. Kennedy, John, and I were the chief participants, although Mrs. Kennedy and Joe, Jr., often broke in with comments. It was clear to me that John had a far better historical and political mind than his father or his elder brother; indeed, that John's capacity for seeing current events in historical perspective and for projecting historical trends into the future was unusual. After the family conclave broke up, John and I continued an animated conversation into the early morning hours.)

Had John Kennedy been nominated for Vice-President in 1956, he would have gone down to disastrous defeat along with Stevenson. That year Eisenhower carried even more of the South than he had in 1952. Both the elder Kennedy and John are reported to have felt that this poorer showing by the Democratic national ticket in 1956 would have been attributed to the continued vitality of anti-Catholic sentiment, thus rendering Kennedy unavailable for the 1960 nomination. It seems that this is a sound judgment.

Despite the fact that more Americans were registered as Democrats than as Republicans, the chances for Republican success in 1960 looked rosy indeed until after the dramatic U-2 incident and the collapse of the Paris summit conference. Had the summit accomplished anything at all, the result would have been hailed as the crowning achievement of Eisenhower, the man of peace, and Nixon would have been effectively portrayed as Eisenhower's experienced heir, one who could be both resolute and conciliatory. The explosion of the summit paved the way for Republican defeat and gave plausibility to the kind of 'view-with-alarm' campaign waged by Kennedy. In any general climate favoring Republican victory, even Kennedy's ability to win the Catholic vote would not have elected him.

Will historians be hard on Kennedy for his extravagant charges during the 1960 campaign that the Eisenhower Administration had been remiss about America's missiles and space programs? (The fact is that the 'gap' in inter-continental missiles was decidedly in favor of the United States.) No, for presidents are rated in history by the records they make in office, not by how they wage their campaigns. In his first campaign for the Presidency, Lincoln assured voters that the South would not secede; Wilson promised his New Freedom but in office wound up closer to Theodore Roosevelt's New

Nationalism; and Franklin Roosevelt pledged economy and a balanced budget but became the founder of the New Deal. Kennedy's zeal will likely be put down as no more than excessive 'campaign oratory'. Oddly enough, it may be Eisenhower who will be blamed for failing to 'nail' Kennedy and to tell the nation bluntly the true state of its defenses, for missing the opportunity to add credibility to America's nuclear deterrent. Liberal historians, impressed by Kennedy's domestic promises and, except for Cuba, his more liberal program than Nixon's in foreign policy—Quemoy and Matsu, emphasis on foreign economic aid, stress on international arms control— will not be prone to hold Kennedy accountable for the alarmist flavor of his campaign.

Of 1960's 'issues', only the religious one will loom large in history. It was the religious implication which gave Kennedy the victory. Democratic gains in the pivotal Catholic cities in the states with the largest electoral votes were greater than Democratic losses in the Protestant rural areas. It was the Democrats, not the Republicans, who actively exploited the religious aspect. In the Protestant areas, citizens were made to feel they were bigots if they voted against Kennedy. But Catholics were appealed to on the grounds of their Catholicism. Any evidence of Protestant intolerance was widely publicized to stimulate Catholics and Jews to go to the polls to rebuke the bigots. But history will treat these Democratic tactics—a kind of bigotry in reverse—with kindness. The means may have been objectionable, but the good achieved was enormous. For the first time in American history a non-Protestant was elected President. The old barriers were downed. Now that an Irish-Catholic had been elected president, the way was opened for the election of an Italian Catholic, a Polish Catholic, a Jew, eventually a Negro. A basic American ideal had at last been implemented at the very pinnacle of American society. (In emphasizing the religious issue as affecting the outcome of the campaign, I incline to the conclusions reached by Elmo Roper in 'Polling Post-Mortem', *Saturday Review*, November 26, 1960; the Gallup figures in 'Catholics' Vote Analyzed, a 62 per cent. Switch to Kennedy', New York *Herald-Tribune*, December 6, 1960; Richard M. Scammon, 'Foreign Policy, Prestige Not a Big Election Factor', Washington *Post*, December 15,

1960; Louis Bean comment in Anti-Defamation League of B'nai B'rith press release, January 14, 1961. These coincide with my own findings as the result of interviews with voters in certain sensitive election districts during the campaign of 1960. However, behavioral statisticians differ about this, and doubtless a number of more definitive studies will be forthcoming. Whatever the reasons for the election of Kennedy, the fact that for the first time a Catholic was elected President is what has made the large and permanent impact on history. Even so, every Kennedy biographer must of necessity be concerned with the old question of means and ends, the moral implications of using a religious prejudice in reverse to break the old Protestant monopoly on the Presidency. A striking example of appealing to religious emotion in the guise of opposing it is found in Robert Kennedy's Cincinnati address of September 13, 1960, which was climaxed by this: 'Did they ask my brother Joe whether he was a Catholic before he was shot down?')

The second permanent contribution of the 1960 election lies in its underscoring the large degree to which presidential pre-convention campaigns and election campaigns have been geared to democratic mass behavior. Kennedy and his team wisely recognized that a mere pursuit of the politicians and delegates was not enough, that beginning with 1928, conventions had nominated the outstanding national favorite as indicated by the primaries and the polls. In Kennedy's case, winning the primaries and the polls was especially necessary to convince the doubters that a young man and a Catholic could be elected President. Hence Kennedy organization, money, and high-level experts were directed not merely to bagging delegates but even more to winning mass support, primaries, and high ratings in the polls. In this they succeeded marvelously well. In effect, the Democratic convention merely ratified the choice already made by the primaries, the polls, and the mass media. The revolution in the presidential nominating process had been in the making for over three decades, but it took the Kennedy campaign to make the public and even the pundits aware of it.

During the election campaign itself, Kennedy kept alive his personal organization; brother Bob, his personal manager, was more important than the chairman of the Democratic National

Committee; the nominee himself made all the meaningful decisions and virtually monopolized the limelight; other party leaders were dwarfed as never before. The TV debates further spotlighted the nominees. Again, as in the pre-convention campaign, the Kennedy team did not create the trend to a personalized campaign, to glamorous celebrity politics. The trend and the techniques to make it work had been on the way for decades. Basically these emerged from the increasingly mass nature of American society. But Kennedy exploited the trend and the techniques in conspicuously successful fashion; he widened, intensified, and accelerated them; he made the nation aware of them; he did much to institutionalize them.

Thus the Kennedy campaigns will always be remembered for the dramatic way they contributed to the personalized and plebiscitic Presidency.

IV

No administration in history staffed the executive departments and the White House offices with as many competent, dedicated, and brilliant men as did Kennedy's. Kennedy paid little attention to party qualifications at top level; the emphasis was on ability, drive, imagination, creativity. Politicians made way for specialists and technicians; but Kennedy was on the lookout for specialists *plus*, for men who had not only technical competence but intellectual verve. Kennedy himself was a generalist with a critical intelligence, and many of the most prized of his staff were men of like caliber—Sorensen, Goodwin, Bundy. After the brilliance of the Kennedy team, and with the ever-growing complexity of government problems, no administration is ever likely to want to go back to the pedestrian personnel of earlier administrations, although few presidents are apt to have the Kennedy sensitivity and magnetism capable of gathering together so scintillating an administration as his. FDR will be known as the founder of the presidential brains trust, but Kennedy will be known as the President who widened and institutionalized it.

In contrast to his performance in the executive departments, Kennedy's relations with Congress can scarcely be said to have been successful. The dream of enacting a legislative program comparable to that of Wilson and FDR soon vanished. The one outstanding legislative achievement of Kennedy was the Trade Expansion Act of 1962. All of Kennedy's other major goals—farm legislation, tax reform, a civil rights law, medicare, federal aid to schools—bogged down in Congress.

Since 1938, major welfare legislation had repeatedly been smothered in Congress at the hands of a Republican-conservative–Southern Democratic coalition. During the bobtail, post-conventions session of 1960, both Kennedy and Johnson, the Democratic party's new standard bearers, had met humiliating legislative failure when they found themselves unable to budge the Democratic Congress. Kennedy had explained that once the powers of the Presidency were in his hands, things would be different. But when he achieved the Presidency and still failed with a Democratic Congress, Kennedy apologists contended that after Kennedy's re-election in 1964 he would be in a position to press more boldly for legislation. This argument stood experience on its head, for most presidents have secured much more legislation during their honeymoon first years than during their lame-duck second terms.

Kennedy will not escape all blame for his legislative failures, for despite his awareness of the stalemate since 1938, he had promised a 'strong' legislative leadership like that of Wilson and the second Roosevelt. Moreover, in various ways Kennedy contributed to the personalized and plebiscitic Presidency: by the manner in which he waged his 1960 campaign, by his assigning to key posts not party leaders but men personally chosen for their expertise and creative intelligence, and by his monopolizing of the limelight. Kennedy and his family naturally made exciting publicity, but the President seemed to go out of his way to get even more—holding televised press conferences, for example, and permitting TV cameras to capture the intimacies of decision-making in the executive offices and of private life in the White House. All of this further exalted the Presidency, further dwarfed politicians, party, and Congress, and added to Congress' growing inferiority complex.

Now, Kennedy was not unaware of the susceptibilities of Congress. He carefully cultivated individual congressmen and senators, frequently called them on the phone, had them up for chats, extended them an unusual number of social courtesies and parties in the White House. His legislative liaison team, headed by Kenneth O'Donnell and Lawrence O'Brien, was diplomatic and astute, pumped and twisted congressional arms, applied both the carrot and the stick. But Kennedy left too many of the congressional chores to his liaison team. He simply did not give this aspect of the Presidency enough attention. Foreign affairs interested him intellectually much more than domestic measures. Despite his years in Congress and his love of politics, Kennedy did not really like or feel at home with small-bore politicians and congressional 'types', and he was not skillful in his personal bargaining with them.

Moreover, Kennedy made no attempt to initiate and in-stitutionalize new devices for easing presidential-congressional relations, nor did he even explore this problem intellectually. The breath of life to politicians is publicity, but no effort was made to share the presidential glory, of which there was a superabundance. What could be done to enhance the publicity and prestige of congressional leaders and committee chairmen who consented to carry the administration ball in Congress? How give them credit for 'creating' and 'initiating' the admin-istration's legislative measures? How let them become spokes-men before the nation of the administration's legislative goals? True, other presidents had made no such probings, but in recent years, with a legislative log-jam piling up, the president-ial-congressional deadlock had reached crisis-like proportions. The President did not give this question, inherently baffling at best, his full creative effort.

Kennedy's Presidency will be known as the time of the Negro revolution, when Negro aspirations widened to include desegregation in the private sector and were spectacularly supported by sit-ins and street demonstrations. As President, Kennedy not only gave full executive backing to the enforce-ment of court decisions but personally identified himself with the goals of the Negro revolution and gave them the full moral support of the Presidency.

By 1960, Kennedy had become an aggressive fighter for Negro rights. With the South lined up behind the Lyndon Johnson candidacy, Kennedy's nomination depended on the support of the Northern liberals and the metropolitan areas outside the South. During the election campaign, Kennedy's strategy was geared to winning the Negro vote in the big cities of the states with large electoral votes. Kennedy's new militancy carried over to his Presidency.

But by 1963, it appeared that what had been a political advantage might turn into something of a political liability. 'The Kennedys' were denounced in the South, and the President faced the loss of much of that section in 1964. More serious, there were indications that the civil rights issue would cost Kennedy many votes in the North, where considerable opposition to the Negro drive had developed. However, by this time Kennedy had chosen his course, and while there might be temporary shifts in tactics, there could be no turning back. Robert Kennedy has stated that at this point the administration really did not have any choice and that, besides, the administration's course was the correct one. He reports the President as saying: 'If we're going to lose, let's lose on principle.'

There seems little question that Kennedy would have been re-elected in 1964, but the civil rights issue would have been his biggest worry. In sizing up Kennedy as a politician, it is significant that he appears not to have anticipated the extent to which his position on civil rights might become politically hazardous. Otherwise it is difficult to explain the appointment of his brother as attorney general, upon whom the brunt of enforcing the civil rights court decisions would necessarily fall. Astute rulers take care to divert the political lightning of an offended public from themselves to subordinates. But in appointing his brother attorney general, the President left himself no 'out'. Those hostile to the Negro revolution could not say: 'President Kennedy is all right; it is that attorney general of his.' Instead, they blamed 'the Kennedys.' With another attorney general, President Kennedy might well have escaped some of the venom of the opposition. And incidentally, Robert Kennedy, in some other important job, would have been made better available for high politics in the future.

V

In foreign policy, the first two years of Kennedy were ambiguous. In the third year, there was a clearer sense of direction, one which promised to harmonize American policy with emerging new realities in the world.

At the time of the Kennedy accession, the post-war world was disintegrating. Bipolarization was giving way to depolarization. The Sino–Soviet rift was widening. With the single exception of little Vietminh, all the old European colonies that had recently gained their independence had escaped Communism, although there were Communist guerrilla activities in some of them. The trend was to a new pluralism, a new diversity. The nuclear revolution in war and the American-Soviet nuclear deterrents had rendered an ultimate military showdown unthinkable. The United States was ahead in the nuclear arms race.

In Europe, despite Khrushchev's bluster about West Berlin, the existing arrangements in East and Central Europe were ripening into a more overt *modus vivendi*, by way of tacit understanding rather than formal political agreements. Trade and intercourse between East and West Europe were increasing, the satellites were operating more independently of Moscow, and an all-European economic and cultural co-operation seemed slowly to be replacing the post-war's clear-cut division between the 'two Europes'. West Europeans were becoming less interested in NATO because they were more and more convinced that there would be no Soviet military aggression in Europe, due to the nuclear deterrent and other reasons. The drive to West European political integration was slackening, owing to the decline of external pressures and to De Gaulle's opposition to the supranational approach. Forces within the Six, composing the Common Market, were honestly divided over whether they wanted an inward-looking European community or an outward-looking Atlantic one.

In short, Kennedy was confronted with a new fluidity, a necessity and an opportunity for a reappraisal of American foreign policy. How much of the old foreign policy was still applicable? What aspects required a new orientation? To what degree was it safe, realistic, and advantageous to strike out in new directions? In some ways this ambiguous situation was more agonizing to decision makers than the obvious crisis situation with which Truman and Acheson had had to deal in the late 1940's and early 1950's. It is no wonder that some aspects of the Kennedy record in foreign affairs seem somewhat confused, even contradictory.

The chief stumbling block to an American-Soviet *detente* continued to be Berlin, the two Germanies, and the territorial arrangements in East and Central Europe. Kennedy rejected explorations of a definite settlement, and if in the future a genuine American-Soviet *rapprochement* develops, this rejection is likely to be held against him. However, he did move informally in the direction of a more openly tacit recognition of the existing arrangements in East and Central Europe. He deferred less to Adenauer's views than previous administrations had done. In his interview in *Izvestia*, remarkable for its clarity and candor, he agreed that it would not be advisable to let West Germany have its own nuclear weapons. After the Communists built the Berlin Wall, Kennedy resisted all pressures to use force to tear it down.

Nevertheless, during his first two years in office, Kennedy seems needlessly to have fanned the tensions of the dying Cold War. (It may be that 'needlessly' is too strong a word; perhaps Kennedy thought he needed to arouse the country to obtain a more balanced military program, more foreign economic aid, the Alliance for Progress; perhaps he thought, too, that a truculent tone was necessary to convince Khrushchev that America would stand firm under duress for its rights in Berlin.) His inaugural address was alarmist, already historically off key, more suited to the Stalinist era than to 1961. His first State of the Union Message was even more alarmist. The nation was told that the world tide was favorable, that each day we were drawing near the maximum danger. His backing of the Cuban invasion in April, 1961, further fanned the Cold War. His statement to newspaper publishers and editors gathered at the White House in May—that the United States was in the most critical period of its history—increased the popular anxieties. He over-reacted to Khrushchev's Vienna ultimatum in June, for in recent years Khrushchev's repeated deadlines and backdowns over West Berlin had become a kind of pattern. But for Kennedy, Vienna seems to have been a traumatic experience. On his return home he appealed to Americans to build do-it-yourself bomb shelters, and this produced a war psychology in the country and all manner of frenetic behavior, caused right-wingism to soar (1961 was the year the membership and financial 'take' of the right-wing organizations reached their peak[5]), and weakened confidence abroad in Kennedy's judgment.

There are no defenders of the Cuban fiasco of April 1961. Even had the expedition of the Cuban exiles been given American naval and air support and forced a landing, there is scant evidence that the Cubans, at that time devoted to Castro, would have revolted *en masse* and welcomed the invaders as deliverers. More likely a nasty civil war would have followed, with the Americans, giving increasing support to the invaders, cast in the role of subjugators. The C.I.A. had already rejected the social-revolutionary leadership of the anti-Castro Manuel Rey for a non-leftist leadership, and this would have made the task of overthrowing Castro even more difficult. The world would have looked on with dismay, and outside the United States the whole affair would have come to be regarded as 'another Hungary.' It is ironical that Kennedy, the generalist with a critical intelligence, the politician with a feel for popular moods, should on this occasion have been taken in by the bureaucrats and the 'experts.' Prodded by his own anti-Castro stand during the election campaign, Kennedy must have wanted desperately to believe in the reliability of those dossiers of the intelligence agents.

With respect to Western Europe, the Kennedy administration underestimated those forces within the Common Market that wanted a European community rather than an Atlantic community, at first regarded De Gaulle as a kind of maverick without group support for his position, and framed the Trade Expansion Act of 1962 in such a way that the most decisive tariff cuts between the United States and the Common Market would depend upon Britain's inclusion in the Market. Nevertheless, the Act as written still allowed for much liberalization of trade, even with Britain outside the Market, and the responsibility for failure to take advantage of this opportunity must be borne by parochial-minded groups and interests inside the Market.

The Kennedy Administration's contributions to national defense were notable. It emphasized a balanced and diversified establishment—both strategic and tactical nuclear weapons, conventional arms, and guerrilla forces—so the nation would never have to make the choice between the ultimate weapons and no other adequate defense. It was realistic in its shift from bombers to missiles as the chief nuclear carriers of the future, and in its dismantling of the intermediate missiles bases in Britain, Italy, and Turkey as the Polaris submarines and inter-continental missiles became increasingly operational. Its attempt to find a formula for a NATO multilateral nuclear force was a way of countering De Gaulle's blandishments to the West Germans and of balancing the possibility of a *detente* with Russia with reassurances to Bonn. Its experiments with massive air-lifts of ground troops was in part a response to the desires of many of America's NATO allies for less rigidity, less insistence on fixed ground quotas, and more flexibility. How-ever, NATO was plainly in transition, and while the Polaris submarines and inter-continental missiles were making the United States less dependent on European bases, ways were not yet actually implemented to share America's nuclear weapons with European allies on a genuine multilateral basis and satisfy their desires for less centralized direction from the United States.

There was an honest facing up to the terrible responsibilities inherent in the nuclear deterrent. That deterrent was put under tighter control to guard against accident and mistake, and the 'hot line' between Washington and Moscow was set up. A much more determined effort was made to get arms-control agreements and a treaty banning nuclear-weapons testing than had ever been made by Kennedy's predecessors. Negotiations with the Soviet Union had been going on for years, but the Americans now so yielded in their former demands for strict international inspection as to put the Russians on the defensive, making world opinion for the first time believe that it was the Russians and not the Americans who were the obstructionists. Kennedy's administration believed that the United States and Russia had an enormous common interest in preventing the spread of nuclear weapons to other countries, that the Sino-Soviet rift gave Khrushchev a new freedom and a new urge to make agreements, and that the increasing accuracy of national detection systems made the possibility of cheating on a test-ban treaty, even one without international inspection, 'vanishingly small'.

Kennedy's regime also showed its international-mindedness

in its firm support of the United Nations. It defended the Secretariat, the executive, from Soviet attacks, and in practice the activities of the Secretariat were widened. The organization was saved from bankruptcy by American financial aid. The operation of the United Nations military force in the Congo, backed by the United States, showed that the American government had no sympathy for 'neo-colonialism' as practised by the Katanga secession, and it added another successful precedent for international enforcement of international decisions.

With respect to the underdeveloped nations, the Kennedy policies paralleled the trend of history. Anti-colonialism and self-determination were more valiantly espoused than in the preceding administrations. The Dulles doctrine that neutralism is 'immoral' was abandoned, and neutralism was cordially accepted for nations which wanted it. Neutralism was positively encouraged in Laos and in the Congo. Help to South Vietnam was so hedged as to prevent the guerrilla war there from escalating into another Indo–China war, another Korea. Foreign economic aid was increased. The Food-for-Peace program was expanded. The Peace Corps was launched. The Alliance for Progress, an ambitious economic-aid program in Latin America coupled with domestic reforms, an experiment in 'controlled revolution', was undertaken.

However, Kennedy, like his predecessors, did little to make the average American understand foreign economic aid—that it is not only an attempt to raise living standards, prevent Communism, and contribute to the world's economic well-being and stability, but is also a substitute for those obsolete ways in which the old colonialism supplied capital to the underdeveloped areas. Until an American president takes to television and in a series of fireside chats explains to Americans in simple terms the real meaning of the foreign-aid program, that program will be in jeopardy.

The Cuban crisis of October 1962, provoked by the discovery of secret Soviet intermediate missiles in Cuba, was the high point, the turning point, in the Kennedy Administration. Could this crisis have been avoided? This will be debated by future historians. True, Khrushchev could not have declined giving Castro economic aid, technical assistance, and some military help, even had he desired to do so, for to have refused this would have been tantamount to surrendering Communist leadership to the Chinese. But why did he go to the length of planting intermediate-missile bases in Cuba? As an appeasement to the Stalinist and Chinese opposition? As a countermeasure to American missile bases in Turkey (which were soon to be dismantled)? As a means of blackmailing Americans into making a compromise on Berlin? To extract a promise from the Americans not to invade Cuba? Whatever the causes, some future historians will have nagging questions: Might this terrible gamble in nuclear brinkmanship have been prevented had Kennedy previously shown more disposition to come to a *detente* with the Soviet Union by a somewhat clearer recognition of the two Germanies and other *de facto* boundaries and arrangements in East and Central Europe; and if so, did this Kennedy reluctance, coming in part out of regard for West German opinion, represent a realistic appraisal of the world situation?

Anyway, when the crisis came, even neutralist opinion seemed to feel that Khrushchev's attempt to compensate for his own inter-continental-missiles lag and the open and avowed American intermediate missiles in Turkey did not justify the sneaky Soviet operation in Cuba. America's quiet, deliberate planning of counter-measures, both military and diplomatic, was masterly. America's prudent use of force, enough but not more than enough to achieve its objective, won world-wide acclaim. Khrushchev and Castro lost face. The Chinese denounced the Soviet backdown, and Chinese–Russian relations worsened. Most important, the peak of the crisis, a spectacular nuclear brinkmanship, cleared the atmosphere like a bolt of lightning. The lunacy of an ultimate nuclear showdown was traumatically revealed. Khrushchev's personal correspondence to Kennedy, reputedly revealing a highly emotional state and a genuine horror of nuclear war, the President had the grace, sportsmanship, and wisdom to keep secret.

Thereafter Khrushchev spoke even more insistently about the need to avoid nuclear war and pursue a policy of peaceful but competitive co-existence. From then on Kennedy gave more public recognition to emerging new international realities, the world's escape from monolithic threats, the trend to pluralism and diversity. In his address at American University in June 1963, Kennedy spoke as if the Cold War scarcely existed and emphasized the common stake both the United States and the Soviet Union had in world peace and stability. This address, one of the noblest and most realistic state papers of our time, will be remembered long after Kennedy's inaugural address is forgotten.

The new spirit in world affairs expressed itself concretely in the consummation of the limited nuclear test-ban treaty in the summer of 1963, the first real break in the American-Soviet deadlock. After this, Kennedy proposed a joint American-Soviet effort to explore the moon, and he agreed to permit the Soviet Union to purchase American wheat.

By 1963, then, Kennedy had come to much awareness that the post-war world was ending and to a determination to attempt more shifts in American foreign policy in harmony with the emerging fluidity. By this time, too, he had developed close personal relations with a large number of premiers and heads of state the world over. It was felt that after his re-election in 1964 he would be in an unusually strong position to give American foreign policy a new direction, that the test-ban treaty was but a foretaste of more significant measures yet to come, measures which might lead to an American-Soviet *detente*, eventually even to a *rapprochement*. Thus the President's life ended in a tragic sense of incompleteness and unfulfillment.

Every twentieth-century American president with a flair for world politics and in power in time of momentous international decision has been felled by sickness or death before his term was over, before his work was completed. First Wilson. Then Roosevelt. Then Kennedy. For sheer bad luck, this is a record unique among nations.

VI

Because of the vividness of his personality and the shortness of his tenure, Kennedy will be known more for the intangibles —a taste-maker, a symbolic embodiment of the values of his time, a romantic folk hero—than for his achievements in statesmanship.

Government requires pageantry, and rulers are expected to

put on a show. The Kennedys put on a superb one. Never before, not even under Dolly Madison, was the White House the scene of such a dazzling social life, one which combined beauty and intelligence, radiance and creativity. There were, to be sure, crabbed Mrs. Grundys who derided 'peacock opulence' and looked back longingly to the decorous days of Lucy Webb Hayes. But most Americans were fascinated, pleased as punch that even Elizabeth and Philip appeared a bit dowdy in contrast to those two young American thorough-breds in the White House. They figuratively crowned Jacqueline Queen of Hearts. This aspect of the Kennedy reign has been inimitably described by Katherine Anne Porter, and no historian will ever record it with more grace, insight, and tenderness.[6]

Kennedy's contributions to the cultural life of the nation also belong to the intangible, and they are difficult to measure. Now of course President Kennedy did not engage in as wide-ranging an intellectual life as President Jefferson or President Theodore Roosevelt. He did not carry on a voluminous and polemical correspondence with American and foreign intellect-uals as these men had done, even when they were in the White House. And Kennedy himself realized that his 'little promotions' did not help young and struggling artists and writers in the direct and material way the New Deal works projects had done.

But never before Kennedy's time had the White House paid so much personal and social attention to the nation's writers, artists, musicians, scientists, and scholars. At first some of the public was inclined to take a snidely skeptical view of all this. Was not this celebrity-hunting, highbrow name-dropping, a further drive to presidential glamour? The recipients of these attentions did not think so. Only William Faulkner, in bad-tempered petulance, rebuffed the President. For the rest, a chat with the President or an invitation to an event in the White House was an occasion of a lifetime, and these felt that Kennedy was not merely honoring them but the creative work they represented. As Richard Rovere has pointed out, Kennedy was tremendously concerned that the American society become a good, even a brilliant, civilization. He thought of himself as a promoter, an impresario, of excellence in every phase of

American life, and he hoped that future presidents would emulate him in this.[7]

To latter twentieth-century Americans, Kennedy will be a kind of beau ideal reflecting what they consider admirable in the politician—a shunning of corniness and hokum, an accent on youth and wealth, the glamorous videographic personality favored by Hollywood and TV, a contrived casualness in dress and manner, the sophistication and urbanity of the ivy league, direct and clear speech sprinkled with wit, an avoidance of doctrine and dogma, a pragmatism just emotionally enough involved to be effective, the capacity for using expertise and Madison Avenue techniques, the ability to create and sustain an 'image.' In these, most of them externals, Kennedy will have many imitators.

The Kennedy elan will not be easy to imitate. Even more difficult of imitation will be the Kennedy mind—rational and balanced thinking, objectivity, the ability to see all around a question, resilience, elusiveness, the capacity for keeping judgment in suspense, a detachment reaching to one's self and one's own image, an avoidance of absolute commitment combined with genuine intellectual involvement, a general critical intelligence brought to bear on the findings of the specialists. The Kennedy magic lies in its combination of the various elements: the externals, the verve with which the externals were carried off, and the cast of mind.

There is still another Kennedy intangible, perhaps the most important, one which belongs to the non-rational. Kennedy is becoming a folk hero, a subject of myth and legend, one of those few in history who capture the poetic imagination and affection of the masses. Solid achievement may have something to do with arriving at such a place in history, but very often it has little or nothing to do with it. Indeed, the titans who have wrought most mightily and in the end been felled by tragedy inspire awe and reverence more frequently than they do folk affection. They are too mature, their lives too devoid of colorful gallantries and foibles, their achievements too overwhelming for the average man to identify himself with such figures. To this class belong Caesar, William the Silent, Lincoln. Increasingly Lincoln has become a father image and 'the martyred Christ of the democratic passion play'.

The folk hero in the affectionate, indulgent sense is one who leaves behind him an over-all impression of elan, style, beauty, grace, gaiety, gallantry, bold and light-hearted adventure, valor—mingled in one way or another with the frail, the fey, the heedless, the mystic, the tragic. This is the romantic tradition, the tradition of Achilles, David, Alcibiades (despite his damaged soul), Arthur, Roland, Abelard, Richard the Lion Hearted, St. Francis, Bayard, Raleigh, Henry of Navarre, Gustavus Adolphus, Byron. Alexander the Great is often put in this tradition, but his exploits were so dazzling, so epoch-making, that he became more a god than a hero.

Kennedy's death has in it the touch of religious epic, of man pitted against fate. Here surely was one favored by the gods, one possessed of power, wealth, youth, the aura of manly war heroism, zest for living, personal charm and beauty, glamour, imagination, keen insight, intelligence, immense popularity, the adoring love of family and friends. Great achievements were to his credit, and even greater ones seemed in store. Then in the fullness of his strength, he was cut down in a flash. History has no more dramatic demonstration of the everlasting insecurity of the human condition. (Although the folk think of Kennedy as a child of fortune, actually he suffered much physically. He seems never to have been robust; the state of his health often concerned his father; in my own brief Kennedy files are letters from the elder Kennedy which speak of Jack's poor health in periods prior to World War II. Following his service in the war, Jack was plagued with malaria and his serious back injury. Even after the successful operation on his back, it would appear that he was rarely free from pain. When this comes to be realized, Kennedy's place as president will appear even more gallant.)

Was Kennedy himself a romantic? In some ways, mostly in appearance and manner. There are photographs of him, for instance several public ones taken in Tampa five days before his assassination, which reveal him in a kind of narcissistic euphoria. (Those who understand how wondrously flexible human nature can be will see nothing damaging in this.) James Reston once observed that the effect Kennedy had on women voters was 'almost naughty'. In his personal relations—and this is a matter not of appearance but of substance—Kennedy had an outgoing freshness and (there is no other term for it) a sweetness of temper. But basically Kennedy was not a romantic. He was a rationalist with a critical intelligence, a realist who knew the hard and subtle uses of power.

However, one need not be a romantic to become a romantic hero of history. Many romantics miss it—sometimes for a variety of reasons just barely miss it: Bolivar, Garibaldi, Gambetta, Jaurès, Michael Collins. In modern times romantic heroes have become rare. Kennedy is the first in this tradition in a long time, and he is the only American in its top echelon. Strange that he should have come out of the America of the machine and mass production. Or is it? People in our prosaic age, particularly young Americans, were yearning for a romantic hero, as the James Dean cult among our youth revealed. Now they have an authentic one.

NOTES

(1) Kennedy made a number of speeches in the South in 1957. Illustrative of their tone is the commencement address at the University of Georgia and the address at the Democratic state dinner at Jackson, Mississippi.

(2) See John P. Mallan, 'Massachusetts: Liberal and Corrupt', *The New Republic*, 13 October 1952.

(3) See an interview granted by Senator Kennedy to Irwin Ross, the New York *Post*, 30 July 1956.

(4) For the Kennedy–Eleanor Roosevelt by-plays over McCarthy, including the incident here mentioned, see Ralph G. Martin and Edward Plaut, *Front Runner, Dark Horse* (Doubleday, 1960), pp. 74–75; J. M. Burns, *John Kennedy —A Political Profile* (Harcourt, Brace, 1960), p. 153; Eleanor Roosevelt, *On My Own* (Harper, 1958), pp. 163–164; Alfred Steinberg, *Mrs. R.: The Life of Eleanor Roosevelt* (Putnam, 1958), p. 343.

(5) Donald Janson and Bernard Eisman, *The Far Right* (McGraw–Hill, 1963), pp. 56 and 127.

(6) Katherine Anne Porter, 'Her Legend Will Live', *Ladies Home Journal*, March 1964.

(7) See Richard Rovere, 'Letter from Washington', *The New Yorker*, 30 November 1963.

Guide to Further Reading

The following books are suggested for further reading on the subjects mentioned below. English editions are noted where these are available.

ON JOHN F. KENNEDY

BURNS, J. MACG., *John Kennedy: A Political Profile*, New York: Harcourt, Brace, 1959.

SCHLESINGER, A. M. JNR., *A Thousand Days: John F. Kennedy in the White House*, London: Andre Deutsch, 1965.

SORENSEN, T. C., *Kennedy*, London: Hodder & Stoughton, 1965.

WHITE, T. H., *The Making of the President, 1960*, London: Cape, 1962.

THE OFFICE OF PRESIDENT

BINKLEY, W. E., *The Man in the White House*, Baltimore: John Hopkins U.P., 1958.

BURNS, J. MACG., *Presidential Government: Crucible of Leadership*, Boston: Houghton Mifflin, 1965.

CORWIN, E. S., *The President, Office and Powers*, New York: New York University Press, 1957.

NEUSTADT, R. E., *Presidential Power: the Politics of Leadership*, New York: Wiley, 1960.

ROSSITER, C., *The American Presidency*, London: Hart-Davis, 1963.

SORENSEN, T. C., *Decision Making in the White House*, New York: Columbia U.P., 1964.

WARREN, S., *The President as World Leader*, Philadelphia: Lippincott, 1964.

PRESIDENT AND CONGRESS

BELOFF, MAX, *American Federal Government*, London: O.U.P., 1959.

BINKLEY, W. E., *President and Congress*, Magnolia: Peter Smith, 1965.

CLAPP, C. L., *The Congressman: his work as he sees it*, London: Faber, 1963.

GRIFFITH, E. S., *Congress: its contemporary role*, New York: New York University Press, 1961.

WHITE, W. S., *Citadel: the story of the U.S. Senate*, New York: Harper & Row, 1957.

CIVIL RIGHTS AND CIVIL LIBERTIES

DORMAN, M., *We Shall Overcome*, New York: Dell, 1965.

GOLDEN, H., *Mr. Kennedy and the Negroes*, Greenwich: Fawcett, 1964.

HANDLIN, O., *Firebell in the Night: the Crisis in Civil Rights*, Boston: Little, Brown, 1964.

KING, M. L., *Why we can't wait*, New York: Harper & Row, 1964.

MYRDAL, G., *An American Dilemma*, New York: Harper & Row, 1962.

FOREIGN POLICY OF THE UNITED STATES

ALMOND, G., *The American People and Foreign Policy*, New York: Praeger, 1960.

BELOFF, MAX, *Foreign Policy and the Democratic Process*, London: O.U.P., Baltimore: Johns Hopkins U.P., 1955.

FULBRIGHT, W. J., *Prospect for the West*, London: O.U.P: Cambridge, Mass.: Harvard U.P., 1963.

BAILEY, T. A., *A Diplomatic History of the American People*, New York: Appleton-Century-Crofts, 1958.

ROSTOW, W. W., *The United States in the World Arena*, New York: Harper & Row, 1960.

BOOKS BY JOHN F. KENNEDY

Why England Slept, New York: Doubleday, 1961.

Profiles in Courage, London: Hamish Hamilton, 1960.

A Nation of Immigrants, London: Hamish Hamilton, 1964.

Index